The New Science of Asset Allocation

The New Science of Asset Allocation

Risk Management in a Multi-Asset World

THOMAS SCHNEEWEIS
GARRY B. CROWDER
HOSSEIN KAZEMI

WILEY

John Wiley & Sons, Inc.

Published by John Wiley & Sons, Inc., Hoboken, New Jersey.
Published simultaneously in Canada.

Limit of Liability/Disclaimer of Warranty: While the publisher and author have used their best efforts in preparing this book, they make no representations or warranties with respect to the accuracy or completeness of the contents of this book and specifically disclaim any implied warranties of merchantability or fitness for a particular purpose. No warranty may be created or extended by sales representatives or written sales materials. The advice and strategies contained herein may not be suitable for your situation. You should consult with a professional where appropriate. Neither the publisher nor author shall be liable for any loss of profit or any other commercial damages, including but not limited to special, incidental, consequential, or other damages.

For general information on our other products and services or for technical support, please contact our Customer Care Department within the United States at (800) 762-2974, outside the United States at (317) 572-3993 or fax (317) 572-4002.

Wiley also publishes its books in a variety of electronic formats. Some content that appears in print may not be available in electronic books. For more information about Wiley products, visit our web site at www.wiley.com.

Library of Congress Cataloging-in-Publication Data:

Schneeweis, Thomas.
  The new science of asset allocation : risk management in a multi-asset world / Thomas Schneeweis, Garry B. Crowder, Hossein Kazemi.
    p. cm.
  Includes bibliographical references and index.
  ISBN 978-0-470-53740-4 (cloth)
  1. Asset allocation. 2. Risk management. I. Crowder, Garry B., 1954- II. Kazemi, Hossein, 1954- III. Title.
  HG4529.5.S3366 2010
  332.6--dc22

                                                                    2009047243

Printed in the United States of America

10 9 8 7 6 5 4 3 2 1

Contents

Preface   xi

Acknowledgments   xix

CHAPTER 1
A Brief History of Asset Allocation   1
  In the Beginning   3
  A Review of the Capital Asset Pricing Model   4
  Asset Pricing in Cash and Derivative Markets   6
  Models of Return and Risk Post-1980   11
  Asset Allocation in the Modern World   14
  Product Development: Yesterday, Today,
    and Tomorrow   15
  Notes   17

CHAPTER 2
Measuring Risk   20
  What Is Risk?   22
  Traditional Approaches to Risk Measurement   24
  Classic Sharpe Ratio   26
  Other Measures of Risk Assessment   28
  Portfolio Risk Measures   30
  Other Measures of Portfolio Risk Measurement   33
  Value at Risk   34
  Notes   37

CHAPTER 3
**Alpha and Beta, and the Search for a True Measure
of Manager Value**   39
  What Is Alpha?   39
  Issues in Alpha and Beta Determination   46
  Problems in Alpha and Beta Determination   48
  Multi-Factor Return Estimation: An Example   50
  Tracking Alternatives in Alpha Determination   54
  Notes   56

CHAPTER 4
Asset Classes: What They Are and Where to Put Them   **58**
  Overview and Limitations of the Existing Asset
    Allocation Process   59
  Asset Allocation in Traditional and Alternative
    Investments: A Road Map   61
  Historical Return and Risk Attributes and Strategy
    Allocation   66
  Traditional Stock/Bond Allocation versus Multi-Asset
    Allocation   70
  Risk and Return Comparisons Under Differing
    Historical Time Periods   71
  Extreme Market Sensitivity   74
  Market Segment or Market Sensitivity:
    Does It Matter?   82
  How New Is New?   84
  Notes   88

CHAPTER 5
Strategic, Tactical, and Dynamic Asset Allocation   **91**
  Asset Allocation Optimization Models   92
  Strategic Asset Allocation   99
  Tactical Asset Allocation   101
  Dynamic Asset Allocation   107
  Notes   109

CHAPTER 6
**Core and Satellite Investment: Market/Manager
Based Alternatives**   **110**
  Determining the Appropriate Benchmarks and
    Groupings   111
  Sample Allocations   117
  Core Allocation   119
  Satellite Investment   120
  Algorithmic and Discretionary Aspects of
    Core/Satellite Exposure   120
  Replication Based Indices   122
  Peer Group Creation—Style Purity   126
  Notes   132

CHAPTER 7
Sources of Risk and Return in Alternative Investments   **134**
    Asset Class Performance   135
    Hedge Funds   139
    Managed Futures (Commodity Trading Advisors)   143
    Private Equity   148
    Real Estate   153
    Commodities   160
    Notes   166

CHAPTER 8
Return and Risk Differences among Similar Asset
Class Benchmarks   **167**
    Making Sense Out of Traditional Stock and
        Bond Indices   168
    Private Equity   170
    Real Estate   173
    Alternative REIT Investments Indices   179
    Commodity Investment   179
    Hedge Funds   185
    Investable Manager Based Hedge Fund Indices   185
    CTA Investment   189
    Index versus Fund Investment: A Hedge Fund Example   189
    Notes   194

CHAPTER 9
Risk Budgeting and Asset Allocation   **195**
    Process of Risk Management: Multi-Factor Approach   195
    Process of Risk Management: Volatility Target   200
    Risk Decomposition of Portfolio   202
    Risk Management Using Futures   203
    Risk Management Using Options   206
    Covered Call   206
    Long Collar   208
    Notes   210

CHAPTER 10
Myths of Asset Allocation   **212**
    Investor Attitudes, Not Economic Information,
        Drive Asset Values   213
    Diversification Across Domestic or International
        Equity Securities Is Sufficient   214

Historical Security and Index Performance Provides a
Simple Means to Forecast Future Excess
Risk-Adjusted Returns   215
Recent Manager Fund Return Performance
Provides the Best Forecast of Future Return   215
Superior Managers or Superior Investment Ideas
Do Not Exist   216
Performance Analytics Provide a Complete Means
to Determine Better Performing Managers   216
Traditional Assets Reflect "Actual Values"
Better Than Alternative Investments   217
Stock and Bond Investment Means Investors
Have No Derivatives Exposure   217
Stock and Bond Investment Removes Investor
Concerns as to Leverage   218
Given the Efficiency of the Stock and
Bond Markets, Managers Provide No Useful Service   218
Investors Can Rely on Academics and Investment
Professionals to Provide Current Investment Models
and Theories   218
Alternative Assets Are Riskier Than Equity
and Fixed Income Securities   219
Alternative Assets Such as Hedge Funds Are
Absolute Return Vehicles   220
Alternative Investments Such as Hedge Funds
Are Unique in Their Investment Strategies   221
Hedge Funds Are Black Box Trading Systems Unintelligible to
Investors   222
Hedge Funds Are Traders, Not Investment
Managers   222
Alternative Investment Strategies Are So Unique
That They Cannot Be Replicated   223
It Makes Little Difference Which Traditional or Alternative
Indices Are Used in an Asset Allocation Model   223
Modern Portfolio Theory Is Too Simplistic to
Deal with Private Equity, Real Estate, and
Hedge Funds   223
Notes   225

CHAPTER 11
The Importance of Discretion in Asset Allocation Decisions   **226**
The Why and Wherefore of Asset Allocation Models   226
Value of Manager Discretion   230

Manager Evaluation and Review: The Due Diligence Process   232
Madoff: Due Diligence Gone Wrong or Never Conducted   233
Notes   239

CHAPTER 12
Asset Allocation: Where Is It Headed?   **240**
An Uncertain Future   241
What Is the Definition of Order?   243
Costs and Benefits   246
Today's Issue   246
Possible Governmental and Private Fund Responses
    to Current Market Concerns   247
Note   249

Appendix: Risk and Return of Asset Classes and Risk Factors Through Business Cycles   **251**

Glossary: Asset Class Benchmarks   **271**

Bibliography   **279**

About the Authors   **285**

Index   **287**

Preface

Without reservation, everything we believe about asset allocation and the perceived science surrounding its application is not necessarily true. The corollary to this statement is that a complete understanding of asset allocation is impossible. First, all beliefs are based on perceived fact; unfortunately sometimes those perceptions stem from a misreading or misunderstanding of the relevant material, or on the reliance of oral communications from a trusted advisor or source. Often our beliefs are a function of intellectual laziness or a failure to properly question.

Second, we do not even know all the facts associated with any asset investment. What *is* known is that the market disturbances of 2007 and 2008 have brought into sharp relief the failure of past beliefs—and the facts upon which they rest—relating to financial models, the institutions that create and distribute these models, and the regulatory and legislative oversight designed to protect investors as well as the financial system as a whole. As such, this is a seminal period in asset allocation. It is a period where once again the approach to asset allocation and risk management has an opportunity to be re-examined and where a new appreciation of the changing nature of asset allocation approaches and the importance of discretion in creating and managing the preservation of wealth can be established.

Asset allocation is perhaps the only investment tool that provides investors with an inherent "free lunch." It focuses on proven practices where equal risk assets with less-than-perfect correlation lead to higher long term returns than if those assets are held individually. What recent history has shown is that many of the benefits of asset allocation have been lost due to oversimplified approaches and a less-than-rigorous understanding of the risks and sources of return of differing asset classes. This is particularly true of "new" asset classes such as hedge funds, private equity, real estate, and commodities, as well as so-called structured products. For example:

- Many simplified approaches to asset allocation are based solely on historical index data. Unfortunately, times change. Benchmarks change. Index composition changes. Today's Dow Jones Index holds a different set of firms and associated risks than those that existed even 10 years ago. This is even truer for emerging markets. Again, while holding a diverse set of assets may reduce risk in certain market environments, historical evidence alone may not provide the basis for deciding which assets to hold (the benefits of emerging markets shown in historical data may simply be due to the unique currency moves of that time period).

- Practitioner research generally focuses on a limited number of asset classes (stocks, bonds, cash, real estate; and so forth), largely because these are the asset classes that most practitioners have to sell. As shown during 2008, those asset classes do not provide the range of assets necessary to provide adequate diversification. Moreover, those asset classes do not contain many of the assets or investment approaches that provide today's investors the ability to manage risk (however you define it). Just as important, many of the historical correlations reported by these asset classes are, in fact, not representative of correlations between many modern asset vehicles in current market environments. For instance, the historical low correlation numbers between stocks and bonds and real estate is due in part to the fact that real estate prices generally have not represented their true market value but their accounting value, which may not change over time, in contrast to their true sale price, which may often change over time. Similarly, private equity returns and the returns of many hedge fund strategies are model driven. The message sent is clear—beware of past data and doubly beware of bad past data.

- Today's market and trading environment is fundamentally different than that of even five years ago. Today, tradable ETFs exist that provide access to a wide range of investment sectors and risk/return scenarios. Tradable forms of private equity, real estate, hedge fund, managed futures, and commodity indices also exist. Moreover, the degree to which these new investment tools are offered and how they are presented to investors is often based on the business model of the firm offering the investment or investment advice. Investors often fail to take into account that the underlying business models of the firms offering asset allocation advice directly impact their product mix, their approach to asset allocation, and the relative return and risk scenarios they use in their asset allocation processes.

In summary, asset allocation is a dynamic yet reflective process. While it is based in part on a fundamental understanding of the underlying assets, the markets in which they trade, and the pros and cons of the various asset allocation and risk models used to manage those assets, it also requires *discretion*. Simple reliance on past model based approaches, past data, or past success does not suffice. By definition the asset allocation process assumes change in both expectations and results. It cannot be viewed in a vacuum and must be viewed against what "can and/or should happen" to asset holdings. Meaningful analysis or reflection cannot be derived from simply reading the top 10 investment books on the *New York Times* nonfiction list. Often these books promote an investment theme that in some way ignores the fundamental rules of the marketplace (e.g., the belief that certain managers can and do defy the laws of financial equilibrium and can make money in all market environments) or ignores the benefits managers may offer by suggesting that successful investment can be accomplished by simple, systematic rules based approaches. Either approach is doomed. Neither discretion without an investment framework nor an investment framework without discretion is sustainable.

OVERVIEW OF THE BOOK

This book's focus is simply to bring a sense of reality back into the investment process. Chapter 1 focuses on a very short history of asset allocation. In the early 1920s, several finance books warned of investment in stocks (and were proven right in the late 1920s). Equity investment however, provides a meaningful way to share in the growth of the world economy, and despite the stock market crash of the 1930s, individual stock investment became commonplace by the 1950s. However, until Markowitz's article in 1952, many investment books concentrated on individual stock selection instead of portfolio creation. Times have changed dramatically since then. In the 1960s, theoretical tools such as the CAPM offered ways to understand expected risk and return. In the 1970s, markets expanded to provide a range of risk management tools (currency futures, bond futures, and stock options, to name a few) that permitted managers to move significantly away from long only based portfolio analysis. In the 1980s, stock index futures and index options were developed. New forms of dynamic risk management, such as portfolio insurance, also came into existence. In the 1990s, new asset sectors such as mortgages, new approaches to asset management such as hedge funds, and a wider range of investment vehicles such as Collateralized Debt Obligations (CDOs) were developed. By 2000, financial engineers had come into their own, developing even more complex investment instruments and vehicles, each designed to further cauterize and trade market risk. Unfortunately, few investors considered that each of these new investment forms or vehicles fundamentally changed the relationship between assets and how those assets would perform and respond in extreme economic environments. This chapter provides a brief history of how each of these major market changes affected the approach to asset allocation and how asset allocation has had to evolve to meet changed economic conditions.

At the core of asset allocation is a view of the expected return to risk relationship. However, when investors actually confront and contemplate the concept of risk, quickly the risk of measuring risk is revealed. Each investor has a different definition of risk. Most academics describe risk in terms of standard deviation and beta—most practitioners have little real understanding of either concept, and risk becomes some amorphous concept based on past experience or the reliance on mathematical models and company practice. Chapter 2 offers investors a better sense of what risk measurement is and what it is not. Differences among investors as to what risk is and how risk measurement affects asset allocations are several of the sources of differential approaches to asset allocation.

Since we monitor only what we can measure, Chapter 3 concentrates on reviewing the principal tools (alpha and beta) governing the determination of fundamental asset risk as well as the ability of managers to create value. We show that even in the simple world of single-factor risk models (standard deviation, skewness, market beta) as well as in more complex models of risk and return determination, the model itself may impede an understanding of the fundamental risks we face. In short, there is risk in assuming we know what risk is, as well as risk in the actual models used for risk estimation.

Chapter 4 provides the building blocks for a multi-asset look at asset allocation. We do not attempt to change accepted approaches to asset class determination as much as to expand it to places it has long wished to go such as a wider range of asset classes including alternative investments. From the very beginning, questions existed as to where non-investable assets fit in the world of the CAPM. For many the question still remains "Do alternative investments provide the average investor with valuable return and risk opportunities beyond that available in traditional stock and bond investments?" In its most simple form, an equal weighted stock (high risk) and bond (low risk) portfolio is in fact a high risk stock portfolio with a little bit of bond risk. The potential addition of a range of other investment classes should at least offer one answer to this stock/bond conundrum.

Moreover, the answer to the benefits of asset allocation in a multi-asset universe may simply be that "more is better than less." Additional assets may provide investors with access to return opportunities that may not exist in other states of the traditional stock and bond world. Many of the limitations of the current asset allocation approaches are that they concentrate primarily on investment in a limited number of assets (stocks, bonds, and real estate). Today, investment in a larger range of investable assets is being addressed through more active asset construction. The increase in potential investment opportunities increases the potential benefit of strategic asset allocation opportunities as well as tactical and dynamic approaches to asset allocation. Chapter 5 addresses those issues.

There are of course numerous approaches to asset allocation. At the heart of asset allocation remains the fundamental set of decisions centered on what and how much to buy, given risk preferences. Chapter 6 ignores individual risk preferences in providing a simple core/satellite approach to asset allocation. This chapter does not emphasize the more complex models of return and risk optimization but focuses on the potential impacts of moving from more liquid, transparent investment vehicles in each asset class to less liquid, less transparent investment vehicles and the potential increase in expected return and risk associated with that movement.

There is a caveat. As noted above, over the last 30 years or so, the underlying characteristics of the asset classes used to measure risks have dramatically changed in composition and delivery. Most books on asset allocation continue to emphasize the return and risk characteristics of traditional stock and bond investments. Given the amount of research and information on the return and risk characteristics of traditional stock and bond investment, Chapter 7 travels a new road and focuses on other major forms of alternative investments, their source of returns, and their recent performance. Understanding the primary forms of alternative investment does not provide sufficient information as to the investability of various alternative investments. The underlying investments that investors have access to *must* reflect the return and risk characteristics of the traditional benchmarks used in most asset allocation models. Investors forget that even the most traditional stock and bond benchmarks are not strictly investable in their "common index" form. For stock and bond indices, management costs and trading costs make even investable stock and bond products differ slightly from the pure non-investable index products used in most asset allocation research.

Chapter 8 provides some answers to the relative performance of various non-investable alternative investment benchmarks and their associated investable counterparts. Here, as in most questions of asset management, the devil is in the details. For many portfolios, it is necessary to back into the asset allocation decision by first determining a reasonable set of investment vehicles with the desired liquidity and return characteristics. For most, traditional asset allocation remains the simple choice of mixing various asset classes to provide a mix of assets that offers increased expected return for a particular level of risk tolerance. However, as discussed previously there is no one definition of risk. Before risk can be managed, the fundamental risks impacting a particular investor must be understood. Chapter 9 reviews some of the major risks facing an investor as well as some common methods of managing them. Finally, we provide several examples of how simple approaches to risk management based on futures markets, options markets, and other basic forms of dynamic asset allocation can fundamentally transform the risk exposure of various investment vehicles. These approaches focus primarily on managing price risk. Thus even the simplified approaches to risk management must be viewed as the proverbial tip of the iceberg of risk and risk management.

It is always dangerous to point out one's own failings, when they are generally fairly obvious to others. Despite that, it is always beneficial to point out that when telling a story it is best that the reader know what parts of the story are true and what parts are based on myth. Chapter 10 examines a number of myths of asset allocation. Perceptions are weighed against measurable outcomes in discussing issues such as whether stocks, bonds, and cash provide an adequate means of diversification; or whether hedge funds provide a natural low correlation to traditional assets; or whether economic and risk relationships remain static over time. The list goes on.

Asset allocation is not a simple science. There are a number of risks involved in its use. In Chapter 11 we discuss the benefits and costs of various asset allocation approaches from more algorithmic to more discretionary. In many books on asset allocation, the systematic model driven approach is emphasized. In Chapter 11 the importance of manager discretion is emphasized. This chapter does not detail a model for determining the costs and benefits of manager discretion. Manager discretion can often increase return but at the potential cost of increased risk. However, for many investors, the potential costs and benefits of discretionary management are not fully appreciated. Most investors simply fail to take to heart the axiom that unusual returns can only be obtained from holding unusual risks or paying for means of managing that risk (systematic or discretionary).

Asset allocation exists in an evolving marketplace. Chapter 12 explores various factors affecting the future of asset allocation. There will certainly be a series of choices and each of those choices will have ripple consequences. The existence of a multi-asset world is of benefit only if we can take advantage of it. As these choices are constrained by market forces, government forces, or personal choice, the potential benefits are perhaps reduced. The question, not answered in this book, is whether the potential constraints are balanced by the change in risk. Unfortunately, making no decision as to the impact of potential future events on asset allocation is in fact a decision. At the end of the day, asset choices have to be made. Investors, however, must know the basis for these decisions as well as the basis for disinvesting from these assets. Systematic approaches to asset allocation may help, but in the final analysis the choice is yours and it must contain your personal discretionary beliefs.

The book concludes with additional material that should help the investor to follow the ideas presented herein. Given the constraints of time and space, the actual historical relationship between many of the asset classes discussed in the book and their performance over various market conditions has not been detailed. However, in an appendix we do provide a review of the performance of various investment classes over a range of historical economic conditions. A glossary summarizes the major asset benchmarks used in the book, followed by a bibliographic section that offers references to the source material for many of the ideas expressed in the book.

Of course, any book with three authors is both a debate and reconciliation. Invariably there are points where the differing perspectives must be melded into one. There are also cases where one author believes that something is important, but for the sake of time, civility, or space constraints, it is agreed that that information will be left out or not explored as fully as that author would like. Thus at the outset of this endeavor we fully acknowledge this book does not cover every aspect of asset allocation from either a practitioner's standpoint or that of an academic. Rather, it is the exploration of a number of the primary issues relating to this subject and designed to provide the reader sufficient insight to effectively question market opportunities, products, and ideas.

The reader should also be aware that like most things, the ideas expressed in this book are time sensitive. The writing of this book began in the early spring of 2009 and concluded in early 2010. Throughout this period, extreme events have occurred. If history is to be a teacher, we know that the future will provide additional information where many of the thoughts and questions within this book will be challenged as well as proven incorrect. Also, throughout this book the reader has been cautioned to be wary of historical data, historical thoughts, and historical performance. In other words show little fear in puncturing myths and their companions. History rarely repeats itself in the same manner; and one of the failings of modern portfolio design as well as some of the recent academic and quantitative research is the presumption that it will. Just as important, given the dynamic aspects of the markets, any asset allocation and risk management approach requires both a full understanding of the benefits and risks of various strictly quantitative approaches as well as a discretionary overlay to provide additional insight and experience to the asset allocation and risk management process.

Acknowledgments

We stand on the shoulders of those who preceded us. There are just too many individuals whose words and ideas we simply transcribed to thank them all. For ideas we conveyed correctly, we extend thanks to those who provided them to us. For those whose ideas we have failed to present in suitable fashion, we ask indulgence. We would like to offer special thanks to our editor, Emilie Herman. There are many reasons for starting a book. There are even more reasons for not finishing it. Without her constant support and encouragement, we fear this effort would have met the fate of the latter.

CHAPTER 1

A Brief History of Asset Allocation

For most investors, asset allocation and its meaning seems relatively straightforward, that is, the process of allocating assets. It is the how and the why of asset allocation that has led to an entire asset management industry dedicated to its operation. Given the amount of resources and effort dedicated to understanding asset allocation, it would be reasonable to expect that after almost 5,000 years of human history there would be a suitable solution. The fact that the investment management industry is still groping for an answer is illustrated in the millions of references to "asset allocation" from any Internet search and the fact that there are enough practitioner books and academic articles on "how to allocate assets" to fill any investor's library. This chapter provides a brief history of how major advances in financial theory and investment practice affected investors' approach to asset allocation and how asset allocation has had to evolve to meet changes in economic, regulatory, and technological environments. However, given the range of current and past efforts to diagnose, describe, and prescribe the process of asset allocation, it seems relatively futile to provide any reasonable summary of how we got here, much less what "here" is.

Before reviewing how we have arrived at current approaches to asset allocation, a brief review of what asset allocation is seems appropriate. Simply put, the ability to estimate what the future returns and risks of a range of investors' acceptable investments are and to choose a course of action based upon those alternatives is at the heart of asset allocation. As a result, much of asset allocation is centered on the quantitative tools or approaches used to estimate the probabilities of what may happen (risk) and the alternative approaches to managing that risk (risk management). While the concept of risk is multi-dimensional—including various types of market risks as well as liquidity risk, operational risk, legal risk, counterparty risk, and so on—for many it is simply the probability of a bad outcome. There is simply no single approach to asset allocation that covers all individuals' sense of risk tolerance or even what risk is. In the world of asset allocation, we generally concentrate on the concept of statistically driven risk management since those risk measurements are often centered on statistical estimates of probability (which is measurable) rather than on the concept of uncertainty (or possibility management), on which our empirically driven asset allocation models have little to say.

As a consequence, there is risk or uncertainty even in the most basic concept of asset allocation. Much of what we do in asset allocation is based on the tradeoffs between the risks and returns of various investable assets as well as the risks and returns of various aspects of asset allocation, including alternative approaches to return and risk estimation. Choosing among the various courses of action lies at the heart of a wide range of asset allocation approaches, including:

- Strategic asset management (allocation across various investment classes with the goal of achieving a desired long-term risk exposure)
- Tactical asset management (allocation within or across investment classes with the goal of maximizing the portfolio's short-term return-risk profile)
- Dynamic asset management (systematic changes in allocation across assets with the goal of fundamentally changing the portfolio's risk exposure in a predetermined way)

Asset allocation is not about solely maximizing expected return. It is a central thesis of this book as well as years of academic theory and investment practice that expected return is a function of the risks taken and that those risks may not be able to be measured or managed solely through systematic algorithmic based risk management. Thus, asset allocation must focus on risk management in a broader context, including the benefit of an individual asset allocators's discretionary oversight in order to provide a suitable return to risk tradeoff consistent with an investor's risk tolerance or investment goals. The story of the evolution of our understanding of that return to risk tradeoff is the subject of this chapter. It is important to emphasize the "evolution" part as our understanding of the expected return to risk relationship keeps changing. First, because through time we learn more about how individuals react to risk and second, because the world itself changes (the financial world included).[1]

An individual's or institution's approach to asset allocation depends of course in part on their relative understanding of the alternative approaches and the underlying risks and returns of each. For the most part, this book does not attempt to depict the results of the most current research on various approaches to asset allocation. In many cases, that research has not undergone a full review or critical analysis and is often based solely on algorithmic based model building. Also, many individuals are simply not aware of or at ease with this current research since their investment background is often rooted in traditional investment books in which much of this "current research" is not included.[2]

IN THE BEGINNING

It should be of no surprise to investors that the two fundamental directives of asset allocation: (1) estimate what may happen and (2) choose a course of action based on those estimates have been at the core of practitioner and academic debate. For our purposes, the timeline of that debate is illustrated in Exhibit 1.1. The advent of Modern Portfolio Theory and practice is often linked to the publication of Harry Markowitz's 1952 article "Portfolio Selection." For many the very words "Modern Portfolio Theory" are synonymous with Markowitz. It is important to point out that Modern Portfolio Theory is now almost 60 years old. As such, and not merely as a result of age, MPT (Modern Portfolio Theory) is really IPT (Initial Portfolio Theory) or OPT (Old Portfolio Theory). Moreover, the fundamental concept expressed in Markowitz's article (the ability to manage risk based on the expected correlation relationships between assets) was well known by practitioners at the time of its publication.

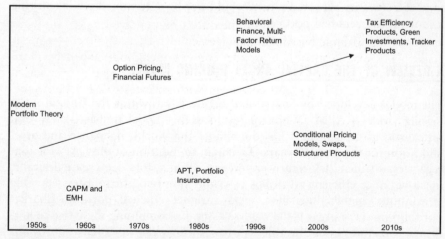

EXHIBIT 1.1 Timeline of Financial Advances in Asset Allocation

Markowitz formalized the return and risk relationship between securities in what is known today as the mathematics of diversification. If expected single-period returns and standard deviations of available securities as well as the correlations among them are estimated, then the standard deviation and the expected return of any portfolio consisting of those securities can be calculated. This means that portfolios can be constructed with desirable standard deviation and expected return profiles. One particular set of such portfolios is the so-called mean-variance efficient portfolios, which have the highest expected rate of return for a given level of risk (variance). The collection of such portfolios for various levels of variance leads to the mean-variance efficient frontier.[3] In the mid 1950s, James Tobin (1958) expanded on Markowitz's work by adding a risk-free asset to the analysis.[4] This brought into focus an individual's ability to hold only two types of assets (risky and riskless) and to lend or borrow such that those two assets provided the tools necessary to match a wide range of investor return and risk preferences.[5]

The next major advancement in asset allocation expanded the work of Markowitz and Tobin into a general equilibrium model of risk and return. In this work, academics treated volatility and expected return as proxies for risk and reward. In the early 1960s, academics (Sharpe, 1964) proposed a theoretical relationship between expected return and risk based on a set of assumptions of individual behavior and market conditions. These author(s) proposed that if investors invested in the mean-variance efficient market portfolio, then the required rate of return of an individual security would be directly related to its marginal contribution to the volatility of that mean-variance efficient market portfolio; that is, the risk of a security (and therefore its expected return) could not be determined while ignoring its role in a diversified portfolio.

A REVIEW OF THE CAPITAL ASSET PRICING MODEL

The model developed by Sharpe and others is known as the Capital Asset Pricing Model (CAPM). While the results of this model are based on several unrealistic assumptions, it has dominated the world of finance and asset allocation for the past 40 years. The main foundation of the CAPM is that regardless of their risk-return preference, all investors can create desirable mean-variance efficient portfolios by combining two portfolios/assets: One is a unique, highly diversified, mean-variance efficient portfolio (market portfolio) and the other is the riskless asset. By combining these two investments, investors should be able to create mean-variance efficient portfolios that match their risk preferences. The combination of the riskless asset and the market portfolio (the Capital Market Line [CML] as shown in Exhibit 1.2) provides a solution to the asset allocation problem in a very simple and intuitive manner: Just combine the market portfolio with riskless asset and you will create a portfolio that has optimal risk-return properties.

In such a world, the risk of an individual security is then measured by its marginal contribution to the volatility (risk) of the market portfolio. This leads to the so-called CAPM:

$$E(R_i) - R_f = [E(R_m) - R_f]\beta_i$$

$$\beta_i = Corr(R_i, R_m) \times \frac{\sigma_i}{\sigma_m}$$

where

R_f = Return on the riskless asset

$E(R_m)$ and $E(R_i)$ = Expected returns on the market portfolio and a security

σ_m and σ_i = Standard deviations of the market portfolio and the security

$Corr(R_i, R_m)$ = Correlation between the market portfolio and the security

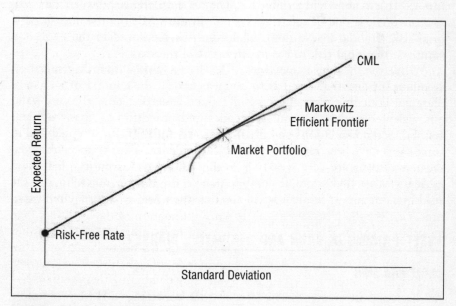

EXHIBIT 1.2   Capital Market Line

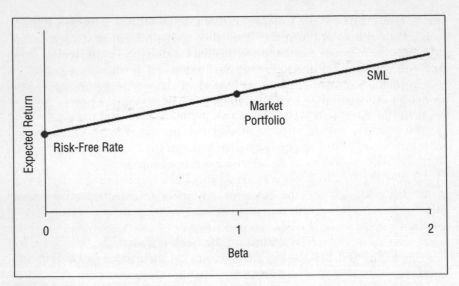

EXHIBIT 1.3   Security Market Line

Thus, in the world of the CAPM all the assets are theoretically located on the same straight line that passes through the point representing the market portfolio with beta equal to 1. That line is called the Security Market Line (SML), as shown in Exhibit 1.3. The basic difference between the CML and the SML is one of reference system. In the CML the risk measured is total risk (standard deviation), while the risk measured in the SML is a security's marginal risk to the market portfolio (beta).

While the most basic messages of MPT and CAPM (that diversification is important and that risk has to be measured in the context of an asset's marginal contribution to the risk of reference market portfolio) are valid and accepted widely by both academics and practitioners, many of their specific recommendations and predictions are not yet fully accepted and in some cases have been rejected by empirical evidence.[6] For instance, observed security returns are very weakly, if at all, related to a security's beta, and most investors find a simple combination of the market portfolio and the riskless asset totally inadequate in meeting their risk-return requirements.

ASSET PRICING IN CASH AND DERIVATIVE MARKETS

CAPM and EMH

As discussed in greater detail later in this book, the CAPM profoundly shaped how asset allocation within and across asset classes was first conducted. Individual assets could be priced using a limited set of parameters. Securities could be grouped by their common market sensitivity into different risk classes and evaluated accordingly; and, to the degree that an expected market risk premia could be modeled, it would also be possible (if desired) to adjust the underlying risk or beta of a portfolio to take advantage of changes in expected market risk premia (i.e., increase the beta of the portfolio if expected market risk premia is high and reduce the beta of the portfolio if the expected market risk premia is low). Here, market risk premia is defined as the difference between the expected rate of return of the market portfolio and the "riskless rate of interest."

While the CAPM is at its heart a model of expected return determination, it quickly became the basis for a number of asset allocation based decision models. The rudimentary nature of computers in the early 1960s is often forgotten and, while the mathematics of the Markowitz portfolio optimization model were well known, the practical application was limited due primarily to the number of numerical calculations. Specifically, the amount of data needed to obtain reasonable estimates of the covariance matrix is significant. For instance, if we have 100 securities, then to estimate the covariance matrix, we would need to estimate 100 variances and $(100^2 - 100)/2$ covariances, which add up to 5,050 parameters, have to be estimated. This would be computationally difficult and would have required many hours of work. As an alternative, the number of calculations can be significantly reduced if it is assumed that returns are driven by only one factor (e.g., the market portfolio). Note that this does not assume that CAPM holds. In other words, suppose we use a simple linear regression to estimate the beta of an asset with respect to a well diversified portfolio.

$$R_{it} = \alpha_i + \beta_i R_{mt} + e_{it}$$

The rate of return on the asset at time t is given by R_{it}, the rate of return on the diversified portfolio is given by R_{mt}, the intercept and the slope (beta) are given by α_i and β_i respectively. Finally, the error term for asset i is given by e_{it}. Suppose we run the same regression for another asset, denoted asset j. If the error term for asset j is uncorrelated with the error term for asset i, then the covariance between the two assets is given by

$$Cov(R_i, R_j) = \beta_i \beta_j Var(R_m)$$

Notice that to estimate covariance between the two assets, we need an estimate of the variance of the market portfolio as well ($Var(R_m)$). However, this term will be common to all estimates of covariance. The result is that the number calculations required to estimate covariance matrix is now reduced to $(2 \times 100 + 1)$.

It is important to note that the above regression model, known as the market model, has nothing to do with the CAPM. The above regression makes no prediction about the size or the sign of intercept. It simply a statistical relationship used to estimate the beta. On the other hand, the CAPM predicts that the market model intercept will be $(1 - \beta_i)R_f$.

It is fair to say, however, that almost 40 years ago most academics and professionals knew that the CAPM was an "incomplete" model of expected return. We now know that Sharpe and his fellow academics had unwittingly created a sort of "Asset Pricing Vampire," which rose from their model and, despite 30 years of stakes driven into its heart lives to this day for many practitioners as the primary approach to return estimation.[7] In the early years of the CAPM, financial economists were like kids with a new hammer in which everything in the financial world looked like a nail. For example, if an asset's expected return can be estimated, then that estimate could be used as a basis for determining if an individual could consistently choose assets that were fundamentally underpriced and offered an ex post return greater than that consistent with its underlying risk. In sum, it provided the basis for determining if managers could obtain an alpha (excess return above that consistent with the expected return of a similar risk-passive investable asset).

The combination of the full information assumptions in the CAPM, along with the "presumed" ability to measure expected returns consistent with risk, offered academics the chance to measure the true informational efficiency of the marketplace. Initial studies by academics indicated that active managers underperformed similar risk passive indices. This empirical result helped give rise later to the creation of a series of passive non-investable and investable indices that would form the basis for the asset allocation consulting industry. As important, the combination of presumed informational efficiency with the ability to measure expected return led to the development of the Efficient Market Hypothesis (Fama, 1970) in which assets' prices were described relative to the degree to which their current prices reflected various types of information; that is, an asset's current price may be consistent with (1) past price information (weak form efficiency); (2) public information (semi-strong efficiency); and (3) private information (strong form efficiency). If market inefficiencies existed, this implied that investors could earn returns that would exceed what is predicted by the asset's underlying risk as if there were some violation of information efficiency (similar to a monopoly or oligopolies). However, if the Efficient Market Hypothesis (EMH) is true, most investors should not waste their time trying to pick individual stocks using well-known public information but concentrate on risk determination and the proper set of assets to capture the expected risk that matches their risk preferences.

Today it is realized that the Efficient Market Hypothesis would be more correctly named the "Excess Return if We Only Knew How To Measure Expected Return Hypothesis"; it did provide the impetus for moving from a "Managers Only Matter" state of mind to an asset allocation process based on "Managers May Matter But Let Us Measure It First" plus a "Passive Approach to Asset Class/Security Selection." Again, it is important to come to terms with what the EMH says and does not say. EMH does not say that prices fluctuate randomly. EMH states that prices randomly fluctuate with a drift; that is, tomorrow's expected price is equal to today's price times the asset's expected return where expected return is based on current information (risk assessment). EMH says that there are no free lunches. Such profit opportunities are quickly eliminated, and the only way one can earn a high rate of return is through assuming a higher level of risk.

The quintessential problem is that there is no firm understanding of how people determine expected risk-adjusted return since there are no conclusive models that demonstrate how people price risk. All we can say is whether a manager has been able to create excess return (return above some arbitrary chosen expected return model). The EMH does not say that an investment manager cannot make a gross return in excess of a passive approach. The EMH only says that if a manager makes such an excess return (e.g., because of access to technology or information), the investor may be charged a fee equal to the excess return such that the net return will be similar to that of investment in the passive index (e.g., manager returns – manager fee ≥ return on passive index). The manager's fee is supposed to cover the cost of acquiring the technology and/or information plus the investment made in time and effort to use that technology and information.

The combination of the CAPM and the EMH gave the market place the twin academic pillars required for the development of the asset allocation industry. All that was needed was a third pillar, a business model capable of developing the infrastructure required to market this new industry. Fortunately, computers and information technology had advanced such that in the late 1960s the investment industry witnessed the expansion of the index business. Both within the United States and overseas, monthly and even daily data series of domestic and global stock indices were being created. These indices could be used to provide estimates of the benefits of various approaches to asset allocation. For instance, newly developed global stock indices were used in a number of studies to illustrate the potential benefits of combining domestic stock indices (asset classes) with foreign and international stock indices (Grubel, 1968; Levy and Sarnet, 1970).[8]

Lost, of course, in this academic and practitioner euphoria were some of the practical realities relating to the underlying assumptions of the CAPM and EMH. First, the available empirical evidence had not strictly supported the CAPM's expected return and risk relationship. There was no means to estimate the "True Market Portfolio," so any empirically estimated betas were only estimates subject to unknown measurement errors. More complex multi-factor models were required to capture expected return processes. While the market for financial products aimed at providing such multi-factor models came into existence (e.g., Barr Rosenberg and Barr's better betas), most academics remained wedded to single-factor models. As academics came to appreciate the statistical problems associated with using underspecified single factor (beta) models of return determination or the data problems associated with the use of international data (e.g., timing of data or liquidity), attempts were made to "tweak" the CAPM. Throughout the 1970s, various forms of zero beta and multi-beta APT models came into existence—better to explain the previously unexplained residual error of the single factor models of return estimation. These models provided additional statistical tools for measuring the efficacy of the EMH.

As with most people, when given the choice between the familiar and the unfamiliar, academics and practitioners kept using the hammers they had (CAPM and EMH) to nail down the problem of expected return estimation and the degree to which individual managers provided returns in excess of similar risk passively produced portfolio returns. In truth, the CAPM and EMH models did an excellent job of describing most market conditions. For the most part, markets do work. It should be expected that for financial markets with low-cost information (e.g., Treasury Bill market), asset prices would reflect current information and a common risk based return model. Other markets and/or assets may require enlarged risk based factor models that capture an enlarged set of underlying risks and therefore expected returns. Small firms with few analysts following them, with less ability to raise capital, with a less diversified client base, limited legal support, and so on may be priced to reflect those risks. Many assets are simply not tradable or have high transaction costs (e.g., housing, commodities, employment contracts, or distressed debt). How they could or should be priced in a single-factor or even a multi-factor model framework was explored, but a solution was rarely found.[9]

Option Pricing Models and Growth of Futures Markets

We have spent a great deal of time focusing on the equity markets. During this period of market innovation, considerable research also centered on direct arbitrage relationships. Arbitrage relationships in capital and corporate markets were explored during the 1930s (forward interest rates implied in yield curve models)[10] and in the 1950s (corporate dividend policy and debt policy). Similarly, cost of carry arbitrage models had long been the focal point of pricing in most futures based research. In the early 1970s Fischer Black and Myron Scholes (1973) and Merton (1973) developed a simple-to-use option pricing model based in part on arbitrage relationships between investment vehicles. Soon after, fundamental arbitrage between the relative prices of a put option (the right to sell) and a call option (the right to buy) formed a process to become known as the Put-Call Parity Model, which provided a means to explain easily the various ways options can be used to modify the underlying risk characteristics of existing portfolios. Exchange based trading floors soon came into existence, which helped eventually to develop a market for a wide range of option based financial derivatives. While a range of dynamic futures based approaches should provide similar risk management opportunities, options provided a direct and easily measured approach to fundamentally change the risk composition of an asset or a portfolio. As important, the model allowed one to estimate the cost for modifying the risk of a portfolio.

The growth of options as a means to provide risk management was centered primarily on equity markets. The 1970s also witnessed the creation and growth of new forms of financial futures, including currency futures in the early part of that decade and various forms of fixed income futures in the latter half (Treasury Bond futures). The creation of the Commodity Futures Trading Commission (CFTC) in the mid 1970s provided the additional government oversight necessary for the growth and development of new forms of financial futures as well as options products based on them. It is well known that futures provide a means to directly track underlying investment markets as well as to provide risk reduction opportunities. Futures contracts offer the ability to reduce or increase the underlying variability of an asset but futures alone do not permit one to fundamentally change the risk structure of the asset. The ability to directly change the distributional form of an asset is left for options. It can simply be said that the creation and development of options and futures trading in the 1970s led the way for the creation of an entire new industry dedicated to new means of managing risk.

MODELS OF RETURN AND RISK POST-1980

Models of investors' behavior as well as models of return and risk relationships, like so much of modern finance as well as life, are evolutionary. Given the tools and information at hand, various theories of expected return and risk relationships were put forth and were tested against the available data and technology of the period. Whether realized or not, none of the theories presented offered stopping points. They were in fact evolutionary steps with each reaching a conclusion within the confines of their stated parameters. As noted above, the EMH only states that expected return is a function of expected risk, which is a function of expected information. Nothing says that individuals do not get it wrong ex post or even that they had it right ex ante. In any market there is a process of information discovery and market reaction. The fact that, on average, individuals do not correctly value factors such as ratings or real estate payment cycles is less a critique of market efficiency than the process by which individuals assess information. Whatever the criticisms of the EMH, it became a staple of the investment jargon along with the CAPM as the benchmarks by which products were designed or marketed. Even other markets and products were discussed in terms of their performance or risk attributes relative to EMH or CAPM. For example, in the early 1970s the benefits of commodity futures were even discussed in terms of their equity market betas (Dusak, 1973). Fixed income securities (while developing their own multi-factor jargon such as duration and convexity) were also discussed with regard to offering expected returns in terms of their betas with some weighted stock and bond market portfolio.

By the early 1980s a range of financial products and databases had come into existence that provided the ability to empirically test asset allocation decision rules (Ibbotson and Sinquefield, 1979). Options trading had grown and financial futures markets had evolved (S&P 500 futures contracts came into existence in the mid 1980s). Other changes had taken place in terms of technology, regulation, and market structure to provide an enhanced set of conditions that supported further development of asset allocation within a risk-controlled environment. During this period, systemized approaches to tactical asset allocation were being developed and marketed. By the mid 1980s concepts such as alpha transfer (Schwarz et al., 1986) and dynamic portfolio insurance (Leland, 1988) were well understood. In addition, during the 1980s advances in computer technology and software (e.g., Lindo) made available for the first time a series of self-serve portfolio management tools that enabled investors the ability to directly manage and adjust portfolio risk exposure.

It is fair to say that throughout the 1980s and 1990s markets continued to expand, which provided additional investable products that further expanded the available investable set. As technology advanced and markets expanded, the ability to dissect and reset asset flows led to the development of a wide range of new structured products and investment vehicles designed to meet the unique return and risk profile of individual investors. Financial regulation made it profitable for banks to offload certain trading processes, and new forms of external product based hedge funds and managed futures programs were developed. By the mid 1990s, globalization had led to the development of new forms of emerging market securities, new commodity products, as well as new forms of non-exchange traded financial products such as swaps to manage investor unique risks not fulfilled by more general exchange based products. The development of these non-exchange traded products culminated in the growth of various fixed income products (e.g., credit default swaps), which helped manage not only the exposure to interest rates but also the credit risk as well.

The evolution, if not revolution, in the market structure and trading also impacted the way practitioners and academics viewed the asset pricing process. Concerns over the deviations from the strict CAPM process led to new research focused on issues that have been expanded under the topic "behavioral economics," which offers for some a more plausible picture of investor behavior. As these alternative models became popular, alternative views as to the underlying process by which excess return was determined evolved. Fama and French (1992, 1995) and others developed a series of empirical models that indicated that sources of returns could be related to firm size as well as style (growth and value).

Although behavioral economics and other expanded models of return to risk models dominated the market, the challenge remained on how to hang on to the baby as the bathwater is thrown out. The development of more behavioral approaches to risk and return determination did focus on a more activist approach to asset price determination and the fact that the process of price determination is not instantaneous.[11] Arguments about the benefit of such behavioral approaches to asset pricing in some cases missed the point. EMH does not say that there are no risk free $100 bills lying on the street, rather it states that there are unforeseen risks in attempting to pick them up. Moreover, the fact that there exist "irrational investors" may have little impact on market prices. The current price is always only a clearing price. There are other individuals who will pay more but do not have to and others who would sell it for less but do not have to. The market price mostly reflects those with the most money and does not generally reflect small rational or irrational investors who for the most part are price takers. Also, people may behave predictably when faced with simple choices in a psychology lab, but when faced with extreme amounts of money, especially in arbitrage markets, it is rare that ex ante market prices do not reflect the best of the brightest; there is just too much money to make or lose.[12]

ASSET ALLOCATION IN THE MODERN WORLD

Looking back over the past decade, the issues in asset allocation had less to do with the theoretical models underlying return determination than the changes in market and trading structures that have led to a rapid increase in the number of available investable alternatives. Today, the number of investment choices has expanded beyond that available in traditional stock and bond investment to a wider range of alternative investments, including traditional alternatives such as private equity, real estate, and commodities, as well as more modern alternatives such as hedge funds and managed futures. In the past 10 years, academics and practitioners have also come to appreciate that both traditional stocks and bonds as well as alternatives (real estate, commodities, private equity, hedge funds, and managed futures) have common risk factors that drive returns and that those risk factors are conditional on changing market conditions. Moreover, global and domestic regulatory forces as well as market forces have created a new list of investable products (exchange traded and over the counter). These products include more liquid and readily available forms of traditional stock and bond investment (e.g., ETFs, OTC forward and options contracts) as well as more liquid and readily investable alternative investment forms (e.g., passive investable benchmark products).

The addition of new investment forms has permitted individuals to more readily access previously illiquid or less transparent asset classes (e.g., private equity or real estate) and has increased the number of assets that provide the potential for risk diversification in various states of the world. In fact, risk itself has become a more tradable asset. While options had always provided a means for individuals to directly manage risk, previous attempts to directly trade risk had not met with success. In the mid 2000s, various forms of VIX (VIX is the ticker symbol for the CBOE Volatility Index) began to be traded directly on central exchanges. In addition, advances in various forms of structuring along with algorithmic based trading products have offered investors a broader set of domestic and international vehicles by which to manage asset portfolios. Lastly, the development of the Internet, along with the expansion of data and product availability as well as computer technology have permitted the development of a wide set of new approaches to asset allocation and risk management.

The problem still exists that we do not know what we can reasonably expect from these new products as well as the various asset allocation systems. Investor asset choices exist under a wide range of investment constraints. Regulation prevents some individuals from investing in certain forms of asset classes except in the most rudimentary form. Investment size restricts certain investors from taking advantage of more cost efficient asset classes (e.g., swaps may be the preferred form of accessing a particular asset class but many investors are limited to investing in exchange traded variants, which do not have the same statistical properties). As pointed out, the market is never efficient for everyone; that is, transaction costs differ, borrowing costs differ, taxation differs such that the actual after-tax return for individuals and institutions varies greatly. Finally, the ability to process and understand information and its consequences differs.

The very unpredictable nature of risky asset pricing raises the issue of how best to manage that risk. Certainly, the Markowitz model based on estimates obtained from historical figures continues as a primary means by which individuals attempt to estimate portfolio risk; however, the 2007 and 2008 market collapse illustrated the fundamental flaw of the Markowitz diversification approach; that is, Murphy's Law of Diversification—assets and markets only offer diversification benefits when you do not need them.

Until recently, investors felt secure that they had available to themselves not only a wide range of potential assets to invest in but also a wide range of risk management tools to manage that risk. It is not that investors are unaware of the potential issues in risk management. While many practitioners continued to concentrate on return maximization, many academics focused on the conditional risk, and, therefore, changing return to risk properties of various investments. Portfolio rebalancing based on the conditional nature of risk appeared to offer a more consistent approach to managing a portfolio's risk. However, even these models were incapable of anticipating the risk exposures of typical portfolios under extreme economic conditions witnessed in 2008. The market collapse of 2007 and 2008 provided conclusive evidence that while risk could be understood and in certain cases even managed, it could not be eliminated. The real problem remained now among market participants—what is risk and how to manage it?

PRODUCT DEVELOPMENT: YESTERDAY, TODAY, AND TOMORROW

The touchstone of evolution is that an entity has to develop to survive within its environment. Understand that the operative word is survive, and survival does not carry an optimization requirement. So we will not find the perfect theory or grouping of products as change comes to the corporate or investment world or, for that matter, to academic research. Rather, we will find that we have a better understanding of risk and return relationships. Today's growth in off-exchange and screen-traded markets, in contrast to floor-traded markets, is only one example of such understanding and change. There can be, however, a gulf between reality and perception. A delay in an investor's (and here the term is used broadly to incorporate regulators and corporate boards) understanding or market awareness of new research or market relationships often results in a delay in an appreciation of these changes and leads to a significant disadvantage in the marketplace.

Change comes from many sources. Modern investment products grew out of economic necessity, regulation, and technological innovations. Currency derivatives came into existence out of the failure of the United States to manage its own currency; thus the market had to devise an approach to facilitate international trade in a world of uncertain currency values. Individual options grew in the early 1970s as risk management tools, partly in response to the collapse of the stock markets of the late 1960s and the demand for new means of equity risk management. In the 1980s the expansion of interest rate futures and the development of equity futures followed, in part, from earlier ERISA laws, which created the pension fund asset base that required investment managers to hedge their asset risks. During the 1990s and into the current era, new product creations (e.g., swaps) were part of the changing world of technology and the resulting increasing ability to manage and monitor an ever more complex series of financial and nonfinancial products.

Thus, while we know very few fundamental truths, one, however, that we can collectively agree upon is that the evolution of asset allocation draws upon the aforementioned changes flowing from a dynamic world in which new forms of assets and risk management tools are constantly being created. Relative risks and returns and the ability to monitor and manage the process by which these evolving assets fit into portfolios will change and will be based on currently unknown relationships and information. Certainly today the challenge is greater, not only because we are working in a more dynamic market but the number of investment vehicles available to investors has increased as well. Hopefully, the following chapters will provide some guidance to meet this challenge.

WHAT EVERY INVESTOR SHOULD REMEMBER

- Much of what we do in asset allocation is based on the tradeoffs between the costs and returns of various approaches to return and risk estimation. Choosing among the various courses of action based on those risky alternatives lies at the heart of a wide range of various approaches to asset allocation, including strategic asset management, tactical asset management, and dynamic asset management.

- MPT (Modern Portfolio Theory) is really IPT (Initial Portfolio Theory) or OPT (Old Portfolio Theory). The CAPM and Efficient Market Hypothesis, as well as more modern multi-factor risk approaches to asset pricing, while providing a basic framework for addressing return and risk dynamics in the marketplace, are in most cases 60, 40, 30, or 20 years old. In short, the sources of asset returns and risks are known to be more dynamic than currently considered in the most basic asset allocation models such that a more nuanced and in some cases discretionary approach of the return and risk process must be considered when viewing the asset allocation process.

- The continued evolution of market structure, regulatory oversight, and trading technology has produced an increasing number of investable products as well as the means to monitor those products' interactions. Asset allocation is more than a simple breakdown of investment alternatives into stocks and bonds and now includes a broader range of traditional alternatives (private equity, real estate, and commodities) along with new alternatives such as hedge funds and managed futures. In addition, the ability to provide a greater number of unique targeted products designed to meet investors' needs has increased the asset allocation choices to investors.

NOTES

1. One of the least emphasized parts of asset allocation is that an asset's marginal risks to a market portfolio may change when assets that were once noninvestable are added to the investable pool, since the marginal risks change when the composition of the investable portfolio changes.
2. Most current investment textbooks (Bodie, Kane, and Marcus 2008; Reilly and Brown 2008) provide an excellent review of basic investment concepts, but for the most part they do not deal in great depth with the wide range of asset alternatives available to investors or with the range of alternative approaches to return and risk estimation. As discussed earlier, a book (including this one) published in 2010 was often written two years earlier (2008) using research material published in 2006, which was written in 2004 based on data from an even earlier period. In short, basic textbooks often emphasize material that is 6 to 10 years old.
3. By the 1950s, other economic concepts such as the existence of pure securities were also commonplace (Arrow and Debreu 1954).

4. An example of the continued debate as to the development of asset pricing is the debate as to whether the MPT and the CAPM are positive or normative in construction. The author(s) will leave it up to the readers to decide. As to the basis for positive and normative models, see Milton Friedman (1953), *Essays in Positive Economics*, University of Chicago Press. Note that Friedman gave proper credit to John Maynard Keynes. Friedman starts his introduction by pointing out that "In his admirable book on *The Scope and Method of Political Economy* John Neville Keynes distinguishes among '*a positive science* ... a body of systematized knowledge concerning what is; a *normative* or *regulative science* ..., a body of systematized knowledge discussing criteria of what ought to be.'"

5. This concept was later expanded with the growth of the capital asset pricing theory and the development of the capital market line in which the investment choice was really between two assets (the risk-free asset and the tangent risky portfolio).

6. The initial tests indicated that while the empirical return to risk relationships derived from the CAPM were superior to similar single-factor volatility based models, the residual error (unexplained return volatility) was so large as to question whether the underlying CAPM fit practice. The decade following the CAPM's introduction saw numerous articles (Roll, 1978) that detailed the problems with empirically testing the CAPM, which—while not denying the significant contributions of the CAPM—did imply that a more complete and dynamic process of risk estimation and return determination would more adequately describe the expected return and risk tradeoff.

7. For example, the Sharpe Ratio, defined as:

$$S_i = \frac{(\overline{R}_i - R_f)}{\sigma_i}$$

was meant to provide evidence of the relative benefit of two efficient risky portfolios on the capital market line and became the performance measurement vehicle of choice. Note that the Sharpe Ratio for an individual asset or portfolio merely provides evidence of the number of standard deviations the mean return of a portfolio/asset is from the risk-free rate.

8. It is hard to remember the importance of the initial studies which demonstrated the return to risk benefits of international investment. However the studies failed to emphasize the point that if the two international financial markets were separated to any great detail, the historical risk relationships may not tell us much about the expected return to risk relationships after the two countries became integrated (e.g., new market portfolio). The implications of that simple point—that as markets evolve, historical return to risk relationships may also evolve—has remained a problem for most asset allocation practitioners.

9. While lost to history, in the early 1970s the University of California at Berkeley held a series of seminars discussing the problem of tradable and nontradable assets in a market portfolio context.

10. Research in the 1930s also addressed the ability to manage investment horizon risk in fixed income through the use of duration based modeling. In addition, at the same time that Markowitz was publishing his views on MPT, Frank Redington (1952) was conducting research on how to best manage the risk of bond funds (duration).

11. While a summary of empirical tests of various equity based pricing models is not the focus of this book, the changing market structure and risk and return opportunities are. Just as the CAPM and its empirical variant (e.g., the market model) became a primary expected factor model for decades, the Fama and French three-factor model plus one (momentum) has somewhat dominated the academic world for the past 20 years, despite evidence that the underlying factors may have become less important in terms of explaining return. Thomas Kuhn (*The Structure of Scientific Revolutions*, 2nd ed. 1970) offers one explanation as to why the movement from one mode of explaining market returns to another is so difficult. The point is simple: there is risk in the use of any risk or return model.

12. One can always take this to various extremes. The fact that over time return to risk is correctly priced does not mean that at some point assets may offer known excess to risk opportunities for which others take the anticipated loss (e.g., government policy may force losses on some for the benefit of others); however, this is simply another risk that must be considered when investing. Some markets are more prone to mispricing than others. Fortunately, the markets that are most prone to mispricing are so small in valuation that they have little impact on global valuation, although they make interesting television.

CHAPTER 2

Measuring Risk

As we begin Chapter 2 of this book, it is worth restating our premise: asset allocation is basically the process by which assets are allocated between and among various investments based in part on investors' expected risk and expected return of those investments. In addition, asset allocation is premised on judgment and experience. Quantitative tools and models are simply reference points in our quest. Just as we use a compass to tell us true north, we know and understand that it cannot tell us which particular road to take. If Chapter 1 is any guide, the truth is that almost 60 years after the introduction of Modern Portfolio Theory we are still struggling to find ways to precisely define and measure factors that affect expected returns. However, since expected return is based on risk (however it is measured), the real focus in asset allocation should be on defining, measuring, and managing risk. This chapter offers investors a better sense of what risk measurement is and what it is not, and just as important, what it can do and what it is not able to provide, that is, investment certainty.

In the previous chapter, we determined that the basic message of modern finance is that higher risk should in the long run lead to higher return. Therefore, risk estimation should be the primary driver in asset allocation for the simple reason that an asset's price and therefore its expected return is a function of its underlying risk. Expected risk drives expected return. So what is risk and how do we measure it? Risk is multi-dimensional whereas the often used standard deviation of the historical return of an asset is merely one possible representation of asset risk. In fact, standard deviation merely offers an estimate of the probability of certain outcomes based on assumptions concerning the underlying asset's return distribution. In brief, standard deviation offers an estimate of the degree to which (e.g., the probability) a bad or good outcome is greater or less than the expected outcome.

   It is probably important in a chapter on risk and a book that emphasizes risk management to lay one's cards on the table early. Most of today's retail investor and high net worth industry based asset allocation models are centered on too simple an approach to return and risk estimation. For the most part they are based on portfolio return and risk estimates derived from historical performance with the assumption that the future risk of an asset or a portfolio mirrors that of the past. Moreover, they do not take into account many types of risk (e.g., uncertain changes in inflation or regulatory environment), changing correlations between and among assets, new assets, or the vagaries or herd instincts of investors. These models often assume an efficient market in ideas, information process, company structure and delivery systems as well as regulatory design. More damning, they are right just enough to be seductive, but not enough to protect against the event that can genuinely destroy wealth. They appeal to a central neurosis of the capitalist psyche—the world is fair, all information is understandable, and all asset allocation models exist in an efficient market of ideas in which each model is well reviewed and tested such that—while differing in emphasis—each approach stands on solid ground of academic theory and practitioner experience.

   Many asset allocation programs are developed to meet the expectations of a retail and high net worth market that simply does not have the statistical or theoretical background to use more advanced asset allocation procedures, all of which have their own unique advantages and disadvantages. In the previous chapter we focused primarily on the evolution of return estimation and the necessity of concentrating on the conditional nature of expected returns; that is, if risk changes then return changes. Risk measurement and risk management must therefore be our focus. Here is the hard part. Risk is almost impossible to define and is surely impossible to measure completely. It is simply too multi-dimensional. In this chapter we do not explore the history of risk or even present a framework for its presentation.[1] Instead some of the most basic approaches to investment risk management are reviewed. For more complex approaches to risk estimation at the individual asset or portfolio level, investors are directed to more complete presentations.[2] One reason for the emphasis on relatively simple risk estimation examples is that, for many, risk is simply any factor that may lead to the possibility of losing some or all of an investment. Risk management is simply the means by which one reduces the likelihood of that event as well as its magnitude and duration. The typical measures recommended for review are risk measures that identify various market risks such as beta as well as absolute risks such as standard deviation. While concentration on relatively simple approaches to risk analysis may seem to miss more subtle risk exposures, basic asset and portfolio risks are the foundation of any risk analysis. As pointed out by a famous academic researcher, if you need a sledgehammer to pound a nail, either you have the wrong hammer or you are trying to pound the wrong nail.

WHAT IS RISK?

To see why it may be nearly impossible to measure and define risk, consider the following example. Suppose Fifth National Bank announces that because of unexpected losses in its loan portfolio, it will have much lower earnings over the next several quarters and it has to lay off several hundred employees. The stock price of Fifth National Bank will obviously experience a sharp drop when the news reaches the market. But what does this event say about the riskiness of its stock price? If an employee of the bank has his entire retirement funds invested in the stock of the bank, this event represents a major risk. On the other hand, if a well-diversified portfolio is held where the stock of Fifth National Bank is only 1% of the entire portfolio, the risk posed by this event is rather small. This demonstrates that there cannot be a unique all encompassing measure of risk. Risk of an unexpected event depends on the investor's circumstance as well as the current economic environment. For instance, had this announcement taken place in 2005, its market impact would have been small, with most investors concluding that this represented a unique problem faced by Fifth National Bank. However, the same announcement in 2008 may have sent the entire stock market down a few percentage points since many investors may have regarded the announcement as the first of many other similar announcements by other financial institutions.

As shown in Exhibit 2.1, risk measurement covers a wide range of quantitative and qualitative risk dimensions. Moreover, given the multi-dimensional nature of the investing public (individual versus institutional, public versus private, domestic versus foreign), it is impossible to come up with a single one-size-fits-all asset allocation model. Keep this premise in mind as you read this book and ask yourself a simple question when a particular asset allocation model comes up with a proposed solution: Where is the fatal flaw in this model approach that can kill me?

In fact, as discussed in Chapter 1, a debate exists as to whether we can measure risk at all or at any level of certainty. It may very well be that we live in a world of uncertainty where only limited judgments can be made as to the probability of any single event happening. The understanding that there is "risk in the measurement of risk" has not stopped the financial industry from attempting to measure and quantify its existence. It is rather like the story of the individual asking for help in finding his watch only to

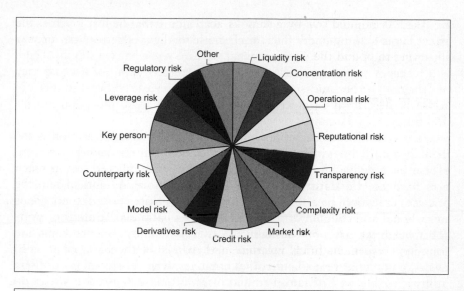

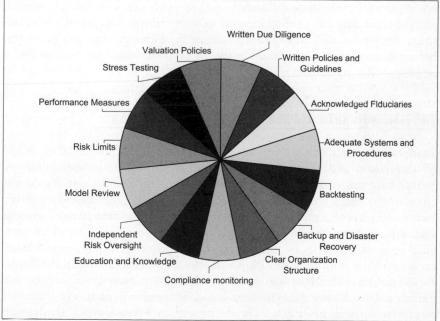

EXHIBIT 2.1 Array of Risk Determinants

be asked: Where did you lose it? When responding that he lost it across the street but is looking under the lamp because the light is better here directly illustrates the point. We measure what we can, not what we should. There is a tendency to measure variance or equity market beta not because they are the only or best measures of risk. They are measured because they are some of the central parameters used within most asset allocation models and they can be estimated based on historical data.

The central issue becomes almost rhetorical. If asset allocation is the primary means by which investors attempt to reach the highest expected return for a defined level of risk, then are investors exposed to too much risk from the standard methods of asset allocation? As anticipated, the answer here would be a resounding yes. In many asset allocation programs operational and counterparty risks related to a particular strategy or portfolio weighting are not considered. Most asset allocation programs use long-term return, historical volatility, and correlations when attempting to evaluate potential return and risk alternatives. The shortcomings of these approaches are well documented and offer little in defense. But where do we go from here? More advanced methods of asset allocation suggest a more dynamic means of tracking and understanding changed risk relationships. For many, this latter point is where the industry is going. However, before getting there let's examine the more traditional approaches for a moment.

TRADITIONAL APPROACHES TO RISK MEASUREMENT

Traditional asset allocation models often concentrate on historical estimates of correlation and volatility due to evidence of their long-run stability—but we also know that when estimates of correlation and volatility do not change over time, the primary driver of comparison portfolios is expected return. A classic example of this phenomenon is in the area of fixed income securities. Current yield to maturity on a one-year note (equal to one-year investment horizon) may be 2% but the historical average annual returns on the note may be 5%. Certainly, we would not use the 5% historical return as the current estimate of this year's expected return; however, many models of asset allocation are based on similar estimates of historical return for various asset classes when an estimate based on current conditions offers a better forecast. Similarly, the riskless Treasury Bill returns based on historical monthly data has a historical average return as well as a historical standard deviation, both of which have little relevance for the current T-Bill yield or its expected volatility going forward (e.g., forward rates).

Other examples associated with historical information are just as perplexing. For example, a classic problem in many basic asset allocation models is that they are unintentionally structured to maximize parameter estimation error; that is, they are often designed to pick the asset with the highest ex post returns and the lowest risk. These high return/low risk assets often have the highest estimation error (an overestimation of the true return and an underestimation of the true risk). As a result, next period's actual returns are often less than expected and next period's actual risk is often greater than expected. In brief, the problem with many of today's popular investor based asset allocation models, especially as they relate to risk management, is their tendency to focus on what we *can* measure in contrast to what we *should* measure. Armies of consultants, computer specialists, and risk managers are focused on technical and quantitative approaches that are easily understood and accepted by the investing public and regulatory authorities. For example, many money managers are forced by regulatory rules or market practice to track a particular benchmark. Here, by limiting the manager to tracking a particular benchmark, both return and risk are constrained. The manager is not permitted to consider a much wider range of risks such as drawdown and changing risk environments. This problem is expressly shown in 2008 when many mutual fund managers lost over 30% because they were required by regulation or convention to track a benchmark that lost 40%. This occurred while volatility on the benchmark rose from 20% to 40%. If managers had been permitted to target volatility while tracking the benchmark, losses could have been dramatically reduced. In the future, managers must focus on the risks they want to control, not necessarily the risk imbedded in the tools readily available to them.

With millions of references and multiple books on risk and risk management, it is statistically easy to choose the wrong book on risk management and asset allocation—even this one.[3] Why not then simply look for investment managers to solve our problem? Most individuals realize how little they know about the future and hope for someone to offer a low cost source of insurance. In fact, there exists an entire set of academic literature "on the manager as a free option." In short, the money we pay managers is in part (1) a payment for operational services and (2) a payment for an option on their services to manage risk such that they provide upside benefits while reducing downside risks. Unfortunately, if such investment wizards do not exist or if they do, they charge too much for their services, and we are left to our own devices. Here is the good news, pundits do not count (any one individual generally has little impact on market prices). A trillion-dollar-asset market with liquidity and transparency has little care for an individual's random beliefs. Only within thinly traded assets can any one individual make any real impact on asset prices, and such assets are such a small part of a global portfolio that they just do not matter to a diversified investor.

So here we transition from the use of well-known systematic algorithmic models of asset allocation that require little investor discretion to the argument for a dynamic approach to asset allocation that may require a larger degree of manager discretion. However, we must be careful that we do not fall back into the belief that the "new" improved model—while eliminating some of the problems and shortcomings of the earlier approach—provides an all-inclusive solution to the risk management problem. While we attempt to summarize some of the issues in many of the traditional model approaches to asset allocation, the size of the asset allocation problem overwhelms any individual approach if for the simple reason that there are too many individuals, each with their own unique set of investment concerns.

CLASSIC SHARPE RATIO

For much of this and the previous chapter we have emphasized the wide range of risks involved in asset allocation and security return estimation; however, for many, when the choice is between two (or more) assets, one way of ranking investments (the Sharpe Ratio) is based on simplifying risk into a single parameter (e.g., standard deviation). This ratio essentially divides the return of the security (after first subtracting the risk-free rate of return) by the price risk (standard deviation of return) of the security. The higher the ratio, the more favorable the assumed risk-return characteristics of the investment. The Sharpe Ratio is computed as:

$$S_i = \frac{\left(\bar{R}_i - R_f\right)}{\sigma_i}$$

where $\bar{R}_i$ is the estimated mean rate of return of the asset, R_f is the risk-free rate of return, and σ_i is the estimated standard deviation. This measure can be taken to show return obtained per unit of risk.

While the Sharpe Ratio does offer the ability to rank assets with different return and risk (measured as standard deviation), its use may be limited to comparing portfolios that may realistically be viewed as alternatives to one another. First, the Sharpe Ratio has little to say about the relative return to risk of individual securities. There is simply too much randomness in the price movement of individual securities to make the Sharpe Ratio of any real use at the individual asset level. Moreover, the

Sharpe Ratio does not take into account that the individual assets may themselves be used to create a portfolio. As discussed previously, the CAPM purports that the expected return of a security stems more from the covariance of the security with the market portfolio than from the stand-alone risk of the individual asset.

The Sharpe Ratio has other well-known shortcomings, including:

- **In periods of historical negative returns, the strict Sharpe comparisons have little value.** The Sharpe Ratio should be based on expected return and risk; however, in practice, actual performance over a particular period of time is often used. In periods of negative mean return, an asset may have a lower negative return as well as a lower standard deviation and yet report a lower Sharpe Ratio (e.g., more negative) than an alternative asset with a greater negative return and with a higher relative standard deviation.

- **Gaming the Sharpe Ratio.** A manager with a high Sharpe Ratio will get a close look from institutional investors even if the absolute returns are less than stellar. Investment managers employ a number of tactics to improve their measured Sharpe Ratio. For most asset classes, increasing the time interval used to measure standard deviation will result in a lower estimate of volatility. For example, the annualized standard deviation of daily returns is generally higher than weekly, which is again higher than monthly. Lengthening the measurement interval will not alter returns but will generally lower the standard deviation. Another trick involves the way returns are reported. If the annual return measure is derived by compounding the monthly returns, but the standard deviation estimate is calculated from the (not compounded) monthly returns, the Sharpe Ratio will be upwardly biased.

- **Options change the return distribution.** Rather than approximating a normal distribution, options produce skewed, kurtotic, or leptokurtotic return distributions, depending on the choice of option types and strikes. For example, writing a 10% out-of-the-money put on a portfolio indexed to the S&P 500 each month would probably generate 2% to 2.5% in annual premiums. Based on the empirical distribution of monthly returns, this strategy has a 2/3 chance of surviving three years without paying off once, and a 50% chance of surviving five years. If the manager is lucky, this strategy will show a significantly higher Sharpe Ratio, as the premiums flow directly to the bottom line with no apparent increase in volatility. Strategies that involve taking on default risk, liquidity risk, or other forms of catastrophe risk have the same ability to report an upwardly biased Sharpe Ratio.

- **Smoothing is also a source of potential bias.**[4] Some illiquid investments are priced using models, which can be used to smooth investment returns. The investment manager (or the pricing model employed by the manager or outside pricing service) may bias returns in ways that understate monthly gains or losses, thereby reducing reported volatility.

OTHER MEASURES OF RISK ASSESSMENT

Security and Asset Risk Measurement

One potential disadvantage of the Sharpe Ratio measure is that even if it is used to compare similar asset class portfolios it may not provide a reasonable basis for comparison when portfolios exist within a multi-asset class portfolio (e.g., commodities, stocks, bonds, private equity) since the Sharpe Ratio is based on a portfolio's stand-alone variance, and not its covariance with other assets that are included in a multi-asset portfolio. Another measure suggested in the literature is the Treynor measure.[5] This measure flows from an understanding of CAPM. The Treynor model is based on the belief that the return of an asset should equal the risk-free rate added together with some "risk premium" multiplied by the asset's sensitivity to the market portfolio, called "beta." The Treynor measure is generally measured as:

$$T_i = \frac{(E(R_i) - R_f)}{\beta_i}$$

As a consequence, the Treynor measure addresses one of the drawbacks mentioned earlier regarding the Sharpe Ratio. The Treynor measure works well when adding assets to a multi-asset market portfolio as the betas of the assets can be used as a surrogate for marginal risk of adding the asset to the multi-asset market portfolio. Unfortunately, as discussed in Chapter 1, the CAPM is not as generally accepted today as it was at its inception —almost 40 years ago. Finding the "market portfolio" is a more difficult task than was initially believed.[6] Proxies may of course be used but it is not clear what that proxy should be (whether the portfolio can be taken as domestic-only for a U.S.-based investor or how much the portfolio should hold of nonequity based assets). Therefore, the Treynor measure also has its potential shortcomings. In short, both theoretical and empirical problems exist in the measurement of beta as indicated in research on the use of multi-factor return estimation and conditional beta estimation.

Skewness and Kurtosis

In much of traditional asset return analysis, an asset's return distribution is assumed to be normally distributed and adequately described by its first two moments (expected return and variance). In fact, securities often exhibit additional return characteristics in which the probability of a security's expected return in the extremes is often greater than that described by a simple normal distribution. An asset's return distribution is often better described not only by its expected return and variance but also by its higher moments of skewness or kurtosis. Skewness and kurtosis are statistical terms that, along with the mean and standard deviation, help describe a probability distribution. The mean (average) of a random variable describes the location, the standard deviation describes the spread of the distribution, and the skewness helps describe the overall shape (left or right), while the kurtosis helps describe the peakedness of the distribution. Relative to a normal distribution, big gains (losses) are more frequent with a positively (negatively) skewed distribution. Relative to a normal distribution, a distribution with significant kurtosis has greater probability of observations around the mean as well as greater probability of outside returns (negative or positive).

There are several issues involved in measuring skewness or kurtosis. First, sample dependent measures of skewness and kurtosis are merely estimates of the skewness and kurtosis of the underlying true distribution. While it is rarely shown, skewness and kurtosis have their own risk parameter; that is, the standard error of skewness is approximated by $\sqrt{6/n}$ while the standard error of kurtosis is approximated by $\sqrt{24/n}$, where n is the number of observations. One should look to see not if the skewness is positive or negative but if it is significantly different from zero. Often what is shown as skewness and kurtosis is simply not significantly different from what would be expected if the true distribution were normal.

This is not to say that the measures are not important. For instance, positive skewness is the goal of most investors. However, even if individual investment returns are often highly skewed, portfolios such as the S&P 500 index or the other investment strategy indices do not exhibit much skewness. The only way an investor can achieve a substantially skewed return is by limiting the number of assets in a portfolio to a few, highly skewed investments (however, the lack of diversification in this portfolio might outweigh the benefits of skewness) or perhaps by creating a skewed distribution through the purchase of insurance (e.g., options), which limits the losses on an investment strategy. Of course, such a strategy will impact other parameters of the distribution, namely, its standard deviation and more importantly its mean.

Semi-variance

Variance is a measure of deviation from the mean. In calculating the variance, we assign the same weight to the returns that are above the mean as those assigned to the returns that are below the mean. Clearly, most investors are only concerned with returns that are below the mean. For this reason, some practitioners have advocated the use of semi-variance. The formula for estimating the historical variance is given by

$$\frac{1}{N} \sum_{t=1}^{N} ((R_t - E(R))^2$$

while the historical semi-variance is estimated using the following formula

$$\frac{1}{N'} \sum_{t=1}^{N} (\min[0, R_t - E(R)])^2$$

where N' is number of observations that are below the mean.

When the return distributions are approximately symmetrical, the two measures of the risk (standard deviation and semi-variance) will be relatively the same. However, when returns are not symmetrical, the two measures of risk will rank asset classes differently. This means that if the portfolio optimization is over asset classes that have skewed return distributions, the composition of the efficient frontier could drastically change.

PORTFOLIO RISK MEASURES

In a world of multiple markets and opportunities, investors are very rarely faced with the choice of just two assets (unless one is investing along the capital market line). When several assets are held together, they behave quite differently from an average of the assets' individual behaviors. One general observation is that the more assets are held in the portfolio, the lower the total risk of the portfolio. Exhibit 2.2 shows how the expected standard deviation of a portfolio composed of equally weighted assets decreases as the number of assets increases. If the number of assets is large enough, the total variance does in fact stem more from the covariances than from the individual variances of the assets. It is, in other words, more important how the assets tend to move together than how much each individual asset fluctuates in value. However, the figure has limitations. First, it assumes equal weighting of the assets. Second, it is an estimation of the expected standard deviation. In short, there is risk even in the estimation

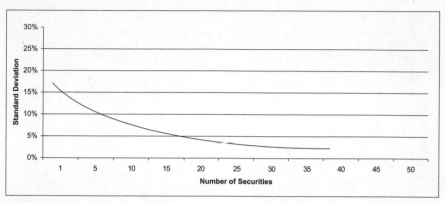

EXHIBIT 2.2 Naïve Diversification—Impact on Variance of Adding Securities/Assets

of risk. In Exhibit 2.2, the line shown is an average of all the sample point estimates of the relationship between portfolio size and standard deviation. For any one sample portfolio of size *n*, the actual standard deviation of that sample could vary widely from that shown in Exhibit 2.2.

Rather than using simple rules based assumptions as to the impact of adding assets to a diversified portfolio, the total risk (variance) of a portfolio of investments can be directly computed as:[7]

$$\sigma_p^2 = \sum_{j=1}^{n} \sum_{i-j}^{n} x_i x_j \rho_{ij} \sigma_i \sigma_j$$

where the x_i and x_j are the weights of each investment, the ρ_{ij} are the correlations between two investments, and the σ_i and σ_j are the standard deviations of each investment.[8] If the level of risk is varied and that maximum return is calculated for each level, the result can be plotted in a diagram that has the form of an arc. The arc is called the efficient frontier, as it shows the most efficient allocation of funds (portfolio) possible at each level of risk. Even the efficient frontier, as shown in Exhibit 2.3, has issues.

There may be a reason that Modern Portfolio Theory is called MPT and not MPF, Modern Portfolio Fact. While the theory of risk reduction of combining two assets that react differently to unexpected changes in economic information is sound, in practice the result may be much different than expected. The word "expected" is important. MPT is based on expectations, that is, expected returns, expected volatility, and expected correlations. Even in the world of expectations, there is really no one expected efficient frontier. Note that the efficient frontier line equates expected return

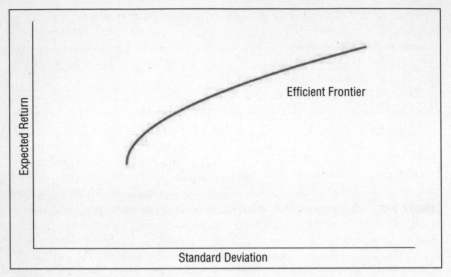

EXHIBIT 2.3   Efficient Frontier

with expected volatility. In fact, there is a distribution of potential returns around the efficient line that are consistent with a particular level of expected volatility.

In short, the efficient line should really look more like an ever increasing band with the probability of return becoming wider and wider as an investor moves up the risk scale. Finally, the end point of the efficient frontier is a single point (a single asset with the greatest return to risk tradeoff). As an investor moves down the efficient frontier, he is generally adding individual assets or combinations of assets to form the efficient frontier. At the lower end of the efficient frontier, the portfolio generally has a greater number of assets in order to find that portfolio with the lowest risk. As discussed above, the estimation error in the actual measured efficient frontier generally declines as an investor moves from the far right to the far left.

This would not be so troubling if there were some assurance that Exhibit 2.3 reflected an investor's actual performance. In practice, we must come up with estimates of the expected returns, standard deviations, and correlations. There are libraries of statistical books dedicated to the simple task of coming up with estimates of the parameters used in MPT. Here is the point: It is not simple. For example, (1) for what period is one estimating the parameters (week, month, year)? and (2) how constant are the estimates (e.g., do they change and, if they do, do we have statistical models that permit us to systematically reflect those changes?)? There are many more issues in parameter estimation, but probably the biggest is that when two assets exist with the same true expected return, standard deviation, and correlation but when the risk parameter is often estimated with error (e.g., standard deviation is larger or smaller than its true standard deviation), the procedure for determining the efficient frontier always picks the asset with the downward bias risk estimate (e.g., the lower estimated standard deviation) and the upward bias return estimate.

As a result, the expected risk based on historical data will generally underestimate the true risk (and the expected return based on historical data will generally overestimate the true return). The investor will generally be disappointed even if things come out as expected in the future based on the true returns and risk (but not the historical). In bringing this discussion to a conclusion, there are two final points. The efficient frontier is based on price risk (standard deviation of return) but not all of the associated risks of holding an asset. While the efficient frontier may offer a collection of top portfolio returns for a level of standard deviation, it tells us nothing about other risks that may be imbedded in a portfolio. Moreover, as noted, not all portfolios are equal in terms of the estimation error in the measured risk. Mind you, the point to the farthest right is a single asset (that asset with the highest return to risk). No diversification there.

The problem in actually using MPT in practice can be mitigated by adding a host of constraints and mathematical corrections, but the problems can never be totally removed. An expanding universe can be reduced to an expanding galaxy, but it is not possible to reduce the universe to a planet. When considering asset allocation, focus on the positives of the model, not just the negatives. The simple truth is that two assets may respond differently to unexpected changes in information simply because they are structured to respond differently (e.g., if personal income stays the same, an unexpected increase in Ford sales probably means a unexpected decrease in General Motors sales), so if the informational release is unknown, better to hold two assets (or in this case two car stocks) rather than one.

OTHER MEASURES OF PORTFOLIO RISK MEASUREMENT

While the standard deviation of a portfolio provides a measure of the total price risk of a portfolio, it fails to provide information on a wide range of the individual factors impacting that risk. As discussed previously, there exists a broad range of definitions of risk. For many, risk is defined as any factor that may lead to the possibility of losing some or all of an investment as well as the magnitude and duration of that loss, while portfolio standard deviation centers on the probability of loss. However, for those who focus on risk measures beyond standard deviation of return, risk analysis at the portfolio level includes a wide range of analysis, including:[9]

- **Market Risk Analysis** (changes in the yield curve or other market-related variables) on the performance of the portfolio as well as the primary asset sectors. Changes in factors such as interest rate movements, yield curve shifts, and other economic factors provide additional information on the macro sensitivity of the portfolio to economic factors.
- **Performance Attribution:** Attribution analysis, which measures the sources of return on an asset class as well as sector selection as a percentage of total return.
- **Correlation Analysis:** Correlation within an asset class (e.g., strategies, security sectors, geographical regions) and across asset classes.
- **Risk Decomposition:** Attributed risk of each investment to total portfolio return standard deviation. Risk decomposition can also be conducted at other levels of risk (credit, higher moments).
- **Tracking Error:** The amount by which a given asset deviates from its benchmark within the asset allocation process. It is important to note that high correlation between an asset and its benchmark may not indicate low tracking error. An asset with a high standard deviation (alone or relative to the benchmark) may have a high level of tracking error despite reporting a high correlation with the benchmark.
- **Risk Factor Sensitivity Analysis:** Measure incremental risk for an individual asset as it relates to specific factors while holding others constant.

Several of the above approaches to risk estimation and control are detailed at greater length in Chapter 9. However, it is important to remind investors that each of us may have a different set of investment goals such that any one risk management approach may not meet our needs. For example, Surplus-at-Risk (SAR)/Liability Driven Investment (LDI) often seeks to minimize risk relative to liabilities, rather than broad, return based benchmarks with the goal of delivering nominal, inflation-linked, or wage-linked defined benefits.

VALUE AT RISK

A chapter on risk and what it is would not be complete (and it never is) without a mention of the concept of "value at risk" or VaR. For a given portfolio, probability, and time horizon, VaR is defined as the loss that is expected to be exceeded with the given probability, over the given time horizon under normal market conditions assuming that there is no portfolio rebalancing. For example, if a portfolio of stocks has a one-day VaR of $1 million at the 95% confidence level, then there is 5% chance that the one-day loss of the portfolio could exceed $1 million assuming normal market conditions and no intra day rebalancing.

If it is assumed that returns are normally distributed and there exists an estimate of the standard deviation then an estimate of the probability of a bad outcome can be surmised. However, the problem then becomes how to measure standard deviation and what if the measured standard deviation depends on the interval used or the historical period of analysis. Thus, one of the principal decisions to be made when measuring risk or any return based statistical parameter is the return interval to be employed and the period of analysis. Exhibits 2.4 and 2.5 present results of the impact on the

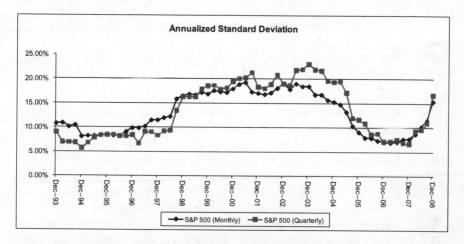

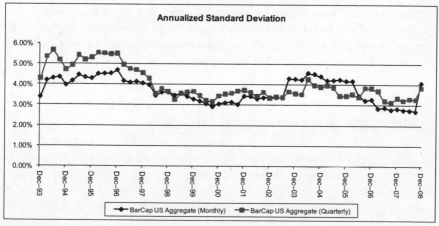

EXHIBIT 2.4 Rolling Three-Year Monthly and Quarterly Interval Standard Deviations

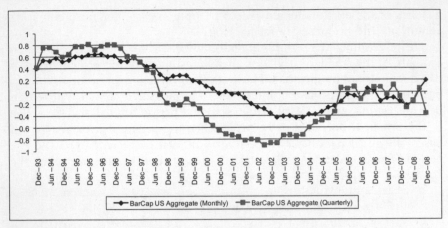

EXHIBIT 2.5   Barclays Capital U.S. Aggregate Rolling Three-Year Monthly and Quarterly Interval Correlation with S&P 500

use of quarterly and monthly return intervals using rolling three-year data on standard deviation of the S&P 500 and Barclays Capital U.S. Aggregate Bond Index and the rolling correlation of the Barclays Capital U.S. Aggregate Bond Index with the S&P 500. Results in Exhibit 2.4 and 2.5 indicate the sensitivity of the parameter (standard deviation or correlation) to the use of return interval and period of analysis. Therefore, Caveat Emptor 1 is that results (different estimates of volatility) may differ when reviewing results from different periods and using different return intervals.[10] Caveat Emptor 2 is that results are also sensitive to the length of the estimation period (one year, two years, three years). Caveat Emptor 3 is that for the period analyzed (1991 to 2008) there are only six periods of independent analysis over 18 years. For all the rest there are periods of common data use.[11]

WHAT EVERY INVESTOR SHOULD REMEMBER

- Since expected return is based on expected risk, the real focus in asset allocation is on defining, measuring, and managing expected risk.
- Risk is almost impossible to define and is surely impossible to measure completely. It is simply too multi-dimensional in nature. Moreover, given the multi-dimensional nature of the investing

public (individual versus institutional, private versus public), it is impossible to come up with a single one-size-fits-all asset allocation model.

- The problem remains that if asset allocation is the primary means by which investors attempt to reach the highest expected return at the lowest level of risk, then investors are simply exposed to too much risk from many of the more simplified methods of asset allocation. Most current asset allocation models use long-term return, historical volatility, and correlation when attempting to evaluate potential return and risk alternatives. The shortcomings of such models are obvious in current global markets in which the dynamics of technology, regulation, and economics make historic data of little use and require a more dynamic means of tracking changing risk relationships.

NOTES

1. For a general history of the development of the concept of risk, see Peter Bernstein (1996).
2. Rather than mentioning any one source, investors are directed to web sites such as www.gloriamundi.com.
3. Thomas Friedman, author of *The World Is Flat* (Farrar, Straus, and Giroux, 2005), was criticized recently for writing a new book that questioned some of his earlier writings. The critic was upset that he had paid $50 for a book that the author later had issues with. Full disclosure: The world changes such that what was right in the past may be wrong in the future, including some of the conclusions expressed in this book.
4. Other means of truncating returns are also available. There is a relatively simple derivative structure that can be set up as a swap: You pay the best and worst returns for your benchmark index each year, and the counterparty pays a fixed cash flow and hedges the risk in the open market. Assuming your portfolio has a low tracking error to the benchmark, this will be equivalent to eliminating your best and worst returns. If no counterparty is willing to take the risk, the strategy can be implemented directly using options.
5. See Treynor (1965).
6. For purposes of clarity, theoretical and empirical issues in the Sharpe Ratio were well known by most individuals from the very start. However, as is often pointed out it is better to light a candle than curse the darkness. The Sharpe model (whatever its known shortcomings) has had a tremendous beneficial effect on focusing investors on the risk component in any investment decision.

7. The market model and the CAPM show the initial importance of beta estimation in initial asset allocation modeling. In the 1960s through the 1980s, computer power was such that minimizing calculations could speed up complex operations. Considerable academic research was dedicated to efficient beta determination. In recent years, the increased speed of computers is such that direct use of correlations and their calculation has become paramount; however, the underlying concern remains the same.

8. It is obvious but it is necessary to point out that an asset can have a high correlation with another asset but a low beta simply if its standard deviation is low or an asset can have a low correlation with another asset but a high beta if its relative standard deviation is high. In short, beta does not equal correlation.

9. This section is presented in terms of individual securities or asset classes. The analysis can also be conducted at the manager level for which each manager provides access to a particular asset class or strategy.

10. Another classic example of how measurement interval impacts return and risk estimation is the case where one used the average yield during a month to measure yield. Two months may have the same average yield and the change between the two months is zero. However, if one used daily end of month data one could see the yield rising in month one and declining in month two such that the end of month yield change would be dramatic.

11. There are various approaches to sample selection (Bootstrapping—random sample selection from past data) or parameter estimation (Monte Carlo simulation—random sample selection from a presumed distribution) that are beyond the scope of this book. Each has its benefits and each has its costs.

CHAPTER 3

Alpha and Beta, and the Search for a True Measure of Manager Value

While asset allocation is basically the process by which an investor allocates assets between investments based on expected risk and return, much of investment analysis is centered on the determination of which individual investments, portfolios, or asset classes may offer superior returns to other comparable securities, portfolios, or asset classes. Chapter 3 concentrates on reviewing the principal tools (alpha and beta) by which we attempt to determine fundamental asset risk as well as the ability of managers to create value. We show that even in the simple world of single-factor risk models (standard deviation, skewness, market beta) as well as in more complex models of risk and return determination, the risk models themselves may get in the way of understanding the fundamental risks we face.

In short, there is hidden risk in assuming that we know how to define risk. There is also what we term model risk imbedded in the actual models that we use for risk estimation or manager alpha determination. For instance, we show that most single-factor risk based models provide only a limited means of exploring asset risk or of determining true manager alpha. As an alternative, we explore the use of multi-factor as well as simple replication/tracking approaches to determine the additional value that a manager may bring to the investment process.

WHAT IS ALPHA?

In most investment seminars and conferences, manager after manager remains intent on proving their ability to produce something they refer to as "alpha," or the excess return relative to a comparable non-manager based investment of comparable risk. This alpha therefore represents the additional return a manager may add to the investment process that does not impact the underlying risk of the portfolio. Each manager and investor has their own unique take on what alpha is and how it should be measured. It should come as no surprise that academics and practitioners have also weighed in on the central questions of this issue:

- What is alpha?
- Since alpha is often measured in terms of beta, what is the best way to measure the beta of an investment strategy?
- Since beta is not an all-encompassing measure of risk, what are its benefits and what are its limitations?
- As one moves from single-factor risk models such as beta, what benefits exist from more multi-factor models of return estimation?
- In recent years, there has been an increase in the use of systematic algorithmic based tracking strategies to capture the expected return process of individual strategies. Is this the future?

In the world of academics, an active manager's performance alpha is generally defined as the excess return to active management adjusted for risk. A better definition of alpha would be the return adjusted for the return of a comparably risky investable "non-actively managed" asset or portfolio. The expected return on a comparably risky non-actively managed investment strategy is often either derived from academic theory or statistically derived from historical pricing relationships. The primary issue, of course, remains how to create a comparably risky investable non-actively managed asset. Even when one believes in the use of ex ante equilibrium (e.g., CAPM) or arbitrage (e.g., APT) models of expected return, problems in empirically estimating the required parameters usually results in alpha being determined using statistical models based on the underlying theoretical model.

As generally measured in a statistical sense, the term alpha is often derived from a linear regression in which the equation that relates an observed variable y (asset return) to some other factor x (market index) is written as:

$$y = \alpha + \beta x + \varepsilon$$

The first term, α (alpha) represents the intercept; β (beta) represents the slope; and ε (epsilon) represents a random error term. In finance, the above equation is often known as the market model. The alpha term is important in finance because it represents the return that the investor would receive even if the benchmark had a zero return or the beta of the investment is zero. Rearranging the above equation (and ignoring the error term for now), we can restate the equation to focus on the alpha:

$$\alpha = y - \beta x$$

Alpha measured using raw returns rather than excess returns is not strictly correct because it assumes that the cost of leverage is zero. Therefore, the return in excess of the risk-free return is the proper estimate of alpha (whether it is single-factor or multi-factor)

$$\alpha = (E(R_i) - R_f) - \beta(E(R_m) - R_f)$$

where

$E(R_i)$ = Expected return on investment i
R_f = Riskless rate of return
$E(R_m)$ = Rate of return on benchmark

Given the knowledge that R_m may not adequately measure the market portfolio, the equation has been expanded to cover a number of additional risk factors that impact expected return.

$$\alpha_i = (E(R_i) - R_f) - \beta_{i1}(E(B_1) - R_f) - \beta_{i2}(E(B_2) - R_f) - \ldots$$

where

$E(B_j)$ = Expected rate of return on investable benchmark j.

Finally, the multi-factor model can be expanded by allowing the betas to change through time. For example, if a manager has market timing skill, then she could increase (decrease) the beta if she anticipates a relatively high (low) rate of return on the market. In some cases the beta may change because of changes in the market environment. For example, to the degree that fund flows increase when markets are rising, cash holdings of fund managers may initially increase during rising markets. The reason is that it may take the fund manager several days to invest the new funds. Under such a circumstance, the beta of the fund will initially decline because of increased cash holdings. This type of conditional model can be estimated as follows (we are going to use the CAPM as an example):

$$R_{it} - R_f = \alpha_i + \beta_{it} \times (R_{mt} - R_f) + \varepsilon_{it}$$

where

R_{it} = Rate of return on investment i at time t
R_{mt} = Rate of return on the market at time t
β_{it} = Beta of the investment with respect to the market at time t.

Next, we need to model the beta. Suppose we believe that a fund manager uses VIX to adjust the beta of her portfolio. Then the beta can be modeled as:

$$\beta_{it} = a + b \times VIX_{t-1}$$

where a and b are parameters of the "beta model" that we need to estimate. Note that the beta is assumed to depend on the lagged value of the VIX. This means we are assuming that the manager looks at the lagged value of VIX to change the beta. On the other hand, if we believe that the manager has some skill in predicting the future value of VIX, we may use the current value of VIX. In its present form the final expression for alpha would look like this:

$$\alpha_i = E(R_i) - R_f - (a_i E(R_m - R_f) + b_i VIX_{t-1} E(R_m - R_f))$$

The same idea can be used to present the conditional version of the multi-factor model. Of course, the key is to identify the relevant factors. For many actively managed portfolios, it may be impossible to determine what the relevant factors are because they represent the skill that the manager is bringing to the table.

While simple or conditional multi-factor models are preferred by the academic community, the problem remains that practitioners prefer to use their own model. This means different investment managers and consultants offer an estimate of alpha that may not be easily comparable across investment managers. Various alternatives used by practitioners are given in Exhibit 3.1.

The equations are all correct under very limited circumstances. However, a few points about measurement of investment performance may be of value:

- The risk free rate benchmark is typically used by edge fund and assumes that the fund has zero beta and that investors do not demand a premium for volatility.

EXHIBIT 3.1 Alpha Determination: Alternative Risk-Adjusted Benchmarks

Alpha Benchmark Model	Alpha Determination	Alpha
T-Bill	$E(R_i) - R_f$	5.26%
CAPM	$\alpha = (E(R_i) - R_f) - \beta(E(R_m) - R_f)$	4.42%
Sharpe Ratio	$\alpha = (E(R_i) - R_f) - \left(\dfrac{E(R_m) - R_f}{\sigma_m} \times \sigma_i \right)$	.68%
Multi-Factor	$\alpha_i = (E(R_i) - R_f) - \beta_{i1}(E(B_1) - R_f) + (\beta_{i2}(E(B_2) - R_f) - ...)$	−0.97%

- The problems with the CAPM based benchmark have already been discussed. It assumes that market risk is the only relevant source of risk.
- The Sharpe Ratio based model assumes in part that there exists a known market portfolio Sharpe Ratio (e.g., .70).
- In the case of multi-factor models, identifying the factors is the most serious problem.
- More modern variants of these models (e.g., the conditional version) pose other problems. For example, because more risk parameters have to be estimated, the estimation error of the parameters will increase unless sufficient return data are available. For instance, since the average life of hedge funds is about five years, most of these models cannot be applied to this asset class.

When considering the benefit of adding an asset to an existing portfolio, an alternative approach known as the break-even analysis is often used. Modern pricing theory emphasizes the risk of an asset as its marginal contribution to the risk of an investor's portfolio. Break-even analysis is often used to test for the potential contribution of an asset to the risk/return profile of an existing stand-alone portfolio. The break-even (R_c) and excess break-even rate of return (EBK) is often computed as follows:

$$E(R_c) = \left(\frac{E(R_p) - R_f}{\sigma_p} \right)(\rho_{cp})\sigma_c + R_f$$

$$EBK = R_c - \left[\left(\frac{E(R_p) - R_f}{\sigma_p} \right)(\rho_{cp})\sigma_c + R_f \right]$$

where

$E(R_c)$ = Break-even rate of return required for the asset to improve the Sharpe Ratio of alternative index p
R_c = Rate of return on asset c
R_f = Riskless rate of return
$E(R_p)$ = Rate of return on alternative index p
ρ_{cp} = Correlation coefficient between asset c and alternative benchmark p
σ_c = Standard deviation of asset c
σ_p = Standard deviation of alternative index p

First, it is important to realize that the above expression is based on the assumption that only mean and variance matter in evaluating the risk-return profile of a portfolio. Second, one must be familiar with the potential problems that can arise in using this expression. For example, if there is a period of high historical R_f, then almost any asset would fail to have a return (R_c) in excess of its EBK. Further, the EBK is dependent on the measurement of correlation. Some investment managers emphasize the non-correlation of their strategy with the S&P 500 and then turn around and offer a comparison of their Sharpe Ratio with that of the S&P 500 to indicate superior alpha performance. Even in this case, the comparison will not indicate its potential alpha benefit relative to other, non-tested, active manager portfolios; nor does it provide an indication of whether another like investment will have produced a similar or even greater increase in the Sharpe Ratio of the newly constructed portfolio. In short, the ability of a manager to achieve alpha is based on the ability to achieve a return via an active strategy, that is, greater than what could be achieved using a passive strategy designed to capture the same risks and hence the same expected returns of the active strategy. If that strategy fits into the existing portfolio and helps the investor achieve his/her unique goals, it should be added to the portfolio as an additional investment in contrast to a similar passive strategy.[1]

As mentioned previously, multi-factor models of alpha determination should be used whenever an investor is concerned with dimensions of risk not covered by the market risk. One of the most common and simplest methods that can be used to build multi-factor models is to use portfolios that represent returns to various factors (they are called factor mimicking portfolios).

In general, these factor portfolios are used for two purposes. First, to measure the exposure of a portfolio or an asset to the factor that is represented by the factor portfolio. For example, by running a regression of the excess return of a manager's return against the return to the factor portfolio that represents the size factor, we measure the manager's exposure to this risk: does the manager have a significant exposure to the performance of small cap stocks? Second, the factor portfolio can be used to measure the return to the factor. For example, the mean return to the factor portfolio representing the size factor can be used to measure the expected return to this factor. If the return to this factor is deemed to be attractive, an investor may decide to shift to a portfolio that has a relatively large exposure to small cap stocks. This can then be used to measure a manager's return from this source.

There are several methods for creating factor portfolios. The most common approach is to rank a large of number of securities according to a characteristic that we wish to represent by a factor portfolio. For example, suppose we wish to create a factor portfolio that represents the inflation factor or risk. Suppose the universe of assets we wish to consider is the U.S.

stock market. First, we calculate the beta of all stocks with respect to inflation rate (this can be done using a simple regression). Second, we rank all the stocks according to size of their betas. Next, we create two equally weighted portfolios. The first one will consist of the 25% of the firms with highest exposure to inflation and the second will consist of the 25% of the firms with lowest exposure to inflation. Finally, we "go short" the low inflation exposure portfolio and "go long" the high inflation exposure portfolio. The return to this position, which requires no investment in theory, represents the return to the factor portfolio representing inflation risk. If the average return on this portfolio is positive, then we may conclude that expected return to inflation exposure is positive. In the same manner one can create factor portfolios representing size, value/growth, P/E, momentum, industry, and others.

One of the most commonly used factor models is the Fama-French 4-factor model. The four factors are:

1. Excess return to the market
2. High book value minus low book value (HML)
3. Small minus big (SMB)
4. Up minus down (UMD)

That is, HML represents returns to a long/short portfolio sorted on book-to-market, with high book-to-market stocks long and low book-to-market stocks short. SMB represents returns to a long/short portfolio, with small cap stocks long and large cap stocks short. UMD represents returns to a long/short portfolio, with past winners long and past losers short.

For our hedge fund indices we estimate the following regression model:

$$R_{it} - R_f = a_i + b_i (R_{mt} - R_f) + h_i \times HML_t + s_i \times SMB_t + u_i \times UMD_t + \varepsilon_{it}$$

That is, we regress the excess returns of our investment, $R_{it} - R_f$, on the excess returns of the market, $R_{mt} - R_f$, and returns on a three-factor portfolio: HML_t, SMB_t, and UMD_t. The residual ε_{it} captures any other variation in excess returns that cannot be explained by the factors.

Again, careful use of the results of these models is required. For instance, returns to some of the factors may not be significant all the time and even the sign may change. Everyone remembers how growth stocks outperformed value stocks during the Internet bubble of 1999 to 2000 and then how value stocks significantly outperformed growth stocks during the post bubble period of 2001 to 2003.

ISSUES IN ALPHA AND BETA DETERMINATION

Extensive academic and practitioner literature exists on asset pricing and return generating models. In general, these expected return models are based on an expected relationship between expected returns and the underlying risk factors driving those expected returns. To the extent that returns to those risk factors can be predicted, then that knowledge can be used to determine asset weighting between various asset classes.[2] Unfortunately, academic research has generally concluded that it is not possible to obtain accurate estimates of future returns to macroeconomic factors such that, as a result, future expected returns are often based on subjective estimates related to long term historical returns to risk factors.

In the investment area one of the primary, if not the essential, questions is the value of active management relative to manager based or security/market factor passive investable indices. Most investors are aware of the number of articles as well as books that attempt to address the value of active versus passive management. For years, this discussion was primarily limited to the traditional stock and bond area as informational and trading costs limited its use in the traditional alternative investments (commodities and private equity) area as well as in the area of modern alternatives (hedge funds and CTAs). Today, as new trading instruments become available, a number of new passive products (ETFs and replication products) have become available that attempt to mimic the performance of various active traditional as well as alternative investment strategies. Exhibit 3.2 displays changes in the market perception of both traditional and alternative assets as more academic research regarding the value added by active management has become available.

In *Alice in Wonderland*, Alice asks the Cheshire cat what path to take. The cat asks in return: Where do you want to go? Alice replies that she has no idea. The cat responds: Then it really doesn't matter which path you take. For managers, however, it does matter which path they take. Is alpha to be used as a marketing device, or as a measure of comparable risk/return performance? If managers wish to define alpha to fit their own marketing purposes and use alpha to sell a product, it is understandable from a product management viewpoint, if not desirable from an academic or investor focus. However, when faced with an alpha estimate in a product marketing document, an investor should never mistake this "marketing alpha" for perhaps a more theoretically defensible "performance alpha."

In sum, if the manager can choose asset positions with a higher return (but the same ex ante risk) to some comparable naive passive investment position, then that person can be said to achieve a positive performance alpha. But performance alpha is all about properly measured return relative

Dominant Paradigm: 1960–2000			Emerging Paradigm: 2000–Present	
Traditional Assets	Alternative Investments		Traditional Assets	Alternative Investments
Beta Return	Beta Return		Beta Return	Beta Return
	Alpha Return			Alpha Return
Alpha Return			Alpha Return	

Traditional Assets			Alternatives
Stock	Gov Bond	Corp Bonds	Traditional and Modern
Alpha	Alpha	Alpha	Alpha
Beta	Beta	Beta	
			Beta
Equity Risks	Interest Rate Risks	Interest Rate and Credit Risks	Multi-Factor Risks

EXHIBIT 3.2 Changing Importance of Alpha and Beta in Return Estimation

to a benchmark. For traditional portfolios such as mutual funds the multi-factor models discussed above tend to do a reasonable job. Of course, the set of factors may be expanded to include factor portfolios representing risks such as inflation, interest rate, or currency risks.

Unfortunately, when it comes to actively managed portfolios that have broad mandates (e.g., hedge funds or CTAs), we have no simple method for establishing this benchmark except under very restrictive situations. But at the very least, we do know that investment decisions involve some risk and that even similar investment strategies often entail different risk exposures (e.g., leverage), so the riskless rate is probably not appropriate as a performance benchmark for hedge funds. How much return should be added and what method should be used to determine the incremental return to add to the risk-free rate to obtain the appropriate return comparison remains open for discussion. For instance, in a recent study (Fernandez, 2009a), the average Market Risk Premium (6.3%) used in 2008 by finance professors in the United States was higher than the one (5.3%) used by their colleagues in Europe. Fernandez also reports statistics for 18 countries, which show that the average MRP used in 2008 ranges from 4.1% (Belgium) to 10.5% (India). Similarly wide ranges exist in estimates of beta. For example, Fernandez (2009b) reports that among various web and database sources the minimum and maximum reported betas for Coca-Cola ranged from a high of 0.80 to a low of 0.31. Similar beta ranges existed for a wide range of other well-known firms.

PROBLEMS IN ALPHA AND BETA DETERMINATION

Perceived wisdom suggests that the growth of the asset management industry is substantially due to the superior returns offered by fund managers. Investors should realize that there is neither consensus on exactly what constitutes "superior" returns, nor is there a methodology to identify and describe such returns on a quantitative basis. To the typical industry participant, "alpha" means the incremental return attributable to a manager relative to a specified benchmark, and as such, attempts to measure that incremental return on an ex post basis by estimating a least squares regression of manager performance against the specified benchmark. The key is that the benchmark must be well specified in measuring the risk of the investment portfolio. To illustrate potential problems in using a benchmark that is not well specified, note that one can write a fund's and benchmark's alphas as a function of average excess returns to each other, their respective volatilities, and their correlation.

As the following equation shows, we are using a benchmark to measure the alpha of the fund and then use the fund to measure the alpha of the benchmark. It may seem odd to use a fund as the "benchmark" for estimating the alpha of a passively managed portfolio such as the S&P 500. However, you may be surprised to know that if these two equations are estimated for a large set of hedge funds, and you will find that a large number of funds have positive alpha with respect to a benchmark while at the same time the benchmark may have an alpha with respect to the same funds.

$$\alpha_{fund} = E(R_{fund} - R_f) - Corr(R_{fund}, R_{bench}) \times \frac{\sigma_{fund}}{\sigma_{bench}} E(R_{bench} - R_f)$$

$$\alpha_{bench} = E(R_{bench} - R_f) - Corr(R_{fund}, R_{bench}) \times \frac{\sigma_{bench}}{\sigma_{fund}} E(R_{fund} - R_f)$$

Such a result should not be obtained if the benchmark was well specified. We can see that a low correlation could lead to a positive alpha and

EXHIBIT 3.3   Relative Directional Move of Asset and Benchmark Alpha

Period	+/+	−/+	+/−	−/−
1998–9/2005	22%	3%	76%	0%
1998–2000	35%	43%	22%	0%
2001–9/2005	11%	5%	84%	0%

Source: Martin (2005).

the low correlation could work in both directions: giving the fund an alpha with respect to the benchmark and giving the benchmark an alpha with respect to the fund. We can investigate the validity of the prevailing economic intuition of alpha as incremental value added by conducting a simple analysis in which we first estimate alpha of a fund relative to a benchmark, and then the converse—the alpha of the benchmark relative to the fund. Characteristic of each of these concepts is the implicit idea that if a hedge fund exhibits alpha relative to a benchmark, then that benchmark should not add alpha relative to the hedge fund. However, for low correlation, and positive excess returns to the fund and the benchmark, fund alpha and benchmark alpha may both be positive. Exhibit 3.3 offers the results of regressing excess returns to 37 hedge fund indices (HFR indices) on the S&P 500, and vice versa, for the periods indicated. The respective columns count the percentage of indices with corresponding signs of their alphas. Thus "+/+" (which we term "weak alpha") means index's alpha with respect to the S&P 500 is positive while at the same time S&P 500's alpha with respect to the index is positive as well. On the other hand, "+/−" (which we may term "strong alpha") means that index's alpha is positive while the S&P 500's alpha with respect to the index is negative—the conventional interpretation of alpha.

The same misspecification could create a problem with regard to ranking of portfolios; that is, suppose Fund A has a positive alpha with respect to a benchmark and Fund B has a larger positive alpha with respect to the same benchmark. Does this mean that Fund B has a positive alpha with respect to Fund A? The answer is no. Indeed, it is possible for Fund B to have a negative alpha with respect to Fund A. So who has the skill? Clearly, in the absence of a well-specified benchmark, any estimate of alpha should be viewed with a great deal of skepticism.

An additional issue within alpha and beta determination deals with the notion of convexity of portfolio returns relative to a benchmark (see Exhibit 3.4). Academics and practitioners have long recognized that a key feature of active portfolio management is the ability to assume nonlinear exposures to market factors, either from dynamic allocation of exposure to market

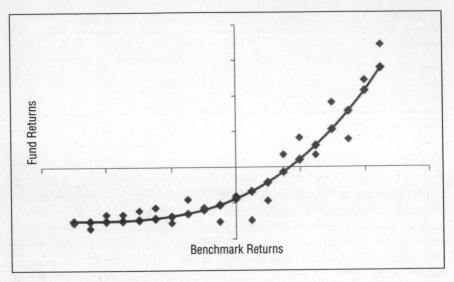

EXHIBIT 3.4   Return Convexity

factors or from the selection of assets with nonlinear payoffs relative to the market in order to deliver improved risk-adjusted returns. In its advantageous form, this dynamic exposure is hypothesized to take the form of increased factor exposure during periods when market factors deliver positive returns, and correspondingly, decreased exposure during downturns in market factors. This payoff profile is generically referred to as "market timing"; however, given the fact that this result may be due either to market timing via dynamic asset allocation, or due to security selection, such terminology is potentially misleading. Early attempts to measure this convexity included a quadratic term in the conventional linear model of performance measurement. In general, we believe that convexity is a more powerful measure of active portfolio management since it is more difficult to manufacture than a linear measure of alpha. As is discussed later in this book, various dynamic and option based approaches to risk management may provide such convexity patterns but not without underlying costs (e.g., insurance).

MULTI-FACTOR RETURN ESTIMATION: AN EXAMPLE

Simple use of average historical returns has been shown to be a poor indicator of future returns. As an alternative, research has shown that underlying market factors (e.g., credit spreads, term structure) are important in determining performance of equity, fixed income, and alternative investment strategies. This means that not only multi-factor models can be used to examine the performance of a portfolio on an ex post basis (to measure its alpha), they can also be used to forecast returns to major asset classes. While a quantitative model is used as a primary basis for strategy return forecasts, actual returns may differ from estimated returns for a variety of reasons, including model misspecification. Strict use of return estimation models at the portfolio level could lead to portfolios that are highly exposed to certain risk factors and inconsistent with current economic conditions to the degree that qualitative factors cannot be incorporated into the model. Qualitative judgments can be used to make marginal adjustments to forecast returns if it is determined that the quantitative model is not capable of incorporating certain aspects of the prevailing economic condition. Simple use of these return estimations without an understanding of the complexities of investment return estimation is not recommended.

In this section, we use a multi-factor regression model to develop estimates of returns. There are many additional approaches to return estimation. In this example, estimated return can be modeled as:

$$R_t = \alpha + \beta_1 \times F_{1,t-1} + \beta_2 \times F_{2,t-1} + \ldots + \varepsilon_t,$$

where

R_t = Investment strategy return;
α = Intercept;
$F_{1,t-1}$ = Lagged value of a relevant factor (e.g., credit spread, term spread, etc.)
β_1 = Coefficient of independent variable 1

It is very important to point out that, unlike previous multi-factor models, factors that appear on the right-hand side of the above equation do not have to represent excess returns on investable portfolios. Next, the variables on the right-hand side are lagged one period because they are used to predict return on the asset class. Finally, it is typically better to use several lagged values of a factor rather than change in the factor. For instance, if credit risk premium is one of the factors, then it may be better to use two lagged values of the credit risk premium rather than the change in the premium. If the contemporaneous values of the factors are used in the above regression, then the idea is that it is easier to forecast factor values than the return on the investment directly. Indeed, in some cases it may be easier to use past experience and professional judgment to forecast certain factors than directly forecasting the return on an asset class.

For example, regression coefficients from an explanatory model for the S&P 500 regressed on credit spread, term spread, and growth in corporate earnings can be used with forecasted values of the independent variables to obtain a forecast of returns for the S&P 500. Similar models have been designed to provide an estimate for expected returns for various strategies depending on the economic environment. We believe these factor estimates reflect current economic conditions; however, other qualitative/quantitative approaches to factor estimation can be used. The factors included in the current model are T-Bill rate (Bloomberg Generic Treasury 3-Month Rate), Credit Spread (Moody's Baa–Moody's Aaa), Term Spread (Bloomberg Treasury 10 Year Rate–Bloomberg Treasury 6 Month Rate), and Growth in Corporate Earnings (corporate profits with inventory valuation and capital consumption adjustments).

Exhibit 3.5 presents an example of forecasted returns for the S&P 500 index. In these examples, historical returns are used to estimate the coefficients. Then using our professional judgment as well as other quantitative models we have obtained forecasts for future values of the factors. Then these forecasted values are used to obtain estimates for expected returns on the S&P 500. Further, instead of using a point estimate for forecasted

EXHIBIT 3.5 Factor Inputs in Regression Model

S&P 500

Variable	Exposure
Intercept	0.04
T-Bill TR	1.61
Credit Spread	−4.81
Term Spread	0.19
Growth in Corp Earnings	0.34

Forecasted Independent Variable

Variable	Exposure
T-Bill TR	1.03%
Credit Spread	0.83%
Term Spreads	1.53%
Growth in Corp Earnings	2.18%

S&P 500 Forecast

Lower	Mean	Upper
4.29%	11.38%	18.47%

factors, we used a range of values and this leads to a range of forecasts for the performance of the S&P 500.

Further improvements can be made to make this multi-factor model more realistic. For instance, we may suspect that the response of the S&P 500 index to changes in the level of risk premium is a function of the level of volatility in the interest rates. Similar to the procedure that was highlighted before, we can assume that the coefficient of one or more factors is related to other factors. For example, the coefficient of the first factor may be expressed as

$$\beta_{1t} = a + b \times Vol_t$$

where Vol_t is an estimate of the volatility of interest rates at time t. This would allow us to estimate the impact of interaction between volatility of interest rates and changes in the credit risk premium.

These are just some examples of what practitioners can do with models of risk and return that account for many factors. There is extensive academic and practitioner literature that discusses expected asset returns as conditioned on a range of factors that may change over time. One important issue that has to be remembered is that more sophisticated models require more data and, if enough data are not available, the estimated parameters will be subject to severe estimation errors. Further, even if enough data are available, the estimated values of the parameters may significantly change if a new factor is added or a factor is dropped from the model.

It should be noted that short run changes in asset values are affected primarily by unexpected changes in information affecting asset values. For instance, the U.S. stock market has been shown to lead future economic conditions; that is, if the markets correctly estimate that economic conditions will improve, then the stock market may immediately rise in anticipation of those expected future "improvements" in economic conditions. It is also true that other asset classes that have economic risks similar to equity (e.g., high-yield debt) may also increase in value before actual changes in economic conditions. As a result, academic research has focused on certain macroeconomic factors that may represent current and future shifts in economic activity. As indicated previously, economic conditions may impact the expected return process; therefore, each of them may be viewed as a risk factor underlying the expected return process of a particular investment class sensitive to that information.

Previous research on conditional performance evaluation has concentrated on the traditional segment of the asset management industry such as equity and fixed income funds. (See Ferson and Khang, 2002, and Ferson,

Kisgen, and Henry, 2003). More recent studies have extended this research to alternative strategies such as hedge funds (Kazemi et al., 2008). In addition, this research has examined whether a conditional performance model that uses a dynamically adjusted portfolio as a benchmark reaches significantly different conclusions compared to those reached by an unconditional linear model.

TRACKING ALTERNATIVES IN ALPHA DETERMINATION

Various investment benchmarks are often utilized to measure the effectiveness and skill with which a manager selects securities. Thus, as an alternative to single- or multi-factor models of return determination, the relative outperformance of a manager in comparison to a predefined benchmark index is often used as a basis for measuring a manager's alpha. One of the principal issues in benchmark determination is the degree to which the comparison benchmark is fully investable. For a manager's alpha to be truly measureable it must be compared to a non-manager based (e.g., passive) investible asset of equal risk. Here, in order to provide a meaningful analysis of the manager and the comparison benchmark the managers fees must be net of all expenses and the fees and expenses associated with directly investing in the benchmark must also be considered. This can be a particularly thorny issue in dealing with alternatives such as private equity, commodities, hedge funds, or real estate, where there are few commonly accepted investable benchmark surrogates. In contrast, there exists a wide range of publicly available investment vehicles (that have been vetted over time) for equity and fixed income that provide access to the returns reflected in their associated benchmarks.

The use of investable benchmark alternatives (futures contracts, ETFs) as vehicles to derive manager alpha has been discussed in a wide range of practitioner and academic studies and is further explored in Chapter 6. In this section, we illustrate the creation of an investable tracking index to provide an investable alternative to the corresponding actively managed investment. One approach is to use investable forms of the risk factors used to describe asset returns in the previous section on multi-factor return estimation. To the degree that these risk factors are investable and capture the underlying risk of the manager's security holdings, the risk factor weightings can be used to create a passive investment alternative. This approach is of course susceptible to the basic issues surrounding any multi-factor return estimation model. In addition, a multi-factor risk model based approach may not capture the unique strategy aspects of an individual

EXHIBIT 3.6 Performance: CISDM Fund of Fund Tracker

Tracking Example (CISDM Fund of Funds)	CISDM Fund of Fund (Tracker)	CISDM Fund of Fund	S&P 500	BarCap U.S. Aggregate
Annualized Returns	0.7%	−7.6%	−26.8%	5.2%
Annualized Standard Deviation	6.4%	7.8%	18.5%	4.9%
Information Ratio	0.10	(0.97)	(1.45)	1.06
Maximum Drawdown	−9.7%	−17.7%	−45.1%	−3.8%
Correlation with CISDM Fund of Funds	0.99	1.00	0.62	0.13
Correlation with S&P 500	0.83	0.62	1.00	0.30
Correlation with BarCap US Agg	0.36	0.13	0.30	1.00

Summary Statistics: May 2007 to Jan 2009.

manager's approach. An alternative approach reflects the use of ETFs with an algorithmic based model to track the comparison non-investable index or comparison fund.

In Exhibit 3.6, a range of investable ETFs are used to create a tracking portfolio that reflects the performance of the CISDM Fund of Fund Hedge Fund index. In this case the correlation between the CISDM Fund of Fund Hedge Fund index and its tracker is over .90. Research (Kazemi and Schneeweis, 2009) has shown investable alternatives can be created from a series of ETFs that offer an investable non-manager based benchmark to the number of non-investable as well as investable manager based indices. There exist, of course, a range of issues in the creation of systematic algorithmic based tracker benchmarks, including the fact that the tracker fund is often based on matching the performance of manager or product over a past historical period, while the current manager portfolio or product may reflect more current asset allocation or security decisions. Finally, there exist a number of algorithmic based trading products that attempt to re-create, at a passive systematic level, the underlying strategy of a particular manager. For example, while each individual manager may regard themselves as unique, most managers within a particular strategy often trade in a similar fashion. These approaches may be regarded as more bottom up strategy tracking based approaches.

WHAT EVERY INVESTOR SHOULD REMEMBER

- An active manager's performance alpha is generally defined as the excess return to active management adjusted for risk, that is, the return adjusted for the return of a comparable investable "non-actively managed" risky asset position or portfolio. The question is, therefore, how to define the expected risk of the manager's investment and how to obtain the return on that investment.

- Use of a single-index model assumes that the single market factor in the model replicates the fundamental risk factor driving the return of the strategy. If not, a multi-factor model should be used to describe the various market factors that drive the return strategy. One of the basic tenets of statistical regression says it is better to over specify a model (include more sources of systematic risk than the fund is exposed to) than under specify (include fewer factors).

- Economic conditions may impact the expected return process and may be viewed as a risk factor underlying the expected return process of a particular investment class sensitive to that information. Research has indicated that a conditional performance model that uses a dynamically adjusted portfolio as a benchmark reaches significantly different conclusions compared to those reached by an unconditional linear model.

- The ability to assume nonlinear exposures to market factors, either from dynamic allocation of exposure to market factors or from the selection of assets with nonlinear payoffs relative to market, may deliver improved risk-adjusted returns.

NOTES

1. There is extensive literature on Sharpe Ratios and alternative relative risk comparison measures (e.g., the Jensen and the Treynor indices). See Bodie, Kane, and Marcus (2008). There have also been additional papers recently on the use of various volatility comparison performance measures in which the volatility of the asset is directly adjusted to equal the benchmark (e.g., Modigliani and Modigliani 1997 and Graham and Harvey 1996). In addition, the use of any average realized return/risk comparison model may not capture manager skill if managers follow conditional risk models (Bansal and Harvey 1996). Lastly, for portfolios in which the underlying return distribution is fundamentally different

from the assumed benchmark or when investors value those parameters in ways different from the assumed theoretical model's derived benchmark, the use of a corresponding naive benchmark may not capture for investors the relative return benefits of active manager choices.

2. In addition to macroeconomic factors driving asset class returns, considerable research exists on microeconomic or firm related factors driving returns on individual assets or asset classes. This brief review does not address issues such as unexpected changes in earnings per share as a basis for individual security valuation.

CHAPTER 4

Asset Classes: What They Are and Where to Put Them

This chapter provides the building blocks for multi-asset allocation. We do not attempt to change accepted approaches to asset class determination as much as to expand it to include a wider set of potential investments including a range of alternative investments (e.g., private equity, commodities, real estate, hedge funds, CTAs). For many, the question still exists: do alternative investments provide the average investor with valuable return and risk opportunities beyond that available in traditional stock and bond investments? In its most simple form, the total risk of an equal weighted stock (high volatility) and bond (low volatility) portfolio is not split equally between the stock and bond investment but is in fact impacted primarily by the high risk stock investment. The potential addition of a range of other investment classes should at least offer one answer to this stock/bond conundrum. The answer to the benefits of asset allocation in a multi-asset universe may simply be that "more is better than less." Additional assets may provide investors with greater access to return opportunities that may not exist in other states of the traditional stock and bond world.

In addition, the crux of asset allocation is reliable and independently verifiable information. The creation of asset classes for which the fundamental return process cannot be monitored or managed is of little use. Black boxes, whether in the form of "investment processes" or in the form of "assets," have proven fertile ground for fraud and nonfeasance. With technological and informational advances, the character and definition of assets have changed. For example, most investors do not realize that returns associated with real estate and private equity are for the most part "accounting" returns based on the business model of the investment vehicle or management firm.[1] Nor do they understand that structured products are conditioned by the balance sheet of the provider and its associated internal rate of return assumptions; or that the returns on hedge funds are heavily influenced by the hedge fund's prime broker and other borrowing relationships. Very little of this information is in the public domain and rarely, if ever, do financial consultants or brokers incorporate these facts into their analyses for clients or prospects.

Thus, as this book moves forward, it is important to revisit definitions and start at the beginning. This chapter provides the building blocks for a fresh look at asset allocation, especially as it relates to a multi-asset class environment. In so doing, it revisits the accepted approaches to asset class determination and seeks to find a place for alternative asset classes. It asks and answers the question of whether alternative investments provide the average investor with valuable return and risk opportunities beyond those easily available in the traditional equity and fixed income markets. In addition, it explores the nature of individual assets and their corresponding benefits in a multi-asset universe and concludes, in relation to asset allocation, that perhaps more is, in fact, better than less. When to add them in the context of strategic, tactical, and dynamic asset allocation is covered in the next chapter.

OVERVIEW AND LIMITATIONS OF THE EXISTING ASSET ALLOCATION PROCESS

Historically, investors' portfolios have been principally weighted towards stocks, bonds, and cash. However, research (INGARM, 2009) has shown that portfolios that allocate up to 10% to alternative investments such as commodities, CTAs, and hedge funds will on average outperform traditional stand-alone stock and bond allocations on a risk-adjusted basis. This research also suggests that the primary basis for the inclusion of alternative investments is that they offer unique return characteristics and risk reduction opportunities not easily found through traditional stock and bond investments. For example, as global economies have become more integrated, the correlation between major asset markets has increased. In addition, as informational efficiency increases, the ability to find traditional investments with true alpha has decreased.[2]

The starting point in explaining the importance of asset allocation is an understanding of both an investor's investment objective and the impact of various investment choices on achieving that objective. The primary goal of many investors is to maximize the long-run rate of return. For some investors, this means concentrating in a few assets or asset classes such as investing primarily in equity markets (Siegel, 2008).[3] Recent performance in traditional stock markets has illustrated the risks of such an allocation process. Given two investment streams with roughly the same expected per period rate of return, the investment stream with the lower standard deviation has the higher long-term rate of return. As a result, for many investors one of the primary goals of multi-asset asset allocation is to hold a variety of investments so as to lower future expected return volatility without drastically reducing expected return.

The asset allocation process often starts with the following three steps:

1. **Description of available investment opportunities.** In this step the relevant asset classes and their risk-return characteristics are analyzed. Considerable academic research exists detailing the unique risk and return attributes of stocks, bonds, private equity, and hedge funds.
2. **Investor's preference, assets, and liabilities.** This step begins by a description of the investor's financial condition (assets, liabilities, financial goals, taxes, etc.) and then proceeds with an estimation of the client's risk capacity and risk tolerance.
3. **Optimal asset mix.** In this final stage the above information is employed to develop an investment policy statement and to recommend a strategic optimal asset mix.

If alternative investments such as private equity and hedge funds are to be included in an investor's optimal portfolio allocation, investors need to determine:

- If alternative investments such as private equity and hedge funds represent a distinct asset class and therefore should be included in the analysis taken place in Step 1.
- If individuals' risk tolerance makes a compelling case for the inclusion of alternative investments in the optimal asset mix as determined from Step 2.
- If, as discussed in Step 3, an asset allocation process that includes investment in alternative assets fits the investment policy guidelines and presents a strategic asset mix of traditional and alternative investments that is consistent with investment policy.

The common denominator within each of these steps or scenarios is unbiased information and research. Neither risk and return characteristics nor preferences nor optimal asset mix can be determined without understanding the economics, liquidity, correlations, and regulatory structure of a particular asset class or its underlying components. For the most part, investments and thus trustee or consultant liability in regard to institutional portfolios is based on the reasonable man theory. This theory asks the question of whether a reasonable person under similar circumstances would place monies at risk. If the answer is yes—no liability. If the answer is no— exposure to prosecution and personal financial liability. The options rather dictate that investment decisions that will be made are centered on the most commonly accepted approach to asset allocation and the most "acceptable" investment choice.

Given that many alternative investments lack the years of scrutiny, in comparison to traditional asset choices to be accepted in most institutional investors' portfolios as a standing allocation, it is not surprising that there is not a broad and substantial body of work that tracks the risks and benefits of alternative investments.[4] In the next section, some of this inequity is remedied as it is clearly shown that certain alternative investments have unique characteristics in the areas of risk and sources of return that qualify them as distinct asset classes.

ASSET ALLOCATION IN TRADITIONAL AND ALTERNATIVE INVESTMENTS: A ROAD MAP

A seminal study by Brinson, Hood, and Beebower (1986) demonstrated that as much as 93.6% of variation in returns in quarterly performance of professionally managed diversified portfolios could be explained by the mix of the asset classes (security selection explains the rest).[5] Recent research however, has also shown, that while over 90% of the return volatility of a diversified portfolio through time is explained by its allocation to broad asset classes, a somewhat smaller portion of that portfolio's total return over the same time period is explained by its allocation to various asset classes. Davis et. al (2007) have shown the portion of total returns on various portfolios that can be explained by their allocations to broad asset classes may vary depending on how actively a diversified portfolio is managed. Whatever the final number, these results indicate that asset allocation is a major determinant of any diversified portfolio's risk-return profile and that any viable asset allocation program should include a wide range of potential asset classes. For example, recent studies (INGARM, 2009) have shown that through the use of alternative investments one can get access to investment opportunities and factor exposures that are not available through traditional asset classes. Alternative investments such as private equity, real estate, commodities, hedge funds, and CTAs offer a variety of return and risk characteristics:

- **Positive alpha:** A risk-adjusted return that exceeds the risk-adjusted return of traditional asset classes. Research has suggested that alternatives often obtain an excess return as providers of liquidity to new investors.
- **Higher rate of return relative to other asset classes:** Certain alternative asset (private equity, real estate) returns are derived from less liquid

investments. These alternative strategies have a higher expected rate of return as a function of the underlying risk of the investment (e.g., late stage private equity investment has a beta of about 1.25 to 1.5).

- **Upside skewness:** Various alternative investments (e.g., hedge funds, CTAs) are structured to limit downside losses but remain exposed to break-outs on the upside.
- **Low correlation with other asset classes:** Certain alternative asset strategies are based on non-equity or non-fixed income based investments. These alternative investments (e.g., commodities, CTAs) tend to have low correlation with returns on traditional asset classes.

These points have been examined in a number of recent studies.[6] Those studies (INGARM, 2009) conclude that alternative investments have a strategic role for investors, particularly those individuals who have some tolerance toward risk. The transition from "should" have a place to "must" have a place within a portfolio and thus an asset allocation model involves some further analysis. The next step is to further develop the asset allocation process and construct sample portfolios using different allocations to various traditional asset classes as well as traditional and modern alternative investments. In finance theory, a pure security is one that provides a unique return and risk opportunity not available in other investment vehicles. Regarding each investment opportunity as an asset class simply because it differs in some unique sense from other assets may be valuable from a conceptual sense but it provides little practical direction for investors. For example, people regard their children as unique and special, but for purposes of education most schools put all third grade children in one class. Similarly, the same approach must be taken in determining whether a strategy or asset falls within or outside of an asset class categorization. A wide range of asset characteristics such as transparency, liquidity, and taxability are all important aspects of the investment decision. But, standing alone or in combination, none of these elements is sufficient to warrant establishment of or inclusion into an asset class. There has to be more.

We get to "more" through a somewhat circuitous route. Here we have to examine whether current quantitative tools take into account how individual assets differ; determine their relative strengths and weaknesses; acknowledge assets' liquidity or ability to trade on the open markets in some type of verifiable context; and examine other risk and return characteristics that require judgment and discretion before determining the assets' contribution to a portfolio's risk, return, and volatility. In part, the core quantitative tools of asset allocation (MPT, EMH, and CAPM) have grown to be seen as the answer, rather than simply a way to frame the approach to modern asset allocation. At one end, the CAPM attempted to link all assets into a single-factor approach in which all assets were priced relative to their common sensitivity to a single common market portfolio. At the other end, various multi-factor models of return expectation, each of which is aimed at producing a manageable set of security groupings such that each group may be said to offer unique characteristics that separate it from other investments, have been offered as alternatives to more basic approaches.

Simply put, what is the place in time and space for each asset? What makes an equity security fit into a unique asset grouping? How is it determined whether assets share some common feature or quality? Or, are the common asset groupings simply a catchall for a wide variety of disparate assets and trading strategies? Once we get past the obvious fact that various investments are labeled "X," do "X" funds really exist as a definable entity? Is there such a thing as "X fundness"? The problem however, cannot simply be addressed by using solely quantitative models. For one, as mentioned previously, measures of risk exposure go far beyond simple quantitative models. Simple CAPM or other quantitative return and risk models fail directly to incorporate a host of qualitative risks (liquidity, counterparty risks, political risks, transparency) that may or may not be reflected in the price risk of a set of tradable assets. Moreover, most models of expected return and risk determination have failed to adequately measure the relative impacts of illiquid assets including the investor's "personal value" in any applicable model of asset class determination. That having been said, there are unique features of some investment strategies (fixed income and exchange traded equities) that have permitted them to be universally accepted as asset classes. Extrapolating these conventions provides an aid in understanding the return and risk properties as well as trading patterns inherent in establishing an accepted asset class.

Beyond taking different approaches, there are also different conventions. Some investors view currencies as a separate asset class while fully understanding that currencies may also be viewed as simple short-term interest rate swap between countries. Some investors refuse to pay managers for cash held in a multi-asset portfolio on the grounds that they should only pay when and where their monies are invested in specific assets and that cash is a placeholder. As we find our way through new terrain, there is a range of issues in determining the taxonomy for asset class determination; however, degree of difficulty must not be the stopping point of establishing a process by which we address asset allocation issues.[7] The approach must be the creation of a map. In designing any map we first look to its purpose and then gauge the level of detail required to make it useful. Here, usefulness is analogous to the risks involved with any particular investment path. Every path has its own risks and every map its faults.

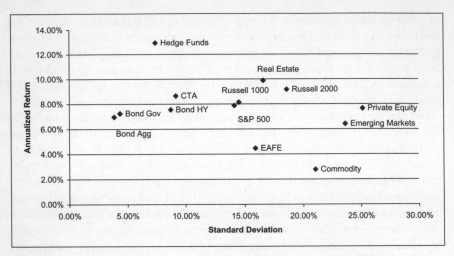

EXHIBIT 4.1   Benchmark Return and Standard Deviation (1991–2008)

Our map looks to proven market tools such as standard deviation, beta, and multiple risk dimensions (liquidity and transparency) for guidance. However, one should not necessarily look simply to past return performance. As shown in Exhibits 4.1 and 4.2, for the listed investment groupings there seems to be differing levels of risk (standard deviation and beta) for the period of analysis (but little relationship between that level of historical risk and historical return).

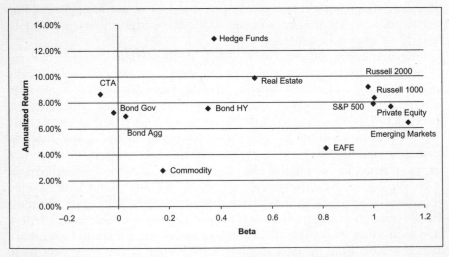

EXHIBIT 4.2   Benchmark Return and S&P 500 Beta (1991–2008)

While investment strategies have often been grouped into asset classes based on absolute risk (standard deviation) or market risks (beta), various investment strategies have also traditionally been grouped into asset classes based on the underlying markets in which they trade (e.g., equity and fixed income). In Exhibit 4.3, we provide one taxonomy for the placement of assets under three principal asset class groupings based on the market segments in which they trade and investment areas into which they have traditionally been classified. Under traditional assets we group both equity and fixed income investments. Traditionally, other less liquid, less transparent, or non equity based investment have been grouped as "traditional alternative investments" since they are viewed primarily as alternatives to the traditional stock and bond asset classes. This group of "traditional alternatives" includes investments such as private equity, real estate (residential and commercial), and commodity investments.[8] In recent years, an additional set of "modern alternative investments" such as hedge funds and managed futures have become increasingly available for both retail and institutional investors.[9]

For purposes of illustration, in this chapter we follow these three primary asset classes illustrated in Exhibit 4.3. It is important to note that the primary emphasis on these three primary asset class groupings is due in part to the necessity to keep it simple. Each of these primary asset classes could be extended to include a wider set of investments. Given the number of external personnel involved in the investment management process, the asset class structure may be by necessity designed to fit a required business model that is workable from an organizational viewpoint.

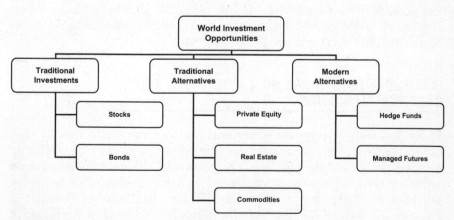

EXHIBIT 4.3 Traditional and Alternative Asset Class Breakdown

Primary Asset Classes
- Traditional Assets
  - Equity
    Domestic Investment
    International Non Domestic
    Emerging Markets
  - Fixed Income
    Government
    Corporate
    Corporate High-Yield
- Traditional Alternative Investments
  - Private Equity
  - Commodities
  - Real Estate
- Modern Alternative Investments
  - Hedge Funds
  - Managed Futures (CTAs)

The list of investment benchmarks used to represent the above asset classes is described in the glossary.[10] In the following section, the benchmarks used to represent the above investment areas are as follows: Domestic Investment (the Russell 1000 and Russell 2000); International Non-Domestic (MSCI EAFE); Emerging Markets (MSCI Emerging Markets); Fixed Income Government (Barclays Capital U.S. Government); Fixed Income Aggregate (Barclays Capital U.S. Aggregate); Fixed Income High Yield (Barclays Capital U.S. Corporate High Yield); Private Equity (Index of publicly traded private equity); Commodities (S&P Goldman Sachs Commodity Index); Real Estate (FTSE NAREIT All REIT); Hedge Funds (CASAM/CISDM Equal Weight Hedge Fund Index); and Managed Futures (CASAM/CISDM CTA Equal Weight Index).

HISTORICAL RETURN AND RISK ATTRIBUTES AND STRATEGY ALLOCATION

In the following sections the return and risk performance of various asset classes is provided for an eighteen year period of analysis as well as relevant sub-periods. In addition we provide return and risk performance results after combining the various asset classes into risk based (standard deviation) portfolio groupings based on commonly used portfolio weightings. As illustrated in Exhibit 4.4, the investment benchmarks used to represent the various investment asset groupings generally reflect different sensitivities to

EXHIBIT 4.4   Investment Strategy—Descriptive Statistics

Index Performance 1991–2008	Annualized Total Return	Annualized Standard Deviation	Information Ratio	Maximum Drawdown	Beta
Equity					
Russell 1000	8.1%	14.5%	.56	−45.0%	1.01
Russell 2000	9.2%	18.5%	.49	−42.9%	0.98
MSCI EAFE	4.5%	15.9%	.28	−49.5%	0.81
MSCI Emerging Markets	6.4%	23.6%	.27	−60.6%	1.14
Fixed Income					
BarCap US Government	7.2%	4.3%	1.66	−5.4%	−0.02
BarCap US Aggregate	7.0%	3.8%	1.81	−5.1%	0.03
BarCap US Corporate High-Yield	7.5%	8.7%	.86	−33.3%	0.35
Traditional Alternatives					
S&P GSCI	2.8%	21.0%	.13	−62.1%	0.18
FTSE NAREIT All REITs	9.9%	16.5%	.60	−58.7%	0.53
Private Equity Index	7.6%	25.1%	.30	−70.3%	1.07
Modern Alternatives					
CISDM EW Hedge Fund Index	12.9%	7.4%	1.74	−21.1%	0.38
CISDM CTA EW Index	8.7%	9.1%	.94	−9.3%	−0.07

various market factors; that is, each equity index generally has a higher level of volatility and a higher equity beta than most fixed income investments. Assets in the traditional alternative investment area (private equity, real estate, commodities) generally have higher volatility and, depending on the asset (private equity), a higher equity beta as well (as will be discussed later, real estate and private equity may not necessarily be regarded as an equity diversifier but more as a return enhancement to equity dominated

EXHIBIT 4.5   Investment Strategy—Correlations

Index Correlation 1991–2008	Russell 1000	Russell 2000	MSCI EAFE U.S. Currency	MSCI Emerging Markets Index	BarCap US Gov
Equity					
Russell 1000		0.79	0.74	0.71	−0.06
Russell 2000	0.79		0.66	0.71	−0.15
MSCI EAFE	0.74	0.66		0.71	−0.08
MSCI Emerging Markets Index	0.71	0.71	0.71		−0.17
Fixed Income					
BarCap US Government	−0.06	−0.15	−0.08	−0.17	
BarCap US Aggregate	0.11	0.00	0.08	−0.02	0.96
BarCap US Corporate High-Yield	0.59	0.62	0.54	0.58	0.04
Traditional Alternatives					
S&P GSCI	0.13	0.19	0.25	0.23	−0.03
FTSE NAREIT ALL REITS	0.48	0.59	0.41	0.42	0.02
Private Equity Index	0.63	0.70	0.71	0.65	−0.19
Modern Alternatives					
CISDM EW Hedge Fund Index	0.76	0.83	0.68	0.80	−0.07
CISDM CTA EW Index	−0.11	−0.13	−0.05	−0.05	0.30

portfolios). Finally, modern alternatives such hedge funds and managed futures both report moderate volatility as well as relatively low equity market betas. In Exhibit 4.5 the correlations between the various investment benchmarks are also presented. The results in Exhibit 4.5 which report less than perfect correlation between most investment benchmarks, indicate the diversification potential for a mixed portfolio of traditional assets as well as for a mixed portfolio of traditional assets and alternatives.

It is important to emphasize that the results in the investment vehicles (indices) used in this analysis reflect that of portfolios of individual securities

BarCap US Agg	BarCap US Corporate High Yield	S&P GSCI	FTSE NAREIT ALL REITS	Private Equity Index	CISDM Hedge Fund EW Index	CISDM CTA EW Index
0.11	0.59	0.13	0.48	0.63	0.76	−0.11
0.00	0.62	0.19	0.59	0.70	0.83	−0.13
0.08	0.54	0.25	0.41	0.71	0.68	−0.05
−0.02	0.58	0.23	0.42	0.65	0.80	−0.05
0.96	0.04	−0.03	0.02	−0.19	−0.07	0.30
	0.26	0.03	0.17	−0.05	0.09	0.23
0.26		0.20	0.60	0.56	0.61	−0.13
0.03	0.20		0.14	0.25	0.31	0.14
0.17	0.60	0.14		0.42	0.42	−0.07
−0.05	0.56	0.25	0.42		0.72	−0.15
0.09	0.61	0.31	0.42	0.72		−0.02
0.23	−0.13	0.14	−0.07	−0.15	−0.02	

or manager based investments. At the individual asset or manager level, individual risk may differ dramatically from that of the portfolio. In addition, within various investment groupings, certain sub-indices may have a high correlation with other primary asset classifications (for example, within the hedge fund asset class, equity based hedge fund strategies such as equity long short may have a high correlation with long equity strategies and distressed debt may have a high correlation with high-yield debt) such that certain sub-asset groupings may be regarded as better diversifiers or return enhancers depending upon the comparison portfolio.

TRADITIONAL STOCK/BOND ALLOCATION VERSUS MULTI-ASSET ALLOCATION

This section provides an analysis of a set of risk (standard deviation) ranked portfolios (aggressive and conservative) within each of three sets of portfolios:

1. MP1 (stock and bond portfolio)
2. MP2 (stock, bond, and traditional alternatives)
3. MP3 (stock, bond, and traditional alternatives as well as modern alternatives)

Results in Exhibit 4.7 show that:

- For each separate set of portfolios, as one moves from an aggressive to more conservative risk based portfolios, the standard deviation decreases.
- Across the three sets of portfolios, when traditional alternatives are added to the stock and bond portfolio or when modern alternatives are added to the comparison risk portfolio, which contains stocks, bonds, and traditional alternatives, the return to risk ratio of the enlarged risk class portfolio increases.

In Exhibit 4.6 the strategy weightings for two separate risk class portfolios are described for each of the three sets of portfolios. Results in Exhibit

EXHIBIT 4.6   Market Segment Based Portfolio Weightings

	Type of Portfolio	Russell 1000	Russell 2000	MSCI EAFE	MSCI Emerging Markets	BarCap US Gov.
Model	Aggressive	25	20	15	10	5
Portfolio 1	Conservative	20	20	10	5	15
Model	Aggressive	15	15	10	5	5
Portfolio 2	Conservative	20	15	10	0	20
Model	Aggressive	15	15	10	5	5
Portfolio 3	Conservative	20	15	10	0	20

Note: Numbers are percentages.

4.7, for the period of analysis and for the asset weighting used, are consistent with previous research that indicates that adding traditional and modern alternative investments to stock and bond portfolios provides the opportunity for improved return to risk tradeoff.[11]

As discussed previously and as shown in Exhibit 4.7 adding additional asset classes (traditional alternatives and/or modern alternatives) for the period of analysis increased the historical return, reduced the standard deviation, increased the information ratio, and reduced the maximum drawdown.

Results in Exhibit 4.8 also show that adding traditional alternatives (MP2) to a traditional stock and bond portfolio (MP1) and adding modern alternatives (MP3) to a portfolio composed of both traditional as well as traditional alternatives (MP2) reduces the equity beta within a particular portfolio grouping. This is consistent with modern alternatives such as hedge funds and CTAs having a relatively low correlation with the comparison equity volatility dominated portfolios.

RISK AND RETURN COMPARISONS UNDER DIFFERING HISTORICAL TIME PERIODS

The results in the previous section illustrate the relative performance of a range of potential portfolios based on their holdings of traditional stock and bonds, traditional alternatives, and modern alternatives. Results, however, reflect the relative performance for one eighteen year period. The question remains as to the performance of the various investments and their

BarCap US Agg.	BarCap US Corporate High Yield	S&P GSCI	Private Equity	FTSE NAREIT ALL REITS	CISDM EW Hedge Fund Index	CISDM CTA EW Index
10	15	0	0	0	0	0
15	15	0	0	0	0	0
10	10	10	10	10	0	0
15	10	0	5	5	0	0
5	10	5	5	5	10	10
15	10	0	2.5	2.5	2.5	2.5

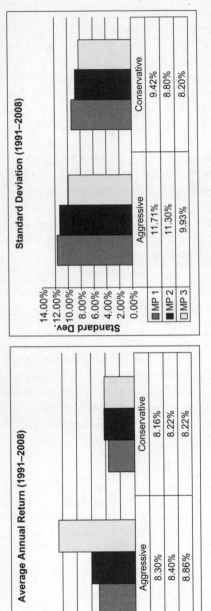

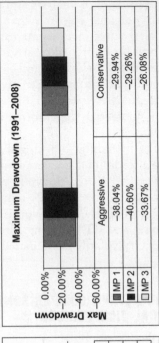

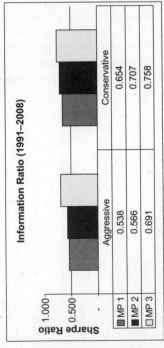

EXHIBIT 4.7 Performance Comparison of Aggressive and Conservative Portfolios (1991–2008)

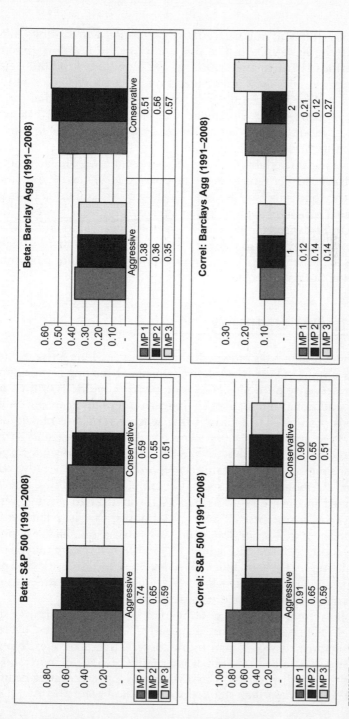

EXHIBIT 4.8 Equity Beta Comparison of Aggressive and Conservative Portfolios (1991–2008)

associated portfolios in alternative historical periods. In Exhibits 4.9 and Exhibit 4.10 the eighteen year period of analysis is broken down into three separate periods (1991 to 1996, 1997 to 2002, and 2003 to 2008). Across all investments, results show a dramatic drop (with the exception of CTAs) in historical returns between the first period (1991 to 1996) and the most recent period (2003 to 2008). Similarly, results in Exhibit 4.10 show that over the most recent six-year period, in contrast to that of the first six-year period, volatility has slightly increased.

As illustrated in Exhibit 4.11, at the portfolio level similar results are reported, that is, higher returns in the first period (1991 to 1996) but lower returns in the following two periods. As shown in Exhibit 4.12, standard deviation also increased slightly in the later two periods; however, results indicate that, as expected, the conservative portfolio's standard deviations were consistently lower than the aggressive portfolio's standard deviations, illustrating the benefits of risk reduction with the addition of modern alternatives to the portfolio choice.

EXTREME MARKET SENSITIVITY

The following results reflect the performance over various six-year periods. The results do not indicate the relative benefits of moving from aggressive to more conservative portfolios in various market conditions or the benefits of adding traditional alternatives or modern alternatives to portfolios in such periods. Exhibit 4.13 indicates that when returns are ranked on the S&P 500, (1) equity sensitive investments (stock and private equity) perform poorly in the worst 72 months of the S&P 500; (2) high-yield corporate bonds, hedge funds, and real estate also reported moderate negative returns in the worst 72 months of the S&P 500; and (3) commodities, non-credit sensitive fixed income, and CTAs had small negative to positive returns. Results reversed in the best 72 S&P 500 months; that is, equity sensitive assets performed well while less equity sensitive assets had less positive returns. In contrast, results in Exhibit 4.14, when returns are ranked on the BarCap U.S. Aggregate Bond Index, fixed income based securities did poorly in down fixed income markets while most equity based investments as well as modern alternatives reported positive returns.

Portfolio returns reflect these individual investment results. As shown in Exhibit 4.15, in periods of extreme negative S&P 500 returns, aggressive portfolios performed worse than more conservative portfolios. However, portfolios that contained traditional alternatives (MP2) or portfolios that also contained modern alternatives (MP3) had lower negative returns in down S&P 500 markets than stand-alone stock and bond portfolios (MP1).

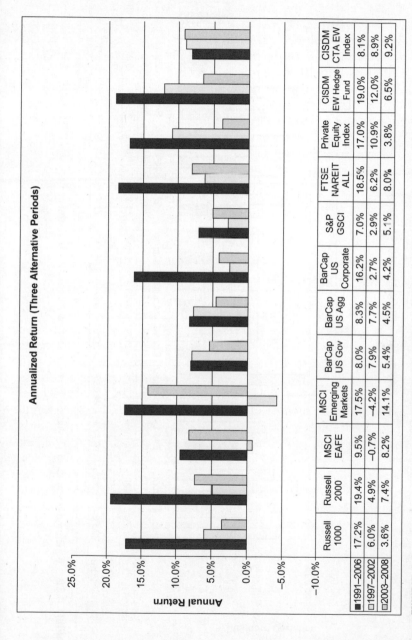

Annualized Return (Three Alternative Periods)

	Russell 1000	Russell 2000	MSCI EAFE	MSCI Emerging Markets	BarCap US Gov	BarCap US Agg	BarCap US Corporate	S&P GSCI	FTSE NAREIT ALL	Private Equity Index	CISDM EW Hedge Fund	CISDM CTA EW Index
■ 1991–2006	17.2%	19.4%	9.5%	17.5%	8.0%	8.3%	16.2%	7.0%	18.5%	17.0%	19.0%	8.1%
□ 1997–2002	6.0%	4.9%	−0.7%	−4.2%	7.9%	7.7%	2.7%	2.9%	6.2%	10.9%	12.0%	8.9%
□ 2003–2008	3.6%	7.4%	8.2%	14.1%	5.4%	4.5%	4.2%	5.1%	8.0%	3.8%	6.5%	9.2%

EXHIBIT 4.9 Benchmark Return Performance in Alternative Investment Periods (1991–2008)

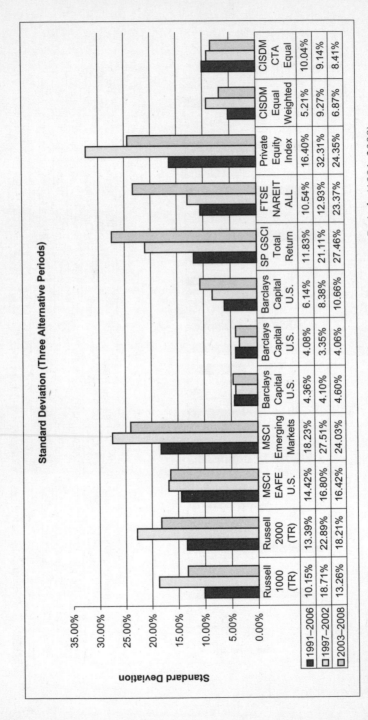

EXHIBIT 4.10 Benchmark Standard Deviation Performance in Alternative Investment Periods (1991–2008)

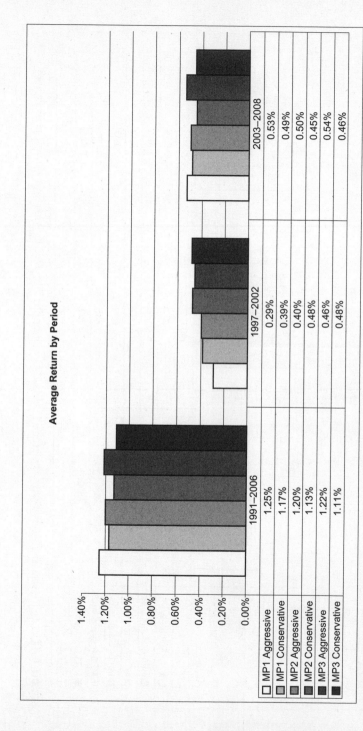

Average Return by Period

	1991–2006	1997–2002	2003–2008
MP1 Aggressive	1.25%	0.29%	0.53%
MP1 Conservative	1.17%	0.39%	0.49%
MP2 Aggressive	1.20%	0.40%	0.50%
MP2 Conservative	1.13%	0.48%	0.45%
MP3 Aggressive	1.22%	0.46%	0.54%
MP3 Conservative	1.11%	0.48%	0.46%

EXHIBIT 4.11 Aggressive and Conservative Portfolio Benchmark Return Performance in Alternative Investment Periods (1991–2008)

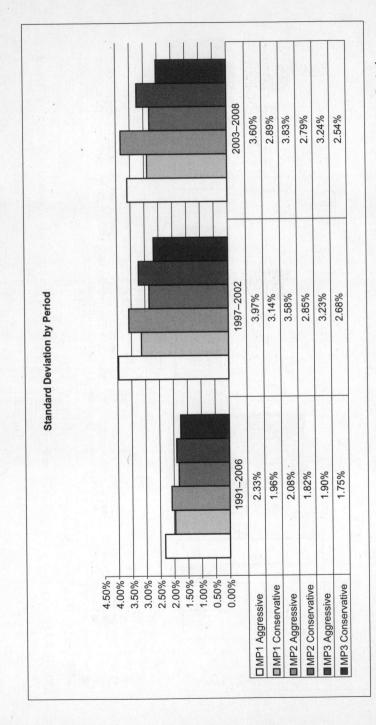

Standard Deviation by Period

	1991–2006	1997–2002	2003–2008
☐ MP1 Aggressive	2.33%	3.97%	3.60%
▨ MP1 Conservative	1.96%	3.14%	2.89%
▨ MP2 Aggressive	2.08%	3.58%	3.83%
▨ MP2 Conservative	1.82%	2.85%	2.79%
■ MP3 Aggressive	1.90%	3.23%	3.24%
■ MP3 Conservative	1.75%	2.68%	2.54%

EXHIBIT 4.12 Aggressive and Conservative Portfolio Standard Deviation Performance in Alternative Investment Periods (1991–2008)

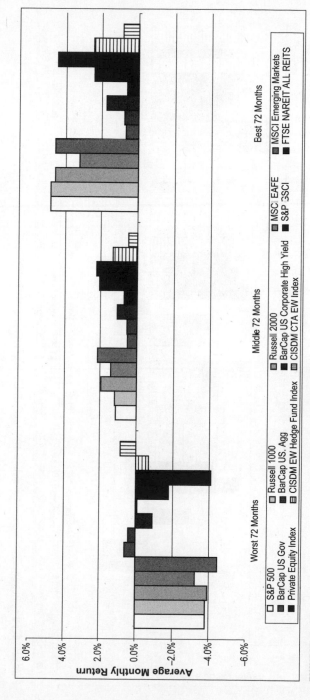

EXHIBIT 4.13 Benchmark Returns Ranked by S&P 500 (1991–2008)

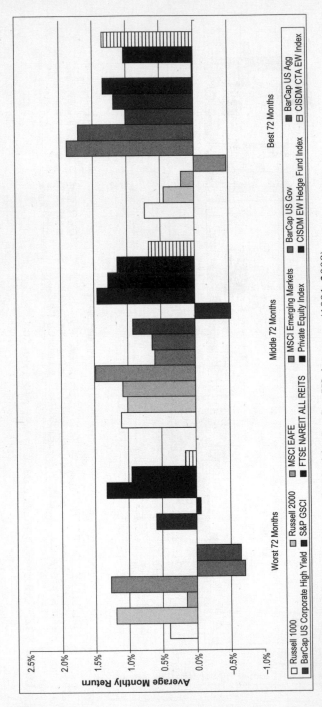

EXHIBIT 4.14 Benchmark Returns Ranked by BarCap US Aggregate (1991–2008)

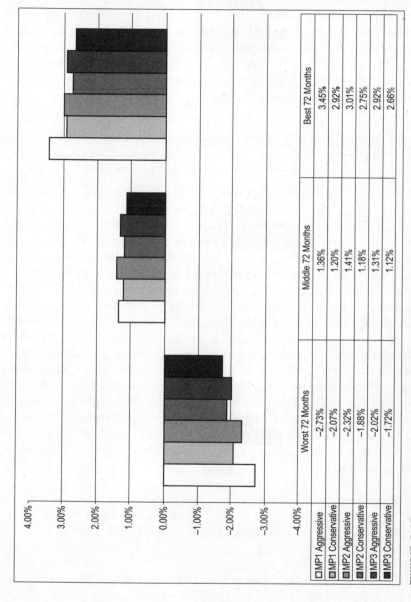

	Worst 72 Months	Middle 72 Months	Best 72 Months
☐MP1 Aggressive	-2.73%	1.36%	3.45%
☐MP1 Conservative	-2.07%	1.20%	2.92%
☐MP2 Aggressive	-2.32%	1.41%	3.01%
■MP2 Conservative	-1.88%	1.18%	2.75%
■MP3 Aggressive	-2.02%	1.31%	2.92%
■MP3 Conservative	-1.72%	1.12%	2.66%

EXHIBIT 4.15 Portfolio Returns Ranked by S&P 500 (1991–2008)

Results are reversed in the best 72 S&P 500 months over this time period; that is, portfolios that are dominated by equity investment (MP1) have superior performance. In contrast, as shown in Exhibit 4.16, when monthly returns are ranked on the BarCap U.S. Aggregate Bond Index, aggressive portfolios that contain a greater percentage of equity based investments generally outperformed conservative portfolios in the worst 72 months. In the best 72 months of the BarCap U.S. Aggregate Bond Index, conservative portfolios that contained a greater percentage of fixed income investment outperformed the aggressive portfolios.

MARKET SEGMENT OR MARKET SENSITIVITY: DOES IT MATTER?

In previous sections, we pointed out that certain alternative investments may have a high correlation with investments in other asset classes. For instance, private equity may have a high correlation with equity markets. In this section, a set of risk (standard deviation) ranked portfolios (aggressive and conservative) within each of three sets of portfolios is constructed. The portfolios differ from those presented in Exhibit 4.6, in that certain investments were combined with other investments for which their equity market sensitivity was similar. For instance, in contrast to Exhibit 4.6, private equity, which has been shown to have a high equity factor component, was grouped with traditional equity investments. Similarly, hedge funds which have been shown to have moderate equity exposure were grouped with assets such as real estate. Lastly, commodities which have low sensitivity with equity markets were grouped with CTAs in the least equity sensitive asset class grouping. Of course, other portfolio groupings could be created based on a range of investment characteristics.

The three portfolios were constructed with a set of risk (standard deviation) ranked portfolios (aggressive and conservative) within each of three sets of portfolios:

1. MP1 (stock, private equity, and non-credit sensitive bond)
2. MP2 (stock, private equity, bond, real estate, and hedge funds)
3. MP3 (stock, private equity, bond, real estate, hedge funds, CTAs, and commodities)

Exhibit 4.17 describes the strategy weightings for the two separate risk class portfolio in each of the three portfolio groupings.

While differences in performance of the market segment based and equity market sensitivity based portfolio groupings are in the eye of the

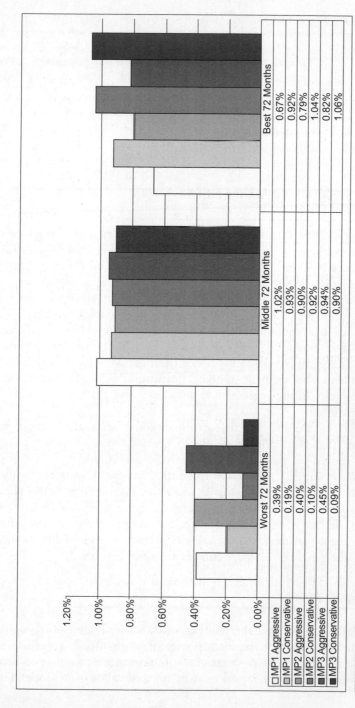

EXHIBIT 4.16 Portfolio Return Ranked on BarCap US Aggregate (1991–2008)

EXHIBIT 4.17 Market Factor Sensitivity Based Portfolio Weightings

	Type of Portfolio	Russell 1000	Russell 2000	MSCI EAFE	MSCI Emerging Markets Index	Private Equity
Model	Aggressive	20	20	15	10	15
Portfolio 1	Conservative	30	20	10	5	5
Model	Aggressive	20	15	10	10	10
Portfolio 2	Conservative	15	10	5	5	0
Model	Aggressive	15	15	10	10	10
Portfolio 3	Conservative	12.5	12.5	10	0	0

Note: Numbers are percentages.

investor, in Exhibit 4.18 we compare the differences in performance measures between the two portfolios—one set of portfolios based on traditional asset (market segment) groupings (Exhibit 4.6), the other set of portfolios based on certain investments being grouped based on equity market sensitivity (Exhibit 4.17). We are not going into detail of each of the comparison portfolios. However, for the market segment and market sensitive MP, the difference in asset holdings impacts a range of the relative performance variables. For example, MP1 aggressive and MP1 conservative market sensitivity standard deviation is greater than the MP1 aggressive and MP1 conservative market segment standard deviation due in part to the addition of private equity in the aggressive and conservative MP1 market sensitivity based portfolio.

In short, results indicate that investors must be aware of the differing approaches that asset allocators use in creating various asset groupings. Investors should be aware of the underlying assets held and the resulting market factor sensitivities derived from those assets. This is especially true for investors who are concerned with extreme movements in market factors. As we discuss in future chapters, strategic, tactical, and/or dynamic asset allocation are based on a thorough understanding of the current portfolio holdings, their market factor sensitivities, and their liquidity (ability to rebalance the portfolio to meet current investor concerns).

HOW NEW IS NEW?

In previous chapters, we cautioned against an over-reliance on empirically based solutions. Results based on historical data are just that—results based on historical data. Also, we stressed the importance of estimation error as well as model error in the inputs used in any asset allocation model. Finally,

BarCap US Gov	BarCap US Agg	BarCap US Corporate High Yield	FTSE NAREIT ALL REITS	CISDM EW Hedge Fund Index	S&P GSCI	CISDM CTA EW Index
10	10	0	0	0	0	0
15	15	0	0	0	0	0
10	10	5	5	5	0	0
22.5	25	2.5	0	15	0	0
10	10	5	2.5	2.5	5	5
25	25	0	2.5	2.5	2.5	7.5

we have pointed out that there exists not only an efficient market in asset pricing but the potential for an efficient market in ideas such that any "new" approach to asset allocation offering new advances often reflects marketing advances more often than an asset management advance. After all of these words of caution, this chapter presented asset allocation as if there existed a simple set of rules for determining a set of risk based investment portfolios as well as a simple set of rules for evaluation of the relative performance of those portfolios. Even worse, in the upcoming chapters on strategic, tactical, and dynamic asset allocation, we again emphasize traditional approaches to creating and comparing alternative methods of passive as well as more active asset allocation.

There are no one-size-fits-all solutions. In this chapter we tried to emphasize that return and risk characteristics of the underlying core portfolios used in the asset allocation process will fundamentally impact the relative benefits of any asset allocation process. If an investor is more comfortable choosing across asset classes where those asset classes are segmented more by the markets they trade than their common sensitivities to various market factors, then there should be an awareness that such an approach comes with a number of benefits (potential for excess returns based on investors' sense of discretionary trading) as well as risks (potential for high correlation between various market sectors). Similarly, emphasis on a set of asset classes constructed on high intra-asset class correlations is sensitive to parameter error as well as the necessity for ensuring that the low inter-asset class correlations remain low. What is important is that the investor know the return and risk characteristics of each asset class and that the models used to determine core asset groupings may also impact how one manages the risk of the groupings (the more style pure a particular asset class, the greater the potential for systematically removing market or sector risks from that asset class).

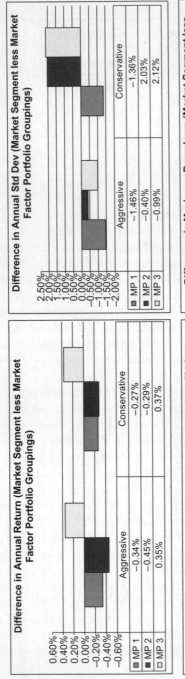

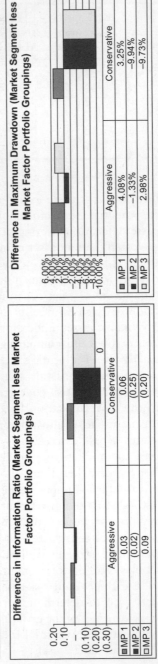

EXHIBIT 4.18 Differences in Aggressive and Conservative Portfolio Performance (Market Segment Portfolios—Market Sensitivity Portfolios)

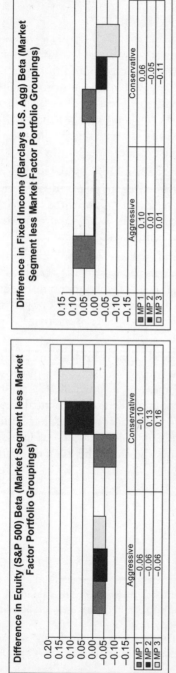

Difference in Equity (S&P 500) Beta (Market Segment less Market Factor Portfolio Groupings)

	Aggressive	Conservative
■ MP 1	−0.06	−0.10
■ MP 2	−0.06	0.13
□ MP 3	−0.06	0.16

Difference in Equity (S&P 500) Correl (Market Segment less Market Factor Portfolio Groupings)

	Aggressive	Conservative
■ MP 1	0.04	−0.02
■ MP 2	−0.05	0.01
□ MP 3	0.00	0.06

Difference in Fixed Income (Barclays U.S. Agg) Beta (Market Segment less Market Factor Portfolio Groupings)

	Aggressive	Conservative
■ MP 1	0.10	0.06
■ MP 2	0.01	−0.05
□ MP 3	0.01	−0.11

Difference in Fixed Income (Barclays U.S. Agg) Beta (Market Segment less Market Factor Portfolio Groupings)

	Aggressive	Conservative
■ MP 1	0.04	0.05
■ MP 2	0.02	−0.22
□ MP 3	0.01	−0.16

EXHIBIT 4.18 (Continued)

WHAT EVERY INVESTOR SHOULD REMEMBER

- Each asset class consists of a number of strategy level investments. There are of course different means for determining the asset class that a particular strategy is grouped within and unfortunately no one single approach seems dominant. Alternatives for asset grouping include (1) standard deviation, (2) beta, and (3) multiple risk dimensions (price variability, liquidity, transparency). In addition, theory rather than simple facts must guide us.

- High equity sensitive alternatives such as real estate and private equity may not necessarily be regarded as an equity diversifier but more as a return enhancement to equity dominated portfolios. Lastly, hedge funds and managed futures both report moderate volatility as well as relatively low equity market betas.

- Over various periods of analysis and extreme market environments, there is evidence that grouping various investment strategies into asset groupings based on traditional asset class segmentation (equity, fixed income, alternatives) provides different performance than typically grouping assets based on various factor sensitivity (equity beta, fixed income beta).

- Portfolio attribution remains the focal point regardless of the means by which asset groupings are determined. It is not the purpose of this book to cover alternative means of portfolio attribution; however, as discussed in future chapters, strategic, tactical, and/or dynamic asset allocation are based on a thorough understanding of the current portfolio holdings, their market factor sensitivities, and their liquidity (ability to rebalance the portfolio to meet current investor concerns).

NOTES

1. The basis for performance fees may impact how assets are valued by general partners. As a result, accounting based performance fees may be determined in part by the business model of the valuing firm.
2. Moreover, recent academic research has shown that individuals' tolerance for risk increases as their wealth increases and as they become more familiar with

a particular asset class. The increasing amount of education on the benefits of alternative investments as well as the increase in personal wealth in recent years further supports the inclusion of alternative investments in investors' portfolios.

3. The classic example is *Stocks for the Long Run* (Siegel 2008), which was popular during the run-up for the stock market.

4. For a review of the return and risk benefits of a wide range of alternative investments, see www.ingarm.org. At this site a series of papers on the Benefits of Hedge Funds, Managed Futures, Private Equity, Real Estate, and Commodities exists that summarizes the return and risk benefits of a range of alternative investment classes.

5. It should not go without saying that research continues to explore the relative importance of security selection and asset allocation. Finally, it is very important to note that all these studies examined well diversified portfolios. None of the results can be extended to concentrated portfolios.

6. There is of course a wide range of approaches to asset allocation. For a review of three basic approaches including market weight, equal weight, and optimization, see Y. Choueifaty and Y. Coignard. "Toward Maximum Diversification," *JPM* (Fall 2008), 40–51.

7. In his *Financial Analysts Journal* article, Bookstaber (September/October 2003, Vol. 59, No. 5) expresses the concern that one may have a difficult time separating the "how" from the "why" in determining the basis for hedge funds. Bookstaber set out his belief that "there is no such thing as a hedge fund. Hedge funds are not a homogeneous class that can be analyzed in a consistent way. The universe of alternative investments is just that—the universe. It encompasses all possible investment vehicles and all possible investment strategies minus the "traditional" investment funds and vehicles." He proceeds to illustrate the problem with viewing hedge funds as a whole when they are managed in the particular. He is looking for the essential in hedge funds.

8. For the most part, these investment strategies are generally each regarded as a separate asset due in part to their differential sensitivities to various market conditions; however, results also show that various forms of private equity and real estate have strong commonalities in sensitivities to equity markets and economic markets, such that they may be regarded as being part of an overall equity sub-class rather than a separate asset class.

9. In recent years hedge funds and managed futures have grown in investor interest. Both of these investment strategies have been shown to have low correlations with equity investments, fixed income investments, and traditional alternatives. However, even in this case, various hedge fund strategies may be better regarded as part of an equity sub class than as a separate asset class providing unique risk and returns unavailable in other asset forms.

10. In the exhibits throughout this book, the benchmark names may have been shortened (e.g., Barclays Capital U.S. Government is often listed as BarCap US

Gov; CASAM/CISDM CTA Equal Weighted Index is listed as CISDM CTA EW Index) for purposes of presentation.

11. This is as good a place as any to remind all readers that the weights used in this example were determined from the STE approach (simple trial and error). All investors should be aware that hypothetical results may reflect manager bias. Investors should always ask themselves if the results are consistent with both theory and other independent empirical research.

CHAPTER 5

Strategic, Tactical, and Dynamic Asset Allocation

One of the limitations of many current asset allocation approaches is that they concentrate primarily on investment in a limited number of assets (stocks, bonds, and real estate). Today, investment in a larger range of investable assets is being addressed through more active asset construction. The increase in potential investment opportunities increases the potential benefit of strategic asset allocation opportunities as well as tactical and dynamic approaches to asset allocation. Chapter 5 addresses those issues.

The term asset allocation means different things to different people in different contexts. For our purposes we have divided asset allocation decisions into three often-used categories:

- **Strategic asset allocation** can be characterized as a long-term asset allocation decision. The objective is to determine the long-term normal asset mix that will represent the desirable balance of risk and return. In developing the strategic asset allocation, the investor's return objectives, risk tolerance, and other investment constraints have to be taken into account. Next, the set of asset classes that are permissible under the investor's investment policy statement are used to establish the optimal long-run mix. If the portfolio's performance is evaluated using a specific benchmark, then strategic allocation would correspond to the mix represented by the benchmark. The investment policy statement would need to spell out if and how the strategic allocation should be altered in light of a new economic environment.
- **Tactical asset allocation** (TAA) represents an active departure from the strategic asset mix. The changes will take place in response to shifts in risk-reward characteristics of different asset classes resulting from changes in the investment environment. Tactical asset allocation is founded on the premise that asset returns are on the average driven by economic fundamentals. There are of course a number of alternative

TAA processes. Some rely primarily on economic based return forecasts, while others are based on historical price movement (e.g., when
the asset prices rise rapidly, a tactical asset allocator may tend to sell,
and when asset prices fall rapidly, the investor will tend to buy).

■ **Dynamic trading strategies** are designed to change the distribution
pattern of the portfolio. The best known of these strategies is the portfolio insurance strategy, which is designed to set a floor for the value
of the portfolio.

Historically, asset allocation has centered on long only stock and bond
investments, but alternative assets are increasingly being considered in the
strategic and tactical areas of asset management as well as underlying assets
in various dynamic trading based structured notes. The unique characteristics of alternative assets also raise a number of issues. For instance, alternative assets are lumpy investments and are typically illiquid, making it
difficult to implement typical strategic, tactical, and dynamic strategies.
Further, while traditional assets are easily accessible through investable
indices, most alternative assets are accessed through selecting active managers, which poses unique issues in asset allocation.

Given the wide range of issues involved in asset allocation, a systematic
approach to its use across traditional and alternative asset classes is important for client education, client marketing, and product creation and management. As discussed in previous chapters, the level of sophistication and
detail may differ for each client. For more sophisticated investors, a wider
range of asset allocation techniques and approaches are often introduced if
for no other reason than to indicate that the firms' modeling processes are
competitive in areas such as tracking error, capacity, and liquidity adjustments. At the basic investor level the simple Markowitz mean-variance asset
allocation is often used simply because of the clients' background with the
methodology. As a consequence, the analysis within this chapter starts with
the use of asset allocation optimization models in portfolio creation and
management.

ASSET ALLOCATION OPTIMIZATION MODELS

Traditional portfolio optimization attempts to find the portfolio with
the lowest possible risk (measured by the variance of the return) for a
target expected rate of return. More formally, the goal is to find the portfolio weights (note that one can eliminated the usual constraint that
weights should add up to one by using returns in excess of a riskless asset)
such that:

$$\min_{weights} \; Var[R_p] \text{ Subject to } E[R_p] = \text{Target} \text{ and } w_i \geq 0$$

Note that the usual constraint that weights should add up to one can be eliminated by using returns in excess of a riskless asset.

The inputs required to perform the above optimization are:

- expected returns
- variance-covariance matrix of returns

As mentioned already, the basic premise of portfolio optimization is quite sensible, and under ideal conditions, it should help create portfolios with attractive risk-return profiles. However, in practice a number of problems have to be dealt with before the results of a quantitative portfolio selection model, whether it is a simple mean-variance optimization or a more advanced model, are put to work. The basic principle that one has to remember is that quantitative portfolio construction models need accurate inputs. Further, the output is typically extremely sensitive to some of the inputs, and unfortunately these inputs are typically the ones that cannot be estimated accurately.

A simple example from the real world can demonstrate this. The annualized rate of return on the S&P 500 for the past 14 years has been around 6.5% while its annualized standard deviation for the same period has been around 16%. Given the long series of returns, one would be tempted to use 6.5% as the long-term return on S&P 500. However, you may be surprised to read that statistically that figure is not significantly different from zero. In fact, all we can say is that with 95% confidence the mean return is between –2.2% and +15%. It turns out that the outputs of portfolio optimization methods are highly sensitive to the estimated values of the means. Even if we decide to use 6.5% as a good estimate of the mean, we must hope that the future will be similar to the past. In other words, we are assuming that the S&P 500 returns of the past 14 years came from the same distribution that is likely to prevail for the duration of our investment horizon.

While generally the estimation of risk parameters can be improved using high frequency data, no such improvement takes place in estimating expected return. For instance, suppose one has five years of data. If annual returns are used to estimate the variance, the potential estimation error will be very high. However, if we use five years of monthly data to estimate the volatility, one would obtain a more accurate estimate of volatility with a lower estimation error. Nevertheless, it makes absolutely no difference if annual, monthly, or daily data are used to estimate the mean return. They will all give the same estimate with the same estimation error. The only way one can reduce the estimation error is to have a longer series. This means that lack of high frequency data for hedge funds and private equity funds affects our estimates of their risks and not their mean return. On the other hand, not having a long return history severely reduces our confidence in the estimated value of the mean. An additional point needs to be mentioned; that is, the use of any historical time period as a basis for parameter estimation assumes that the period examined represents the expected return and risk characteristics of the future anticipated investment horizon.

Estimating the Inputs

The most obvious approach is to use historical averages to estimate expected returns and risk parameters of the investment set. This approach has a number of problems. As discussed previously, one problem often referred to is "maximizing over the errors" because the resulting optimal portfolio maximizes over the errors in estimated parameters.[1] This means that the highest allocation is likely to be made to the investment that has had the highest positive error (e.g., highest realized return or lowest realized volatility). There are five methods for reducing the impact of this problem:

1. **More robust estimation methods:** There are statistical methods that can improve the accuracy of the estimates. However, almost all of these methods deal with estimation of the variance-covariance matrix. Very little can be done to improve the efficiency of the estimated value of the mean.
2. **More robust optimization methods:** There are adjustments that one can make to the classical mean-variance optimization such that the impact of estimation risk is incorporated in the optimization process. These methods require specialized software and typically require specific adjustments to the algorithm to handle some practical problems (e.g., limits on sector exposures or illiquidity of some asset classes).
3. **Bootstrapped or resampled portfolios:** In this case various "versions" of historical data are used to generate various optimal portfolios. Different procedures are available for selecting a representative of simulated portfolios. Though this approach does not yield a unique portfolio, one learns a great deal about the sensitivity of the optimal portfolios to changes in the inputs.
4. **Constraining portfolio weights:** In this case the portfolio manager imposes various constraints on portfolio weights in order to avoid portfolios with extreme weights. This is a rather ad hoc procedure because it is not clear what the constraints should be. However, this simple solution tends to produce portfolios that are sensible, and, according to several studies, they tend to perform well out-of-sample.[2]

5. **Economic model based estimates:** The most famous version of this approach is the Black-Litterman model. This model takes the weights of a well-diversified portfolio as the starting point. The most appealing aspect of this approach is that it uses an equilibrium economic model to estimate expected returns. If one were to use these estimates as inputs, then the portfolio's mix will be similar to the mix of a well-diversified portfolio, which is typically the portfolio's benchmark. We will have more to say about this approach later in this chapter.

Predictability of Risk and Return

There is some evidence that risk and returns of major asset classes and trading strategies are predictable. The evidence on the predictability of risk is very strong and there is virtually no disagreement about its strength and significance. The entire academic literature on what is known as ARCH and GARCH models deals with the issue of predictability in risk. It turns out that most of these models perform rather well in predicting short-term changes in risk. For example, it is well known that financial markets display "volatility clustering." This means that when there is a spike in volatility of asset prices, there will be a tendency for that volatility to last several days. However, these models perform rather poorly when it comes to predicting changes in volatility in the long term. Therefore, when it comes to strategic asset allocation, models that predict volatility are not of great use (they could be useful for tactical or dynamic allocation).

To determine if a return series has predictability in its volatility, one could perform a simple test. Suppose we look at daily returns on the Russell 2000 Index, covering January 1, 2006 through December 31, 2008. We run the following simple regression:

$$R_{t,R2K} = a + b \times R_{t-1,R2K} + \varepsilon_t$$

where $R_{t,R2K}$ is the rate of return on Russell 2000 Index on day t. The parameters that have to be estimated are a and b. If the estimated value of slope parameter is -0.10, then there is a small degree of mean reversion in the daily return on Russell 2000, which may not be significant enough to create a profitable trading strategy.

Now, let's try the above experiment again, but instead of using raw returns, we will use returns squared; that is:

$$R_{t,R2K}^2 = a + b \times R_{t-1,R2K}^2 + \varepsilon_t$$

This time if the estimated value of the slope is 0.37. This means that a high volatility day is likely to be followed by a high volatility day. In fact, about 37% of the previous day's volatility spills over into the following day's volatility. If the same exercise is performed using monthly data, the estimated value of b when raw returns are used may decrease or increase; however, its estimated value when squared returns are used is very likely to decline significantly; that is, long-term volatility is less predictable.

The evidence on the predictability of expected returns is not as strong, and there is a lack of consensus among researchers on whether the apparent predictability is strong enough to be used in asset allocation. During the last several years, a number of studies have demonstrated that a meaningful amount of variation in stock returns be explained by lagged values of variables such as the dividend yield, T-Bill yield, and credit risk premium, among others. Unlike predictability in volatility, which is mostly short-term, predictability in stock returns using economic fundamentals is mostly a long-run phenomenon. In this regard, this predictability could be useful for strategic asset allocation.

There is a perception that if returns are predictable, then market efficiency cannot hold. This is not necessarily correct. It is correct to argue that if markets are not efficient, then asset returns are likely to be predictable and one would be able to earn returns not justified by the risk of the position. However, the opposite is not necessarily true. Asset returns could be predictable in a perfectly efficient market. One reason for this is that the risk premiums on various asset classes are not stable and vary through time as the economy moves through various stages of business cycle. This means that to the extent that one can predict changes in the risk premium, then expected returns will be predictable, and this is completely consistent with efficient markets.

Other Risk Measures

The appropriate measure of risk is dictated by the needs of the investor. Traditionally, variance has been the most common measure of risk in asset allocation programs. Clearly, variance is not an ideal measure of risk in some circumstances. As mentioned above, risk relative to liabilities cannot be captured by variance. Further, in other cases variance may represent only one dimension of the risk. For instance, risk of exposure to unexpected increases in inflation cannot be measured by the variance of the portfolio. Of course, there are many other dimensions to risk (e.g., interest rate risk, credit risk, and currency risk). However, inflation risk poses a special case because it affects real returns; that is, a portfolio with fairly stable nominal return could have a very volatile real return during an inflationary period. In fact, it can be argued that no single variable can ever serve as an accurate measure of total risk.

It is possible to maintain the simple structure of the mean-variance optimization model but instead use measures of risk other than variance. A common approach is to use the semi-standard deviation, which measures the volatility of the portfolio below a target return (e.g., zero). To the degree that return distributions are not symmetric, then the use of semi-standard deviation as a measure of risk could lead to significantly different allocation when compared to classical mean-variance approach.

The next step consists of expanding the classical mean-variance approach to account for multiple measures or sources of risk. For example, suppose one is interested in creating a mean-variance efficient portfolio that would avoid allocation to investments with negative skewness and would favor investments with positive exposure to inflation. Suppose the skewness of the fund is denoted by $S[R_p]$ and the beta of the fund with respect to inflation is denoted by $B[R_p,I]$. Then the classical mean-variance optimization can be changed to the following:

$$\min\{Var[R_p] - a \times S[R] - b \times B[R_p, I]\} \quad \text{Subject to} \quad E[R_p] = \text{Target}, \quad w_i \geq 0$$

Note that the usual constraint that weights should add up to one can be eliminated by using returns in excess of a riskless asset. In this case, the investor minimizes a weighted average of variance, skewness, and beta with respect to inflation, where negative weights are assigned to skewness and inflation beta. The size of a and b are set by the investor. This is where experience and some common sense are needed. Basically, the larger the value of these two parameters, the greater the portfolio's tilt in that direction. This will, of course, come at the expense of a higher variance. After all, there is no free lunch. In a similar fashion, one can incorporate other risk dimensions into the model. However, bear in mind that the more risk dimensions one introduces, the greater the chance that there will be estimation errors in inputs, leading to a portfolio that is only optimal in terms of its allocation to errors.

Tracking Error

As mentioned in the previous section, risk has many dimensions. One of the most common situations in which a multi-dimensional measure of risk is required is in the area of tracking error. Whatever the primary objective of the portfolio optimizer is, the added objective would be to reduce the tracking error of the portfolio relative to a benchmark, liabilities, or an economic factor. In this case, the objective of the optimizer can be expanded such that reducing the tracking error of the portfolio is included in the optimization process. Similar to what was proposed above in dealing with skewness or inflation, this will require the user to assign a value (a loss function) to the tracking error. In other words, the user has to specify how important the tracking error is and how much performance he is willing to give up for a marginal reduction in tracking error. The resulting efficient frontier will naturally suffer from some inefficiency, but the inclusion of the tracking error will have the beneficial effect of reducing variation in optimal weights through time relative to the chosen index.

Other Risk Concerns

Even in an ideal world, the investor's degree of risk aversion has to be taken into account. Therefore, a crucial step in the design of any asset allocation program is the determination of the investor's objectives and constraints. Risk aversion affects the level of volatility or beta that the investor is willing to accept in the long run. Through various simulation procedures, one can educate the investor about the potential impacts of assuming various levels of risk. For instance, value at risk could be used to show the impact of high and low volatility strategies.

Risk aversion, especially at the institutional level, may be highly affected by the investor's liabilities. In this context, risk could be measured with respect to liabilities. For instance, a family business that is expected to fund future generations of a family has potential liabilities with long duration and significant exposure to inflation. Therefore, in this context, an optimal portfolio would need to have significant allocation to long duration assets and assets that provide a hedge against inflation. However, if the portfolio is managed on a stand-alone basis, an optimal allocation may have little or no allocation to those assets.

When an optimal portfolio is viewed in relationship to liabilities, one has to pay attention to the cost of not meeting the liabilities. For instance, for a family business the cost of not meeting the obligations is not as significant as it is for a life insurance company. Therefore, if the cost of not meeting its obligations is very high, the investor must take liabilities into account in designing optimal portfolios.

Another constraint on the portfolio is the cash flow requirements of the investor, which is closely related to the time horizon of the investor. In the case of an endowment, the cash flow requirements are fairly predictable and the time horizon is *very* long. This means the endowment can afford to invest in illiquid assets. On the other hand, a casualty insurance company has unpredictable cash flows and the time horizon is somewhat unpredictable as well. Therefore, the insurance fund must maintain significant liquidity.

STRATEGIC ASSET ALLOCATION

Strategic asset allocation is a major determinant of variability of a portfolio and, to a lesser degree, its total return. Studies have shown that up to 90% of a well-diversified portfolio's return volatility is determined by its strategic allocation. On the other hand, about 20% of its mean total return is determined by its strategic allocation.[3] Therefore, no matter how you look at it, the strategic allocation is a major determinant of a portfolio's risk-return profile.

In the previous sections, we discussed various aspects of asset allocation. In this section we present the basic steps that one has to take to implement a strategic asset allocation.

The first step is to identify the investor's objectives and constraints. We have already discussed attitude toward risk and the role of liabilities as being important factors in this area. If liabilities are not important, then the portfolio is managed on a stand-alone basis. Otherwise, the portfolio allocation will need to take liabilities into account.

In the next step, we need to decide if there is a benchmark that will be used to measure the portfolio's performance. This will help us identify the universe of permissible asset classes. Of course, the portfolio may be allowed to invest in asset classes that are not part of the benchmark; but all asset classes that are included in the benchmark should be available to the portfolio.

In step three, we estimate the risk and return characteristics of the permissible asset classes. As indicated already, estimates obtained from historical return series may not always be the best inputs to the strategic allocation model. This is particularly true for expected returns to asset classes. Here, we can use the basic message of equilibrium asset pricing models to obtain internally consistent estimates, which can serve as our starting point. To implement the equilibrium approach we need to create a benchmark that consists of all the asset classes that we are permitted to invest in. Our job will be much easier if the investment committee has already decided on a benchmark. If not, then we need to come up with one or more potential benchmarks. For example, suppose the set of permissible asset classes consists of equity markets that belong to MSCI Global, bond markets that are covered by Barclay's Capital Global Bond Index, commodities that are covered by Goldman Sachs/S&P Commodity Index, and funds of hedge funds.

Given the investor's risk tolerance, we may decide that a benchmark consisting of 40% in MSCI Global Index, 30% in Barclays Capital Global Bond Index, 10% in S&P GSCI Commodity Index, and 20% in CISDM Fund of Funds Index is a sensible benchmark. Using historical data, we estimate the variance-covariance of the returns on these asset classes. Then the expected return on asset class i that is consistent with the above benchmark is given by

$$E[R_i - R_f] = \lambda \times \beta_i$$

where β_i is the beta of asset i with respect to the benchmark portfolio, R_f is the riskless rate, and λ is coefficient measuring the degree of risk aversion. This last parameter may appear to be rather tricky to estimate, and it is. It is given by the investor's attitude toward risk and is rather difficult to estimate. It basically asks how high the return should be to warrant an allocation to the portfolio. Even if one has no estimate of the risk aversion parameter, one can use the above expression to learn what the relative rates of returns should be. The bottom line is that if one were to use the above expected returns in a mean-variance optimization approach, the resulting optimal portfolio would be the same as the benchmark. In practice, the portfolio manager should experiment with various combinations to determine how sensitive expected returns are to changes in the benchmark. It should be noted that the estimates of expected returns obtained through this procedure represent a starting point for our portfolio manager. Next, the manager will adjust these expected returns to reflect her views on the potential performance of various asset classes. For instance, the portfolio manager may decide that because of easy monetary policies of various central banks, inflation is likely to surprise to the upside and thus commodities are likely to perform better than the equilibrium expected return.

Black and Litterman (1992) describe a quantitative procedure to adjust the equilibrium returns so that the portfolio manager's confidence in her forecast is taken into account. A full description of the Black-Litterman approach is beyond the scope of this book. But it must be pointed out that using equilibrium returns to begin the process of estimating expected returns to various asset classes is highly recommended but is rarely followed.

The final step is to use a combination of quantitative and qualitative methods to determine the optimal allocation. Generally speaking, a purely quantitative approach in most cases does not provide a full solution to the investor's problem. For instance, the presence of alternative investments typically complicates a purely quantitative approach because these investments are bulky and illiquid, and they take time to implement. Strategic asset allocation is normally performed on three- to five-year basis with quarterly rebalancing. If there are major changes in the investor's financial position or the economic environment, the strategic allocation has to be reevaluated.

TACTICAL ASSET ALLOCATION

Tactical asset allocation (TAA) is a dynamic approach to asset allocation where the asset mix is actively adjusted in response to short-term changes in the economic environment. The objective is to adjust the allocation in order to take advantage of temporary pockets of inefficiency. Strategic allocation determines the risk-return of the portfolio while TAA can add value if it is designed correctly and all the potential costs and risks associated with it are taken into account.

Generally, TAA programs are designed to take advantage of temporary changes in market conditions that would favor one asset class over another. The markets, therefore, provide us with the potential opportunity to take advantage of these changing market conditions to improve the performance of a portfolio. It is important to note that the pro forma returns of any tactical asset allocation model are dependent on the actual period of analysis and therefore should be analyzed very carefully in order to decide if the performance is likely to be repeated in the future.

The main source of value derived from a TAA program is the strength and consistency of its signals, which are then used to alter the portfolio mix. The forecasting model of a TAA must possess a number of desirable properties. First, the signals must make economic sense; that is, one should be able to explain in simple terms why the model is able to forecast relative performance of various asset classes. For example, one of the most reliable signals about future performance of equities relative to fixed income instruments has been the slope of the yield curve. An upward sloping yield curve is generally consistent with a period of rising stock prices. The reason behind this is that an upward sloping yield curve is generally observed at the beginning of economic expansion. By examining the economic foundation of the signal, one can avoid using results that have resulted from data mining, that is, the generated signals that are not likely to perform well out of sample.

So what are the economic foundations of a sensible signaling model of a TAA? Clearly, it is difficult to predict risky investment returns. The main reasons are: (1) returns to risky assets are highly volatile and (2) financial markets tend to be highly efficient most of the time. Since the current price of an investment equals the present value of its cash flows discounted by the riskless rate plus a risk premium, the economic model must be able to explain how changes in one or more of these factors are predicted.

TAA models that include a wide variety of assets have more opportunities to identify inefficiencies in various market segments. TAA models benefit from large differences in the alternative asset class choices. The primary problem with TAA modeling is to offer superior return to risk performance while at the same time seeking to avoid allocations that would deviate from the general long-term strategic goals of the investor. One potential problem with many TAA programs is that the client cannot be sure of what possible allocations may be adopted under various scenarios unless the process is constrained so as not to deviate dramatically from the initial strategic asset allocations. In the following, the sample TAA program solution to this problem is achieved to constrain the three alternative portfolios to have somewhat similar stock and bond sensitivities as well as absolute risk.

Outline of a TAA Model

The main features of this program include:

- **Model Portfolios.** Three model portfolios consisting of nine broad asset classes are created for each client. The asset classes are:
  1. Short-term fixed income instruments
  2. Investment grade corporate bonds
  3. Government bonds
  4. High-yield corporate bonds
  5. Large cap equity
  6. Small cap equity
  7. Developed international equity excluding the United States
  8. Emerging markets equity
  9. Alternative investments

    Other asset classes can be added to or removed from this list depending on the client's needs.

    The three model portfolios represent a strategic allocation, a conservative tactical allocation, and an aggressive tactical allocation. The strategic allocation represents the long-term, normal portfolio of the client. Conservative tactical allocation will be adopted should the quantitative model indicate that market conditions do not offer attractive risk-return opportunities and therefore a more conservative allocation is warranted. By the same token, the aggressive tactical allocation will be adopted if the model indicates improved return opportunities in equities and other less conservative asset classes. Since this model works with predetermined allocations, the client knows exactly which allocation will be selected, based on certain market conditions.

- **Quantitative Model.** Expected return models are often based on multi-factor models. In this case, a 4-factor model is used to predict risk and return on each predetermined allocation. The four factors are:

1. Current level of credit risk premium (CR) compared to its histori-cally normal level
2. Current level of term premium (TP) compared to its historically normal level
3. Current level of S&P 500 implied volatility as measured by VIX compared to its historically normal level
4. Recent return to each allocation

- **Estimation Strategy.** A quantitative approach is adopted to estimate the lead-lag relationship between the performance of each allocation and the factors mentioned above.

$$E[R_{t+1}] = f(CR_t, TP_t, R_t, VIX_t)$$

In this case, five years of monthly returns are used to estimate the model. The estimated relationship is back tested to ensure its robustness and stability.

- **Reallocation Strategy.** Once the quantitative model is estimated, we are prepared to use the model to perform tactical asset allocation. The process is systematic and the role of human judgment is minimal. At the end of each reallocation period (in this case monthly), data on predictive factors are collected and then fed into the model. The output would consist of expected performance of the three model portfolios over the next allocation cycle. The allocation that is likely to perform best for the strategic allocation up to the next reallocation point is selected. In the case that no allocation significantly dominates the other two, the current allocation is maintained.

Example

This section demonstrates an application of the TAA approach using the following model portfolios. For this example, asset weights are given in Exhibit 5.1. The indices shown in Exhibit 5.2 are employed to represent the historical performance of these asset classes. The performance of asset classes along with the three allocations are presented in Exhibit 5.3.

It can be seen that the three allocations have each had distinct perfor-mance in the past. The conservative allocation has demonstrated a relatively stable risk (annual volatility of 6.7%) and reasonable return (5% per year). As expected, the aggressive allocation has demonstrated the highest perfor-mance (5.1% per year) with greatest volatility (12.2% per year).

Even though the aggressive allocation has performed better than the other two allocations over this time period, there have been periods during which the conservative allocation performed better than the other two.

EXHIBIT 5.1 Hypothetical Weights

	Conservative Allocation	Strategic Allocation	Aggressive Allocation
Short-Term Fixed Income Instruments	29%	15%	5%
Government Bonds	16%	7%	5%
Investment Grade Bonds	8%	8%	5%
High-Yield Corporate Bonds	4%	5%	5%
Large Cap Equity	17%	25%	28%
Small Cap Equity	3%	5%	7%
International Equity Excluding U.S.	10%	17%	18%
Emerging Markets	3%	3%	7%
Alternative Investments	10%	15%	20%
Total	100%	100%	100%

Using the procedure discussed earlier, we estimated the quantitative model using a five-year rolling window starting with the period between December 1991 and November 1996. The model was used to perform tactical asset allocation starting in December 1996. The reallocation cycle was set at one month. The results are presented in Exhibit 5.4.

Exhibit 5.4 demonstrates the power of tactical asset allocation. Exhibit 5.5 demonstrates that the tactical asset allocation model exceeds the performance of the strategic allocation in the down markets of 2002 and 2008.

EXHIBIT 5.2 Benchmark Alternatives

Asset Class	Index
Short-Term Fixed Income Instruments	BarCap US Treasury Bills
Government Bonds	BarCap US Government
Investment Grade Bonds	BarCap US Corporate Investment Grade
High-Yield Corporate Bonds	BarCap US Corporate High-Yield
Large Cap Equity	S&P 500
Small Cap Equity	Russell 2000
International Equity Excluding U.S.	MSCI EAFE
Emerging Markets	MSCI Emerging Markets
Alternative Investments	CISDM EW Hedge Fund Index

EXHIBIT 5.3 Benchmark Performance

12/1996– 5/2009 Asset Class	Annualized		Beta with Respect to		
	Mean	Std Dev	Government/ Credit Bonds	Large Cap Equity	Information Ratio
Short-Term Fixed Income Instruments	3.7%	0.6%	0.02	0	6.68
Government Bonds	5.7%	5.9%	0.63	−0.04	1.80
Investment Grade Bonds	5.5%	5.9%	1.14	0.09	0.93
High-Yield Corporate Bonds	4.9%	10.3%	0.37	0.37	0.48
Large Cap Equity	3.3%	16.6%	−0.01	1	0.20
Small Cap Equity	4.2%	21.4%	−0.14	1.01	0.20
International Equity Excluding U.S.	1.2%	17.6%	0.13	0.69	0.07
Emerging Markets	4.0%	26.6%	−0.21	1.2	0.15
Alternative Investments	10.0%	8.3%	0.04	0.37	1.21
Conservative	5.0%	6.7%	0.17	0.38	0.75
Strategic	4.9%	9.9%	0.22	0.57	0.50
Aggressive	5.1%	12.2%	0.11	0.69	0.42

These basic features of a tactical asset allocation (TAA) program will adjust strategic allocations to a portfolio of various fund strategies in a predetermined manner. The approach is systematic and quantitative, leading to a menu of allocations that have been agreed upon at the beginning of the process. This is the major advantage of this program when compared to other TAA asset allocation programs offered by other institutions: the investor knows precisely the changes that will take place in the strategic allocation based on possible future market conditions.

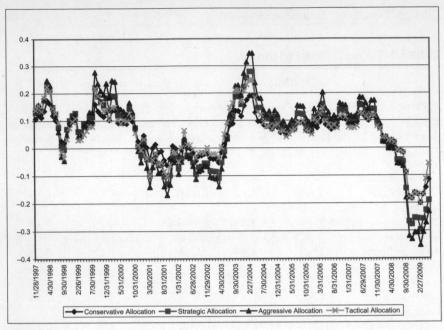

EXHIBIT 5.4 Twelve-Month Rolling Returns: Risk Based Portfolios and Tactical Asset Portfolio

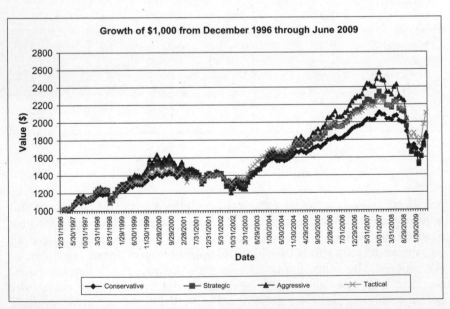

EXHIBIT 5.5 VAMI: Risk Based Portfolios and Tactical Asset Portfolio

DYNAMIC ASSET ALLOCATION

In general, dynamic asset allocation programs are targeted at creating a risk-return profile over time that generally assures a minimum return while preserving the opportunity for potential gains from the risky assets. In the 1980s various dynamic hedging strategies were created that were known by their general title of portfolio insurance. Portfolio insurance should under optimal conditions create a return profile that is similar to a put protected investment strategy. Instead of buying a put to protect the portfolio's value, a dynamic asset allocation model adjusts the mix between a risky portfolio and risk-free asset according to a predefined hedge ratio, which adjusts the amount in the two assets as the fund value rises and falls. As an alternative to dynamic portfolio insurance based strategies, a number of risk management strategies are conducted under the generic concept known as constant proportional portfolio insurance (CPPI). Simply put, under CPPI the exposure to a risky asset is increased as the portfolio rises in value and the exposure to the riskless asset increases as the portfolio value falls. There are a number of constraints in many practical applications of the CPPI, especially in various structured notes or products that have regulatory constraints on what a product can be invested in and how it is invested.

In its simplest form, the CPPI can be represented by the following expression:

$$\text{Size of Risky Position} = m \times (\text{Portfolio Value} - \text{Floor})$$

The portfolio value and floor are typically determined by the client. For example, the floor could be the present value of the portfolio. In this case, the goal is to protect the principal and guarantee a minimum return of zero. The parameter m determines how much risk the investor is willing to accept in terms of violating the floor. For instance, if m is selected to be 5, then the model should work as expected as long as the value of the risk position does not move any more than 20% between rebalancing periods (20% is equal to 1/5). It can be argued that if the rebalancing period is short, then a diversified portfolio of risky assets should not move by more than 20% and the model should work properly. However, it must be borne in mind that there are costs associated with frequent rebalancing and the costs increase rapidly if there are positions in alternative investments. These rebalancing costs and various fees charged by managers of such dynamic allocation products represent a major drag on their performance.

Let's consider a simple example. Suppose a structured note is to be set up where the principal is to be protected. The maturity of the note is 10 years. The underlying assets of the structure are (1) a diversified portfolio of traditional as well alternative assets and (2) U.S. Treasuries. The first step is to calculate the bond floor, which is equal to the present value of the principal discounted using the current term structure of Treasuries. For instance, if the current price of a 10-year zero-coupon Treasury security is .67, this means that for every $100 investment, $67 must be invested in Treasuries to protect the principal. The remaining $33 can be invested in the diversified portfolio. Such a strategy would be free of almost any risk and of course is not likely to provide a meaningful return either.

Alternatively, the investor may be willing to take a small risk and use a CPPI structure to manage the risk. Using a moderate multiplier (e.g., $m = 2$), the investor can have a great deal of confidence that the bond floor will not be violated. In this case, the portfolio manager will invest the following amount in the diversified portfolio:

$$66 = 2 \times (100 - 67)$$

The remaining 34 will be invested in Treasuries. Suppose the bond floor increases to 70, the investment in Treasuries grows 36 and the investment in diversified portfolio grows to 73. The reallocation is determined as follows:

$$78 = 2 \times (36 + 73 - 70)$$

This means that the total investment in diversified portfolio should increase from 73 to 78. The net investment in Treasuries will be $31 = 36 + 73 - 78$. This procedure is followed until the note matures. This simple approach will guarantee that the principal is protected as long as the percentage change in the value of the diversified portfolio between rebalancing does not decline by more 50%, which is the inverse of 2.

The multiplier, m, does not have to be constant. In practice, it could change as the volatility of the underlying portfolio changes. Typically, one would want to decrease the value of the multiplier as markets become more volatile. Finally, simulation can be used to obtain distributional properties of the note under various assumptions regarding the behavior of interest rates, underlying assets of the diversified portfolios, fee structures, coupon rates and so on.

WHAT EVERY INVESTOR SHOULD REMEMBER

- Markowitz based optimization provides suggested strategy weightings that are sensitive to a wide range of issues related to parameter estimation. For example, asset allocations are sensitive to the differential return forecasts (anticipated weightings may therefore be better determined using forecasted returns) and the measurement interval used in calculating the inputs to the various asset allocation procedures.

- Tactical asset allocations benefit from the consideration of alternative core strategy portfolios that differ in the underlying factors used in determining the tactical rebalancing.

- Dynamic asset allocation processes are by their very nature adjustments based on future unforecastable factors and are liable not only to changes in the underlying factors driving the model but to changes in the business and regulatory environment.

NOTES

1. The impact of various optimization models maximizing over errors varies as to the types of assets being considered and the degree to which the errors exist both in return estimation and risk estimation.
2. See P.A. Frost and J.E. Savarino, "For Better Performance: Constrain Portfolio Weights," *Journal of Portfolio Management*, 1988.
3. For a summary of research in this area, see Y. Tokat, et al., "The Asset Allocation Debate: A Review and Reconciliation," *Journal of Financial Planning*, Vol. 19, No. 10 (2006): 52–63.

CHAPTER 6

Core and Satellite Investment: Market/Manager Based Alternatives

Asset allocation consists of a fundamental set of decisions centered on what investments and how much of each investment to buy given an investor's risk preferences. This chapter provides a traditional basic "core" and "satellite" approach to asset allocation. In so doing, it focuses on the potential impact of moving from more liquid and transparent investment vehicles in each asset class to less liquid and less transparent investment vehicles and the potential change in expected return and risk associated with that movement. To reach this end, the chapter first defines the concept of core and satellite portfolios and then goes on to discuss the issues associated with benchmarking the different asset classes critical to the implementation of these concepts. Note that the research and data associated with alternative investments is relatively new and must be carefully managed. Next, the chapter provides examples of an investor's decision making process in moving between and among core and satellite portfolios and offers an overview of sample allocations and expected risk/return scenarios. Finally, the chapter discusses recent issues in replication theory and how these developments can enhance the value of an investor's decision.

Throughout this discussion, the chapter posits that the benefit of diversification is based on the potential for investing in a wide range of assets, each with its own unique return and risk characteristics. A reasoned understanding of the economic and market factors underlying an asset's return and risk profile is critical to the meaningful formulation of investment policies and the exercise of informed judgment.

In a core-satellite approach to traditional stock and bond asset allocation, an investor builds a core consisting mostly of passively managed, liquid, and low cost equity and fixed income assets and adds to this core a set of satellites consisting of actively managed, relatively illiquid, alpha generating assets. The idea is that investors should not spend valuable resources on seeking alpha where it does not exist or is too small to make a difference.

According to Standard & Poor's latest study (Standard & Poor's Indices Versus Active Funds Scorecard, Year End 2008):

- Over the five-year market cycle from 2004 to 2008, the S&P 500 outperformed 71.9% of actively managed large cap funds, the S&P MidCap 400 outperformed 79.1% of mid cap funds, and the S&P SmallCap 600 outperformed 85.5% of small cap funds. These results are similar to that of the previous five-year cycle from 1999 to 2003.
- The belief that bear markets favor active management is a myth. A majority of active funds in eight of the nine domestic equity style boxes were outperformed by indices in the negative markets of 2008. The bear market of 2000 to 2002 showed similar outcomes.
- The difference between the performance of first quartile large cap funds and third quartile large cap funds was 2.73% per year from 2003 to 2008. For small cap funds the difference is 4.1%.
- Similar results are obtained for fixed income funds and international equity funds.

These results indicate that it does not pay to waste time, money, and effort on finding alpha or top managers in the area of traditional equity and fixed income investments. Not only do most managers fail to beat their benchmarks, even when an investor gets lucky and finds a "good" manager, he fails to outperform other managers by a significant amount.

While the return differential between top and bottom quartile equity and fixed income managers is relatively small, the same cannot be said for alternative investment managers. For instance, according to a report by Yale endowment (Yale Endowment Report, 2005), the return differential between the first quartile venture capital funds and third quartile venture capital funds was 43.2% for 1995 to 2005. The result for funds of funds was 7.1%. This means it pays to spend time and effort to identify top performing actively managed alternative investments.

DETERMINING THE APPROPRIATE BENCHMARKS AND GROUPINGS

As noted, understanding the underlying sources of risk and returns of a given investment or its associated "grouping" is essential to a meaningful asset allocation program. In many programs, non-investable benchmarks have been used to provide a basis for determining the potential risks and returns of asset classes from traditional stock and bonds to alternative investments such as private equity, real estate, commodities, and hedge funds. The core asset decision should produce an investable portfolio whose return and market risk characteristics reflect those of the noninvestable benchmark portfolio. Due to the desired matching between the noninvestable benchmark portfolio and the investable core portfolio, the core portfolio provides "market returns for market risk." Investors who desire higher potential returns within each asset class must consider investment alternatives that provide higher return potential consistent with higher risk. These investments may be regarded as satellite portfolios to the comparison passive investments within the core asset class.

For a wide range of reasons (academic and commercial), most asset allocation programs have used different approaches to determine the number of core asset classes.[1] While asset allocation for many investors remains dedicated to traditional stock and bond investment, in this chapter we concentrate on presenting a multi-asset class allocation model that is more suitable for the increasing number of investors who are considering various forms of alternative investment vehicles. For these investors, alternative investments are centered on traditional alternatives such as private equity, real estate, and commodities. For other investors, alternative investments also include various forms of hedge funds and managed futures (often classified as modern alternative investment vehicles). In previous years, most investors were required to find manager based alternative investment products that tracked the performance of the underlying noninvestable benchmarks used in the initial asset allocation analysis. Recently, there has been a growth in various liquid investable products that offer a direct means to access these forms of alternative investment. Today these investable forms include ETFs, strategy-specific algorithmic based trading products, and replication/tracking products that offer the means to invest in liquid transparent vehicles that track the performance of less liquid alternative investment products.

Exhibit 6.1 proposes a brief schematic that indicates one process for determining the potential strategic portfolio based on a range of noninvestable asset benchmark/indices. It indicates the importance of a systematic investment process in determining an investor's approach to overall asset allocation. As stated, a central part of the strategic management process is to establish a set of core portfolio holdings across a set of predetermined investments that provide the basis for meeting one's long term return to risk. While the underlying core assets that are used to capture the expected return and risk attributes of the strategic portfolio may be passive

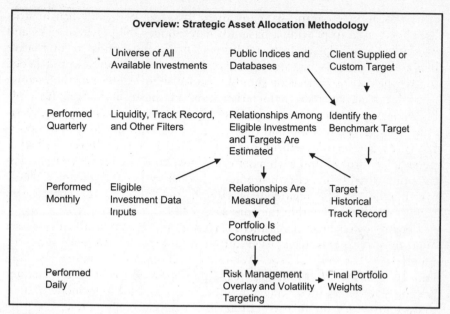

Overview: Strategic Asset Allocation Methodology

EXHIBIT 6.1 Benchmark Strategic Asset Allocation Process

in nature, the process by which these assets are chosen and managed should be active and include discretionary oversight.

Exhibit 6.2 reflects a brief taxonomy for reviewing a set of multi-asset investments facing the typical investor. This overview of the investment choices facing the typical investor is similar to that presented in many asset allocation approaches. First, as indicated above, choices must be made as to the series of asset classes considered for investment when determining the strategic portfolio holdings of the investor. As indicated in the previous chapter, increasing the number of potential asset classes increases both the potential for greater risk management as well as increased return for a predetermined level of risk. As shown in Exhibit 6.2, while the underlying strategic asset allocation may be based on noninvestable benchmarks, an investor's core portfolio should contain investable passive investments which capture the underlying returns of the noninvestable benchmarks. If an investor desires to increase their potential return without dramatically changing one's asset class exposure, then, as shown in Exhibit 6.2, adding additional manager based investments (Satellite I and Satellite II) which track the passive investable assets but also may contain potential manager alpha should be considered.

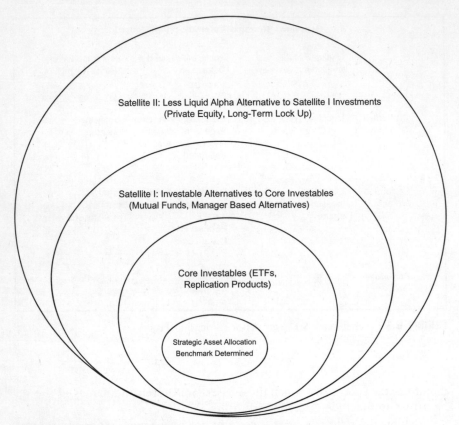

Satellite II: Less Liquid Alpha Alternative to Satellite I Investments
(Private Equity, Long-Term Lock Up)

Satellite I: Investable Alternatives to Core Investables
(Mutual Funds, Manager Based Alternatives)

Core Investables (ETFs,
Replication Products)

Strategic Asset Allocation
Benchmark Determined

EXHIBIT 6.2   Strategic Benchmark, Core, and Satellite Groupings

In Exhibit 6.3, the core investment classes have been broken down into
equity, fixed income, traditional alternatives, and modern alternatives. Each
of these classes of course contains a set of sub-indices (e.g., equity—
value and growth, domestic/foreign, small/large) and each of the relevant
sub-indices may be combined to achieve a unique risk set consistent with
investor needs. In Exhibit 6.3, those potential investments that are both
investable and transparent alternatives to the noninvestable asset classes
investment vehicles are grouped into the core portfolio. These investments
may include a range of investible ETFs as well as closed end funds and/
or passive investable tracking programs (hedge fund and CTA tracking
products).

For investors who are willing to invest in investments within an asset
class which have less liquidity and transparency, a range of investments are

Asset Class	Noninvestable Benchmark	Core	Satellite I	Satillite II
Equity				
Large Cap	Russell 1000	Russell 1000 ETF	Funds	Individual Mgrs.
Small Cap	Russell 2000	Russell 2000 ETF	Funds	Individual Mgrs.
Emerging Mkt.	MSCI Emg. Mkt.	MSCI EM. ETF	Funds	Individual Mgrs.
Non-U.S.- Dev.	MSCI EAFE	MSCI EAFE ETF	Funds	Individual Mgrs.
Fixed Income				
Government/Credit	Barclay Gov.	Barclay Gov. ETF	Funds	Individual Mgrs.
Aggregate	Barclay Agg.	Barclay Agg. ETF	Funds	Individual Mgrs.
High Yield	Barclay HY	Barclay HY ETF	Funds	Individual Mgrs.
Alternative Traditional				
Private Equity	S&P PE Index	S&P PE ETF	Funds	Individual Mgrs.
Real Estate	NAREIT	NAREIT ETF	Funds	Individual Mgrs.
Commoditites	S&P GSCI	SP GSCI ETF	Funds	Individual Mgrs.
Alternative Modern				
Hedge Funds	CISDM EW HF Index	Index Replication	Funds	Individual Mgrs.
Managed Futures	CISDM EW CTA Index	Index Replication	Funds	Individual Mgrs.

Investment Characteristics

Higher	←——— Transparency, Daily Price, Exchange Traded ———→	Lower
Higher	←——— Style Consistency, Scalability ———→	Lower
Lower	←——— Business and Counterparty Risk ———→	Higher
Lower	←——— Alpha ———→	Higher

EXHIBIT 6.3 Alternative Asset Classes in Benchmark, Core, and Satellite Groupings

listed in Satellite I. These investments include various manager based mutual fund investments as well as investable manager based or managed account benchmark products in the alternative investment area. Satellite II is for those investment products for which liquidity and transparency are lower compared to comparison core products and manager based products included in Satellite I. In fact, the lower liquidity and lack of transparency for assets in Satellite II may in some cases form the basis for the excess return for Satellite II products over similar core and Satellite I investment products.

It is important to note that for each product the transition from core to satellite may result in slightly different return and risk characteristics. It is key, however, that these risk characteristics be manager specific and that a portfolio of such assets may provide excess return relative to the core benchmark product but will retain a relatively high correlation with that

EXHIBIT 6.4   Alternative Product Characteristics in Core through Satellite Products

Investment Sector	Core	Satellite I	Satellite II
Product Characteristics	Index, ETF, Replication	Liquid, Fund Based	Manager Based
Fees	Low	Medium	High
Liquidity	High	Medium	Low
Transparency	High	Medium/High	Low
Required Minimums	Low	Low/Medium	High
Diversified Exposure	High	Medium	Low
Regulatory Oversight	Medium/High	Medium/High	Low
Manager Risk	Low	Medium	High
Style Consistency	High	High	Low
Product Flexibility	High	Low	Low
Valuation Frequency	High	Medium/High	Low
Capacity	Medium/High	Constrained	Constrained
Trading	Systematic	Active	Active
Only Exchange Traded	Yes	No	No

benchmark. It is essential again to remind investors that the excess return to a particular form of investment within an asset class may not be due solely to price risk but to a range of potential risks consistent with the underlying investment (lack of liquidity, lack of transparency). A range of those potential risks an investor faces when they move from core to satellite groupings is provided in Exhibit 6.4.

Many investors may doubt the ability of various passive investable core products to reflect the return and risk characteristics of various noninvestable asset class benchmarks. Exhibit 6.5 reports the correlations between the noninvestable benchmarks used in portfolio asset allocation determination and the underlying core investments based on investable ETFs, as well as replication indices that track the underlying noninvestable index (the primary period of analysis is 1999–2008, however, for some paired correlations the period of analysis is less). In all cases, the correlations between the noninvestable benchmarks and the investable core are over 0.70. Note again, that the use of historical benchmarks in any asset allocation program is based on the assumption that the actual investment mirrors the factor characteristics of the benchmark. In this case, the investable core portfolios are designed to be style pure with consistent expected return and risk characteristics. Satellite I portfolios are generally regarded as additions to the investable core sector portfolio but with the potential for the benefits of active management. Satellite I portfolios as indicated in Exhibit 6.5 have correlations with the benchmark indices and with the core such that their use should not fundamentally change the market risk characteristics of the benchmark and/or investable core portfolio.

SAMPLE ALLOCATIONS

The decision that drives the asset allocation process is the underlying risk tolerance of the investor. As discussed in Chapter 4, an investor's risk tolerance may cover a range of desired risk exposures.[2] Typically those ranges have included conservative, moderate, and aggressive risk based portfolios. Within each of these risk tolerance classifications, investors may decide to invest primarily in traditional security investments or they may decide to place additional investments in the alternative investment area without dramatically changing volatility characteristics. These portfolios will reflect an investor's characteristics such as assets, liabilities, time horizon, tax status, and risk tolerance. It is fully expected that increased investment in private equity and hedge funds offer financial consultants the investment products required to provide their clients unique returns that are not available through traditional stocks and bonds; and, just as important, provide financial consultants with a set of assets that enable them to show their unique educational role.

This decision can be broken into the "can" and "will" portion of an investor's asset allocation framework:

- **Can-Risk Capacity:** The investor's objective ability to take financial risks, that is, how much risk the investor is *able* to accept.
  - The investor's ability to take financial risks is externally given by the investor's financial situation. Various academic and practitioner models exist that attempt to map out an investor's current financial situation, their long-term financial needs, and the investor's capacity to take on additional risk.
  - Often various forms of contingent (e.g., minimum asset floor) investment models are used, which permit an investor to feel assured that the minimum investment level is protected while automatically increasing investment and potential return through alternative investments as the minimum investment level is systematically increased and investor wealth or investment levels increase. (Of course, if

EXHIBIT 6.5 Comparison Correlations for Benchmark, Core, and Satellite Groupings

Benchmark	Russell 1000	Russell 2000	MSCI EAFE	MSCI EM	BarCap US Gov	BarCap US Agg
Core	iShares Russell 1000 Index Fund	iShares Russell 2000 Index Fund	iShares MSCI EAFE	iShares MSCI EM	iShares Barclays Government/ Credit Bond Fund	iShares Barclays Aggregate Bond Fund
Correlations to Benchmark	1.00	1.00	0.98	0.97	0.86	0.95
Satellite 1 Investments	Lipper Lg-Cap Core	Lipper Sm-Cap Core	Lipper Non US Stock	Lipper Emerg Mkt Fd	Lipper A Rated Bnd Fd	Lipper Gen US Govt Fd
Correlations to Benchmark	1.00	0.98	0.93	0.99	0.97	0.94
Satellite 1 Investments	Lipper Lg-Cap Core	Lipper Sm-Cap Core	Lipper Non US Stock	Lipper Emerg Mkt Fd	Lipper A Rated Bnd Fd	Lipper Gen US Govt Fd
Correlations to Core	1.00	0.98	0.95	0.97	0.89	0.87

wealth or investment levels decrease, systematic reductions would also be conducted.)

- **Will-Risk Aversion:** The investor's subjective disposition for taking risks, that is, how much risk the investor is *willing* to accept.[3]

  - Know-how: An investor's understanding of the financial market and its products is a major influence. The better the understanding, the higher the risk level an investor will accept. For instance, even though according to objective measures of risk, hedge funds are less risky than long equity positions, individual investors may avoid any allocation to hedge funds because of their lack of familiarity. An important task of a financial consultant is, therefore, to educate high net worth individuals about the risk-return characteristics of the various private equity opportunities and hedge fund strategies.

  - Positive Experience: Positive experiences with different asset classes in the past increase the willingness to take new risks (i.e., invest in unfamiliar asset classes).

BarCap US Corporate High-Yield	Private Equity Index	S&P GSCI	FTSE NAREIT ALL REITS	CISDM EW HF Index	CISDM CTA EW Index
SPDR Barclays Capital High Yield Bond ETF	PowerShares Listed Private Equity Portfolio	iShares S&P GSCI Commodity Indexed Trust	iShares FTSE NAREIT Real Estate 50 Index Fund	HF Replication	CTA Replication
0.95	0.94	0.99	0.99	0.94	0.73
Lipper HI Cur Yld Bd	Private Equity MF	Lipper Nat Res Fd IX	Lipper Real Estate Fd	HF Investable (Mgr. Based)	CTA Investable (Mgr. Based)
0.98	0.68	0.63	0.99	0.90	0.41
Lipper HI Cur Yld Bd	Private Equity MF	Lipper Nat Res Fd IX	Lipper Real Estate Fd	HF Investable (Mgr. Based)	CTA Investable (Mgr. Based)
0.90	0.83	0.85	0.98	0.91	0.73

- Personal Character: Optimism, entrepreneurship, and the discipline of staying with a predefined strategy.

CORE ALLOCATION

Once the risk appetite of the investor is known, decisions can be made as to the core asset allocations as well as the degree to which the investor is willing to hold various satellite portfolios. As noted above, once the underlying strategic asset allocation is determined, the initial problem is to determine which assets to hold that fundamentally track that of the noninvestable assets benchmarks used in the initial strategic asset allocation determination. The economic rationale for investable core traditional and alternative investable products is that while these passive index-based core investment products are designed to generate no alpha; they are designed to provide diversification benefits and help manage underlying risk exposure.

SATELLITE INVESTMENT

Given an investor's desire for greater exposure to manager skill, a series of manager based products in various satellite portfolios can be considered. Satellite investment products are actively managed and may be a source of risk management or manager alpha. The risk exposures of these products are similar to those of the investable core portfolio and thus can be used without fundamentally changing the core portfolio's risk exposure.[4] Satellite investments are generally regarded as less liquid satellite investments that represent the most likely source of alpha in today's marketplace. The degree of alpha is a function of the liquidity and informational transparency of the investment vehicle.

ALGORITHMIC AND DISCRETIONARY ASPECTS OF CORE/SATELLITE EXPOSURE

Most current research has discussed the algorithmic or discretionary aspects of asset allocation across various core asset classes. However, some research has also addressed various tactical asset allocation processes within a particular asset class. In Exhibit 6.6 we have ranked various Russell 1000 and Russell 2000 growth and value indices on changes in VIX. Results show that decreases in VIX have a more positive impact on Russell Growth than on the Russell Value. In contrast, increases in VIX have a more negative impact on Russell Growth than Russell Value. Investments within a Russell 1000 or Russell 2000 core strategy can thus be dynamically managed to achieve desired risk level within a strategy, however, with a bias toward the underlying equity sector that the investor may think will outperform in the expected market environment.

It is also possible that rather than adjusting between core value and core growth, an investor could simply adjust the weighting within an asset class such that when volatility increases relative to traditional risk levels, dynamic asset allocation will adjust weightings to ensure that an asset's returns reflect historical volatility. For instance, an investor can reduce strategy risk exposure in high volatility markets (therefore reducing exposure to decreasing market return factors) and increase strategy risk exposure in low volatility markets (therefore increasing exposure to increasing market return factors).

The strict use of algorithmic models to manage risk within a core set of strategies or across core and satellite programs may not be sufficient to reach desired goals. In certain cases simple heuristic models of decision making based on a fundamental understanding of the relationship between macroeconomic and market information and strategy performance is

EXHIBIT 6.6 Intra-Equity Benchmark Performance: Ranked on Change in VIX

	Low		Medium-Low		Medium-High		High		All Dates
	Min	Max	Min	Max	Min	Max	Min	Max	
Ranking on VIX End-of-Month Change	−15%	−2%	−2%	0%	0%	2%	2%	21%	
				Monthly Mean					
VIX End-of-Month Change	−4%		−1%		1%		5%		0%
Russell 1000 Growth	3.53%		2.12%		0.44%		−3.81%		0.65%
Russell 1000 Value	2.82%		1.79%		1.08%		−2.67%		0.82%
Russell 2000 Growth	4.15%		2.63%		0.24%		−4.61%		0.70%
Russell 2000 Value	3.34%		2.41%		0.79%		−2.63%		1.04%

required. In short, sometimes you simply have to be discretionary in choosing what to hold and when to hold it.

REPLICATION BASED INDICES

While a range of passive based investable indices as well as fund products (ETFs and futures contracts) exist for most of the core investment strategies, for more expansive core/satellite programs additional liquid forms of passive investment are often required. Multiple approaches exist for asset replication including factor based replication, strategy based security replication, and strategy consistent security replication. In this analysis, for creating a suitable replication/tracking investment we use a set of ETFs that reflect the underlying securities used in the representative mutual fund. This ensures that the underlying model captures the relative factor movements of the actual assets held by the representative fund:

- **Liquidity without adverse impact on performance:** Liquid securities (cash and futures equity and fixed income instruments) are employed.
- **Immediate diversification:** ETFs, futures contracts, and other diversified portfolios representing various asset classes are used in the replication product.
- **Transparency of the product:** The algorithm is completely self-contained and transparent. This results in low startup (due diligence) cost. Further, there is very little manager risk or style drift risk.

Therefore, even if a viable replication product does not outperform its corresponding benchmark, it could be an attractive alternative to actively managed hedge fund products. Replication products can be used in a variety of ways.

- **Long-term investment and tactical asset allocation:** Because of its liquidity, the replication product could be used in a TAA program.
- **Hedging of existing positions:** Because the replication product can be shorted, it can be used to hedge illiquid long positions in certain hedge fund strategies.
- **Cash management:** Because of its liquidity, the product can be used to manage cash within existing fund of funds platforms.
- **ETF creation:** The product may be used to create Exchange Traded Funds.

There currently exist a range of replication processes. These processes can be categorized into:

- **Top Down:** Factor based methodologies generally use investable securities that reflect the underlying risks of a particular strategy (e.g., S&P ETFs to reflect equity risk and option straddles to capture market timing). The investment securities may not reflect the actual securities held in a particular strategy.
- **Bottom Up:** Trading process that attempts to directly reflect the actual investment decision process. For instance, by selling high P/E stocks and buying low P/E stocks to replicate a long short strategy.
- **Mixed (Security/Algorithmic Based):** Reflects a mid-point between the top down factor approach and the bottom up security approach. ETFs are used that reflect the underlying holdings of various investment strategies. The holdings of these ETFs vary to reflect the underlying returns of a benchmark and the corresponding changes in the holdings in the benchmark, which are the source of the return patterns.

With each of the approaches to replication, several concerns exist as to the underlying process.

- **Top Down:** May not be appropriate for funds that have low factor exposure; that are discretionary in approach and therefore for which the factor exposures may change dramatically; or that use multiple strategies, due to the low or changing factor exposures of the respective portfolios.
- **Bottom Up:** May not be appropriate for funds that use a range of trading approaches (e.g., earnings forecasts, valuation, cash flow analysis) to determine securities chosen such that a single systematic bottom up approach may not represent the range of strategy approaches offered in some investment strategies or for fund styles that hold relatively illiquid securities such that the bottom up strategy may be selling into similar difficult market environments.
- **Mixed (Security/Algorithmic Based):** May not reflect performance of funds for which the performance gap between replication fund performance and underlying fund reflects asset concentrations in the fund that cannot be replicated by the existing ETFs and/or for which the fund reflects active trading activity undertaken by the manager.

Among the various approaches, the following process is based on an algorithmic model that uses an array of ETFs and futures contracts to track the underlying sector holdings of a particular strategy. While simple linear factor models are often used in fund replication, simple linear regression models are likely to fail to provide attractive risk-return profiles under various market conditions. This could be the case because simple linear factor models may not be able to capture dynamics of funds' exposures and therefore may fail to replicate fund returns as market conditions change significantly and quickly (e.g., August 2007). Further, a replicating strategy that uses a fixed set of asset classes may also fail to replicate funds because risk-premiums of asset classes are not fixed and in some cases structural or momentum changes may occur in the market. For example, historically, value stocks have outperformed growth stocks. This relationship need not remain stable through time and it is conceivable that the differential return between value and growth stocks could decline to zero. Under such circumstances, replicating strategies that involve long and short positions in value and growth stocks will fail to produce meaningful returns. The same can be said about small versus large cap stocks.

Some of the unique features of the following replication approach are:

- A large set of asset classes is initially considered for investment. Currently, over 30 equity, fixed income, and commodity investments are considered.
- A multivariate GARCH model is used to estimate the variance-covariance of these asset classes.
- The estimated variance-covariance matrix is then used to reduce the number of assets to 8 to 15 assets and to estimate optimal weights.
- Other market factors such as credit spread, term spread, and volatility are used to adjust weights between calibration periods. This allows the model to react on a daily basis to changes in the market conditions.

The following reflects the relative costs of an investable approach that uses liquid ETFs to create a portfolio that tracks the risk and return characteristics of a targeted hedge fund benchmark. One of the benefits of an ETF or liquid trading based replication process is that it may reduce the overall costs of product development relative to more manager based vehicles. As shown in Exhibit 6.7, a manager based investment vehicle may require higher gross returns in order to provide the same net returns as a comparable replication product. Moreover, this is before consideration is made for additional operational issues of a manager based vehicle relative to an algorithmic replication product.

EXHIBIT 6.7 Comparison Fund and Replication Product Fees

	Managed Accounts	FOF	Replication
Trading Costs	.20%	.20%	.10%
Management Fee	2.00%	2.00%	1.00%
Performance Fee	20.00%	25.00%	0.00%
Wrap/CPPI	1.10%	1.10%	.70%
Administrative	.40%	.40%	.35%
Break-even Return	12.80%	13.50%	9.00%

The purpose of this replication approach is to:

- Directly capture the changing strategy emphasis of the benchmark
- Provide both low cost and low counterparty risk
- Provide high transparency and trading liquidity

Exhibit 6.8 reflects the performance of the noninvestable CISDM Equity Long Short (ELS) index, a mutual fund ELS Hybrid Benchmark, and an ETF based replication process with volatility targeted to that of the Mutual Fund ELS Hybrid Benchmark. It should come as no surprise, given the relative restrictions on short selling for mutual fund products, that the mutual fund hybrid ELS benchmark has a higher volatility than that of the

EXHIBIT 6.8 Comparison Benchmark, Mutual Fund, and Replication Performance

5/2007–5/2009	Return Annual	Std Dev Annual	Information Ratio	Correlation CISDM ELS	Correlation MF Based Hybrid ELS
CISDM Equity Long/Short Index	−2.2%	8.4%	−0.27	1.00	
Mutual Fund ELS Hybrid Benchmark	−13.1%	14.6%	−0.89	0.65	1.00
ELS Replication	−7.4%	15.1%	−0.49	0.81	0.98
ELS Rep Half Vol/MF	−0.62%	7.23%	−0.09	0.76	0.98

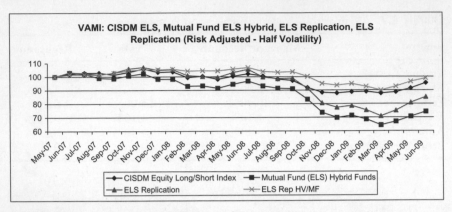

EXHIBIT 6.9   Comparison VAMI

representative CISDM ELS Index. However, as indicated in Exhibit 6.9, the first three representative indices do have a high degree of correlation. If desired, investors can simply adjust the replication product volatility goal to a lower level in order to have the replication volatility closer to that of the comparison CISDM ELS index.

As indicated in Exhibit 6.8 and Exhibit 6.9, when the mutual fund hybrid ELS index is replicated with the goal of one half of the volatility, the results are more representative of the CISDM ELS index. However, investors should be aware that the reported volatility for the CISDM ELS index may not reflect the actual volatility of the index. Research has shown that hedge funds may include a percent of nontradable securities for which historical prices may be smoothed, such that the historical volatility may underestimate the true volatility (Asness, Krail, and Liew, 2001).

PEER GROUP CREATION—STYLE PURITY

Results in the previous sections show the potential benefits of both replication strategies and style pure satellite investments as a means to access the core investable portfolio. As investors wish to access more active manager based strategies, they must ensure that the underlying mix of strategies reflects that of the strategy benchmark. Satellite creation is dependent on the grouping of managers/funds that have factors in common with underlying core products. Peer group creation or style purity is based on the fact that a significant portion of funds and funds of funds returns are driven by market factors representing various sources of risk and return. The basis behind the process is to create a peer group. (A peer group is a set of comparison investments that have risk exposures that are similar to the fund or fund of fund that is to be evaluated.) The following elements are some of the more important factors in this analysis:

- The filtering process employed in creating the peer group is flexible so that it can be customized for each client
- Specific exposures (e.g., credit risk) can be given higher weight than other risk exposures in creating the peer group
- Peer groups can be created for new managers based on their targeted risk exposures
- Risk exposures of the fund being considered
- A peer group clarification and reconciliation which has the following characteristics:
  - Factor exposures of each member of the peer group is reported
  - Other characteristics of the peer group (e.g., length of track record, AUM, and so forth) are reported.

In Exhibit 6.10, two peer groups have been created using the traditional method of finding managers within an asset class that are highly correlated with the comparison benchmark (style pure) and a set of managers with low correlation to the comparison benchmark (non style pure). In Exhibit 6.10 the equity long short style pure peer group has similar exposure to various risk factors as well as the CISDM Equity Long Short (ELS) Hedge Fund index. Thus the portfolio of managers with similar factor exposures to that of the CISDM ELS index also has a higher correlation with the CISDM ELS index than a portfolio of managers who are not style pure.

Head-to-Head Investment Comparison

In certain cases, various passive index and manager based products that may have similar market exposures have been grouped into different asset classes (commodity based equity in traditional equity and direct commodity investment in traditional alternatives). The basis for these differences may vary but include liquidity, regulatory constraints, and transparency. Investors should be aware that these assets are generally not regarded as substitutes and have varying degrees of risk and return characteristics. In Exhibit 6.11 the risk and return performance for comparison investable real estate products is compared. Similarly, in Exhibit 6.12 the risk and return performance of comparison commodity investment vehicles is presented.

EXHIBIT 6.10 Peer Group Performance Comparison: Style Pure and Non Style Pure

Period: 2000–2008	Annualized Return	Std Dev	S&P 500	BarCap US Gov	BarCap US Corporate High Yield	CISDM Equity Long Short (ELS)
					Correlation	
CISDM ELS Index	4.8%	6.6%	0.72	−0.21	0.57	1.00
ELS HF Style Pure	5.8%	14.9%	0.81	−0.25	0.71	0.94
ELS HF Non Style Pure	7.8%	13.8%	0.36	−0.17	0.30	0.45

EXHIBIT 6.11   Head-to-Head Comparison Performance: Real Estate (2001–2008)

	Annualized Return	Std Dev	Maximum Drawdown	Correlation FTSE NAREIT	Correlation S&P 500
FTSE AW Dv Ex US Real Estate TR USD	3.7%	19.7%	−60.5%	0.47	0.70
FTSE NAREIT All REITs	13.7%	15.0%	−27.0%	1.00	0.42
Hedge Fund Research Index: Real Estate	9.2%	15.5%	−6.1%	0.82	0.48
Lipper Real Estate (Mutual Fund)	13.8%	13.8%	−22.9%	0.99	0.45
S&P 500 Total Return Index	−2.9%	10.5%	−40.7%		
BarCap US Aggregate	5.7%	4.2%	−3.8%		
BarCap US Corporate High-Yield	3.2%	4.7%	−33.3%		

For real estate and commodities, results show a relatively high correlation between the comparison assets.

In the preceding exhibits, examples were given of actively managed external products (mutual funds) that offer similar return to risk characteristics to the other investable alternatives (real estate and commodities). In Exhibit 6.13, we extend this analysis to provide a comparison of noninvestable hedge fund indices and investable hybrid mutual funds. With the exception of equity market neutral, which is structured to have little common exposure to market factors, the various hedge fund benchmarks have a moderate to high correlation with the comparison mutual funds.

As discussed previously, it is also possible that various investments such as hedge funds with lockups may be regarded as less liquid alternatives to underlying core investable products. To the degree that an investor may not

EXHIBIT 6.12 Head-to-Head Comparison Performance: Commodities (2001–2008)

	Annualized Total Return	Annualized Standard Deviation	Information Ratio	Maximum Drawdown	Correlation Commodity Index*
Composite Commodity Indices (Energy, Industrial Metals, Precious Metals)	9.4%	17.7%	0.53	−42%	
Composite S&P 500 Indices (Energy, Metals, Gold)	7.5%	24.3%	0.31	−52%	0.67
Lipper Natural Resources	6.5%	24.1%	0.27	−57%	0.69
Commodity Index: Energy	2.0%	30.9%	0.06	−60%	
S&P 500 Energy Index	6.1%	20.6%	0.30	−41%	0.55
Morningstar Energy	5.5%	25.9%	0.21	−58%	0.31
HFRI Energy (Hedge Fund Index)	7.4%	14.6%	0.51	−40%	0.54
Commodity Index: Industrial Metals	9.5%	22.5%	0.42	−52%	
S&P 500 Metals & Mining Index	2.9%	32.1%	0.09	−67%	0.59
Commodity Index: Precious Metals	12.7%	17.0%	0.75	−31%	
S&P 500 Gold Index	8.9%	34.5%	0.26	−57%	0.72
Lipper Gold	19.9%	34.0%	0.58	−61%	0.80

*Commodity Index: Average of three commodity indices (S&P GSCI, DJ-UBS, BCI)

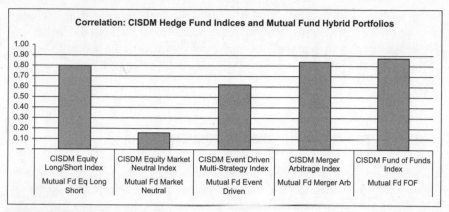

EXHIBIT 6.13   Correlation of Head-to-Head Portfolios and CISDM HF Indices

require liquidity but desires not to fundamentally change the return and risk structure of the underlying core portfolio, decisions must be made as to which traditional or core assets must be replaced when adding various assets. In Exhibit 6.14 we show that hedge funds that have similar market exposures to underlying traditional assets may be used as substitute assets. For example, as shown in Exhibit 6.14, the addition of equity long short

EXHIBIT 6.14   Impact of Incremental Hedge Fund Addition in Asset Management

Hypothetical Portfolio Weights	Traditional Portfolio	Portfolio with HFRI Distressed	Portfolio with HFRI Equity Long Short
U.S. 30 T-Bill	5.0%	3.0%	2.3%
1-Year Treasury	5.0%	5.0%	5.0%
3–7 Year Treasury	5.0%	5.0%	5.0%
10> Year Treasury	10.0%	10.0%	10.0%
Hi-Yield	5.0%	2.6%	5.0%
High Grade Corp.	10.0%	10.0%	10.0%
Russell 1000	40.0%	40.0%	39.9%
Rusell 2000	10.0%	9.6%	8.1%
MSCI EAFE	5.0%	5.0%	4.8%
MSCI Emerging Mkt	5.0%	4.8%	4.9%
HFRI Distressed		5.0%	
HFRI Equity Long Short			5.0%
Total Weights	100.0%	100.0%	100.0%
Annual Return	10.9%	11.1%	11.5%
Annual Std Dev	9.4%	9.4%	8.4%
Sharpe Ratio	0.63	0.67	0.70
Correlation: Original Port.		1.00	1.00

hedge funds can replace traditional equity with little impact on the relative risks of the two portfolios. Similarly, the addition of distressed debt/securities hedge funds can replace high-yield debt with little impact on the risk of the two portfolios.

WHAT EVERY INVESTOR SHOULD REMEMBER

- A central part of the strategic management process is to establish a set of core portfolio holdings across a set of predetermined investments that provide the basis for meeting one's long-term return to risk goals. While the underlying assets may be passive in nature, the process by which these assets are chosen should be active.

- Due to the desired matching between the benchmark portfolio and the core portfolio, the core portfolio is providing "market returns for market risk." Investors who desire higher potential returns within each asset class must consider investment alternatives that provide higher return potential consistent with higher risk. These investments may be regarded as satellite portfolios to the comparison passive investment within the core asset class.

- Little research has discussed the algorithmic or discretionary aspects of asset allocation within a particular core asset class. Investors should be aware of the ability to actively manage security selection within an asset class without fundamentally changing the risk exposure of the core asset.

- As more risky and less liquid investments are considered, an investor should be aware of the comparison assets that provide similar exposure to the comparison asset within an asset group.

- Finally, to the degree that investable liquid core investments may not exist that offer direct investment in benchmark assets, replication technologies exist that permit the creation of liquid investable vehicles which correspond to the underlying core portfolios.

NOTES

1. Different extremes exist. Sharpe (1992) used 12 asset groupings in his analysis of asset allocation. Most of these asset groupings, however, were variants of

various equity markets. In contrast, more recent studies on multi-asset allocation use as little as four asset classes (commodities, currencies, equities, fixed income) or as many as eight (equity, fixed income, private equity, real estate, commodities, hedge funds, CTAs). Similarly, within any individual core asset group, various asset allocation models use a wide range of investment strategies that trade securities consistent with the construction of that core asset class (e.g., value/growth and small cap/large cap within a U.S. equity core allocation).

2. Risk aversion, on the other hand, is difficult to determine. Numerous risk-assessment tools developed by banks, brokers, and psychologists try to give investors help in determining their desired level of financial risk. Studies in behavioral finance and decision making under risk have shown that risk aversion is influenced by recent performance (Sewell, 2008).

3. For a discussion of the determinants of risk taking behavior, see D. Hryshko, M.J. Luengo-Prado, and B.E. Sorensen, "Childhood Determinants of Risk Aversion," www.ssrn.com, 2009.

4. The diversification benefits of less liquid satellite portfolios depend both on the returns drivers of the alternative investments and on the ability of the portfolio to track initial core portfolios (E. Olan, E. Sorensen, and R. Hua, "Global Investing Delivers Diversification: A Multi-Strategy Perspective," *JPM* (Winter 2009): 42–49; and P. Chen, G. Jiang, and K. Shu, "Fund of Funds, Portable Alpha, and Portfolio Optimization," *JPM* (Spring 2009): 79–92.

CHAPTER 7

Sources of Risk and Return in Alternative Investments

Any investment outside of traditional fixed income, equities, or cash is often considered an alternative investment. As such this category occupies a vast space in finance. Most books on asset allocation, however, continue to emphasize the return and risk characteristics of traditional stock and bond investments. Chapter 7 travels a new road and focuses on major forms of alternative investments, their source of returns, and their recent performance. Alternative investments include hedge funds, managed futures, private equity, real estate, and commodities.[1] In this chapter a working definition for each is provided. For a range of alternative investments, the historical performance and correlation with certain performance benchmarks such as the S&P 500 are presented. The overall goal is to demonstrate how these asset classes should perform within a multi-asset portfolio. Throughout the analysis the period 2001 through and including 2008 is used as a reference period. This period was chosen because 2001 corresponds to the end of the dot-com bubble and is perhaps a bit more reflective of future equity and fixed income markets. There are significant caveats, however, with this approach. First, reference periods can always be used to game pro forma return results as well as risk projections. Where a period starts and where it ends can have significant consequences as to whether the performance looks great or whether the risk looks modest. We also examine the behavior of these traditional alternative asset classes in down markets. The focus on down markets is important from the perspective of risk. So long as everyone is making money, there is very little concern about correlations. However, down markets are where the portfolio shock truly takes place and where the diversification decision is truly tested. Throughout this review the chapter focuses within each section on the sources of return and the risks inherent within each asset class. Finally, the book uses this chapter as a starting point for the benchmark issues discussed in Chapter 8.

Keep in mind that this chapter focuses on the general performance of each investment area rather than the performance of individual funds or managers. The performance of a portfolio of style pure managers (managers who consistently trade the same strategy in basically similar ways) is expected to have the same general factor sensitivities as the average manager in that strategy but with lower risk.

ASSET CLASS PERFORMANCE

In Exhibit 7.1, results for the return and risk performance of various traditional and alternative asset classes are presented. Each equity index generally has a higher level of volatility and a higher equity beta than most fixed income investments and modern alternatives. Assets in the traditional alternative investment area (private equity, real estate, commodities) generally have the highest volatility and, depending on the asset, a high equity beta as well (as will be discussed later, real estate and private equity may not necessarily be regarded as an equity diversifier but more as a return enhancement to equity dominated portfolios). Finally, hedge funds and managed futures both report moderate volatility as well as relatively low equity market betas. In Exhibit 7.2, the correlations across the various investment asset groupings are also presented. Results reflect those presented in Exhibit 7.1; that is, benchmarks with equity exposure have relatively high intra-asset correlations. Lastly, asset groups that can easily take long and short positions (e.g., CTA) or which hold assets not directly linked to equity or bond markets (e.g., commodities) report low correlation with other asset classes. Exhibit 7.3, however, indicates that the relative benefits of these asset classes may be time-specific. For example, after ranking performance of various asset classes over the period 2001 to 2008 by the S&P 500, results indicate that in years of extreme negative stock market performance, many of the listed asset classes (with the exception of credit quality fixed income and CTAs) also reported negative returns.

Results at the asset class level may not reflect the potential benefits of various investment options within each class. For instance, within particular alternative asset classes, certain sub-strategies may have a higher correlation with other asset classes than with their own investment class (for example, within the hedge fund asset class, equity based hedge fund strategies such as equity long short may have a higher correlation with long equity strategies and distressed debt may have a higher correlation with high-yield debt than they have with a composite hedge fund index). As a result, certain sub-asset class groupings may be regarded as better diversifiers or return

EXHIBIT 7.1 Benchmark Performance

Index Performance 2001–2008	Annualized Total Return	Annualized Standard Deviation	Information Ratio	Maximum Drawdown	Beta Russell 1000	Beta BarCap US Gov	Beta BarCap US HY
Equity							
Russell 1000	−2.7%	15.28%	−0.18	−41.58%	1.00	(1.25)	0.96
Russell 2000	1.7%	19.55%	0.09	−42.98%	1.13	(1.58)	1.24
MSCI EAFE	−0.1%	17.00%	0.00	−49.51%	0.98	(0.94)	1.05
MSCI Emerging Markets Index	6.8%	24.41%	0.28	−60.60%	1.31	(1.29)	1.54
Fixed Income							
BarCap US Gov	6.4%	4.70%	1.36	−4.64%	(0.12)	1.00	(0.04)
BarCap US Agg	5.7%	3.99%	1.44	−3.83%	(0.03)	0.79	0.08
BarCap US Corporate High-Yield	3.2%	10.96%	0.29	−33.31%	0.49	(0.20)	1.00
Traditional Alternatives							
S&P GSCI	−0.5%	25.57%	−0.02	−62.16%	0.33	(0.64)	0.67
FTSE NAREIT All REITs	6.4%	20.95%	0.31	−58.79%	0.81	(0.42)	1.27
Private Equity Index	−3.7%	26.43%	−0.14	−70.33%	1.44	(1.59)	1.75
Modern Alternatives							
CISDM Hedge Fund EW	5.6%	6.62%	0.84	−21.12%	0.35	(0.37)	0.44
CISDM CTA EW	9.2%	8.75%	1.05	−8.75%	(0.14)	0.49	(0.16)

EXHIBIT 7.2 Benchmark Correlations

Index Correlation 2001–2008	Russell 1000	Russell 2000	MSCI EAFE	MSCI Emerging Markets	BarCap US Gov	BarCap US Agg	BarCap US Corporate High-Yield	S&P GSCI	FTSE NAREIT All REITs	Private Equity Index	CISDM Hedge Fund EW Index	CISDM CTA EW Index
Equity												
Russell 1000		0.88	0.88	0.82	−0.38	−0.13	0.69	0.20	0.59	0.83	0.81	−0.25
Russell 2000	0.88		0.81	0.78	−0.38	−0.15	0.69	0.20	0.69	0.82	0.80	−0.16
MSCI EAFE	0.88	0.81		0.88	−0.26	−0.01	0.68	0.35	0.56	0.81	0.88	−0.09
MSCI Emerging Markets	0.82	0.78	0.88		−0.25	0.00	0.69	0.36	0.52	0.80	0.93	−0.03
Fixed Income												
BarCap US Gov	−0.38	−0.38	−0.26	−0.25		0.94	−0.09	−0.12	−0.10	−0.28	−0.26	0.26
BarCap US Aggregate	−0.13	−0.15	−0.01	0.00	0.94		0.22	−0.02	0.13	−0.06	0.00	0.17
BarCap US Corporate High-Yield	0.69	0.69	0.68	0.69	−0.09	0.22		0.29	0.66	0.72	0.73	−0.20
Traditional Alternatives												
S&P GSCI	0.20	0.20	0.35	0.36	−0.12	−0.02	0.29		0.16	0.29	0.45	0.22
FTSE NAREIT All REITs	0.59	0.69	0.56	0.52	−0.10	0.13	0.66	0.16		0.62	0.52	−0.12
Private Equity Index	0.83	0.82	0.81	0.80	−0.28	−0.06	0.72	0.29	0.62		0.80	−0.14
Modern Alternatives												
CISDM EW Hedge Fund Index	0.81	0.80	0.88	0.93	−0.26	0.00	0.73	0.45	0.52	0.80		0.02
CISDM CTA EW Index	−0.25	−0.16	−0.09	−0.03	0.26	0.17	−0.20	0.22	−0.12	−0.14	0.02	

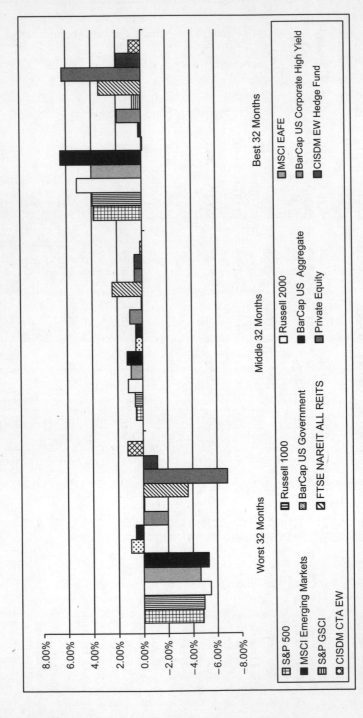

EXHIBIT 7.3 Benchmark Returns Ranked by S&P 500 (2001–2008)

enhancers depending on the portfolio for which they are being considered as potential additions to.

As discussed in the introduction to this chapter, in the following sections we discuss (1) the various sources of return, (2) the return and risk performance, (3) the market factor sensitivity, and (4) the performance in down and up equity markets for each of five major alternative investments that is: hedge funds, managed futures, private equity, real estate, and commodities. Results are presented both at the composite index level as well as, when available, the strategy index level.

HEDGE FUNDS

Hedge funds have often been described as being loosely regulated private pooled investment vehicles that are often levered and generally include a performance fee. There are four principal ways in which an investor can invest in hedge funds. First, direct investments where the investor meets the standards of an "accredited investor" or "qualified purchaser." Second, an investor can invest in a fund of hedge funds. Third, there are investable hedge fund indices. Fourth, recently managers have developed hedge fund replication products. As of the end of 2009, there were more than an estimated 7,000 hedge funds managing approximately $1.5 trillion in assets. Hedge fund strategies generally fall under three primary groupings:

1. Relative value (equity market neutral, fixed income arbitrage, convertible arbitrage)
2. Event driven (merger arbitrage, distressed securities, event multistrategy)
3. Opportunistic (equity long short, global macro)

Sources of Hedge Fund Return

The sources of hedge fund returns are often described as being based on the unique skill or strategy of the trader. Because hedge funds are actively managed, manager skill is important. However, academic research (Fung and Hsieh, 2002; Schneeweis 1998; Schneeweis et al. 2002, 2003) demonstrates that hedge fund returns are also driven systematically by market factors such as changes in credit spreads or market volatility, rather than exclusively by an individual manager's alpha. Therefore, one can think of hedge fund returns as a combination of manager skill and an underlying return to the hedge fund strategy or investment style itself.

Similar to the equity and bond markets, passive security based indices have been created that are designed to capture the underlying returns to the hedge fund strategy (Schneeweis, Kazemi, and Karavas, 2003; Jaeger and Wagner, 2005).[2] If a manager's performance is measured relative to the investable passive hedge fund index, for example, then the differential return may be viewed as the manager's "alpha" (return in excess of a non-manager based strategy similar replicate portfolio). If a manager's performance is measured relative to an index of other active managers, then the relative performance simply measures the over- or underperformance to that index of manager returns.

Hedge Fund Return and Risk Performance

Exhibit 7.4 shows the risk and return performance of hedge funds, traditional U.S. stocks and bonds, CTAs, real estate, commodities, and private equity for the period of 2001 to 2008. Portfolio combinations that include traditional assets and alternative investments for the most recent eight-year period 2001 to 2008 are shown in Exhibit 7.5. Over the period of analysis,

EXHIBIT 7.4 Hedge Fund and Comparison Index Performance (2001–2008)

Performance	S&P 500	BarCap US Aggregate	CISDM Hedge Funds EW Index
Annualized Total Return	–2.9%	5.7%	5.6%
Annualized Standard Deviation	15.0%	4.0%	6.6%
Information Ratio	(0.19)	1.44	0.84
Maximum Drawdown	–40.7%	–3.8%	–21.1%
Correlation with Hedge Funds	0.79	0.00	1.00

Alternative Asset Performance	S&P GSCI	CISDM CTA EW Index	FTSE NAREIT All REIT	Private Equity
Annualized Total Return	–0.5%	9.2%	6.4%	–3.7%
Annualized Standard Deviation	25.6%	8.7%	20.9%	26.4%
Information Ratio	(0.02)	1.05	0.31	(0.14)
Maximum Drawdown	–62.2%	–8.7%	–58.8%	–70.3%
Correlation with Hedge Funds	0.45	0.02	0.52	0.80

EXHIBIT 7.5   Multiple Asset Class Portfolio Performance (2001–2008)

Portfolio	A	B	C	D
Annualized Returns	1.7%	2.1%	2.4%	2.7%
Standard Deviation	7.5%	7.3%	8.4%	8.1%
Information Ratio	0.22	0.28	0.29	0.34
Maximum Drawdown	−21.0%	−21.0%	−25.6%	−25.2%
Correlation with Hedge Funds	0.79		0.78	
Portfolio A	Equal Weights S&P 500 and BarCap US Agg			
Portfolio B	90% Portfolio A and 10% Hedge Funds			
Portfolio C	75% Portfolio A and 25% CTA/Commodities/ Private Equity/Real Estate			
Portfolio D	90% Portfolio C and 10% Hedge Funds			

hedge funds reported higher annualized returns but lower volatility than the S&P 500. Compared to the returns of the Barclays Capital U.S. Bond Aggregate Index, hedge funds reported slightly lower rates of return but with higher volatility. Also, compared to CTAs and real estate, hedge funds reported a lower return but lower volatility. Next, compared to commodities and private equity, hedge funds reported higher returns and lower volatility. Exhibit 7.5 shows that the information ratios for portfolios that include at least a 10% investment in hedge funds dominate those portfolios which do not contain an investment in hedge funds.

The high correlation of the CISDM EW Hedge Fund index with the S&P 500 is due in part to the dominance of hedge fund index returns by equity biased hedge funds. As shown in Exhibit 7.6, hedge funds (equity market neutral, convertible arbitrage, fixed income arbitrage) that have in part removed the impact of associated market factor from their returns have correlations with the S&P 500 of under .60, and global macro, which trades global markets opportunistically, has a correlation of only .30. In contrast, equity long short and emerging markets hedge funds report correlations with the S&P 500 of close to or over .70. This is as expected. As discussed previously, each unique hedge fund strategy trades in particular markets such that their performance is sensitive to the underlying movements of securities in those markets. As a result, hedge fund strategies that primarily trade equity markets (e.g., equity long short) may be viewed as return enhancers to traditional equity portfolios rather than as risk diversifiers. Other traditional hedge fund strategies such as distressed securities, fixed income arbitrage, and convertible arbitrage often trade in high-yield debt. As indicated in Exhibit 7.6, the correlation of these three strategies with the Barclays Capital U.S. Corporate High-Yield Index are all close to

EXHIBIT 7.6 Performance of CISDM Hedge Fund Strategy Indices (2001–2008)

	Annualized Return	Standard Deviation	Correlation S&P 500	Correlation BarCap US Gov	Correlation BarCap US Corporate High-Yield
CISDM Equity Market Neutral	5.6%	2.0%	0.44	−0.16	0.40
CISDM Fixed Income Arbitrage	3.6%	4.8%	0.56	−0.18	0.75
CISDM Convertible Arbitrage	3.3%	6.2%	0.46	0.05	0.69
CISDM Distressed Securities	7.6%	6.0%	0.65	−0.16	0.77
CISDM Event Driven Multi-Strategy	5.6%	6.3%	0.76	−0.27	0.78
CISDM Merger Arbitrage	4.8%	3.4%	0.66	−0.17	0.65
CISDM Emerging Markets	7.9%	10.5%	0.69	−0.17	0.71
CISDM Equity Long/Short	4.4%	6.0%	0.77	−0.32	0.62
CISDM Global Macro	6.4%	3.3%	0.30	0.05	0.28
S&P 500	−2.9%	15.0%	1.00	−0.39	0.68
BarCap US Gov	6.4%	4.7%	−0.39	1.00	−0.09
BarCap US Corporate High-Yield	3.2%	11.0%	0.68	−0.09	1.00

or over .70. Simiarly, hedge fund strategies that primarily trade high-yield debt (e.g., distressed securities) may be viewed as return enhancers to high-yield debt portfolios rather than as risk diversifiers.

In general, hedge funds and their associated strategies cover a broad array of risk/return scenarios. In Exhibit 7.7, the correlation of various hedge fund strategies are given. Note that strategies that trade in similar markets or are exposed to similar risks should have higher correlations (equity long short and emerging markets) than strategies which trade in fundamentally different markets (global macro and merger arbitrage).

Hedge Fund Performance in Down and Up Equity Markets

Exhibit 7.8 depicts the performance of various hedge fund strategies in months in which the S&P 500 had its worst and best performance over the period 2001 to 2008. Results show that, relative to other hedge fund strategies, hedge fund strategies with significant equity bias (e.g., event driven, equity long short, and emerging markets) had the most negative returns in the worst S&P 500 months as well as the highest positive returns in the months in which the S&P 500 had its best performance.

MANAGED FUTURES (COMMODITY TRADING ADVISORS)

The term "managed futures" represents an industry composed of professional money managers known as commodity trading advisors (CTAs) or commodity pool operators (CPOs). Commodity trading advisors or commodity pool operators manage client assets on a discretionary basis, using forwards, futures, and options markets as the primary investment area. Managed futures, through their ability to take both long and short investment positions in international financial and non-financial asset sectors, offer risk and return patterns not easily accessible through traditional (such as long-only stock and bond portfolios) or other nontraditional investments (e.g., hedge funds, real estate, private equity, or commodities).

Investors generally invest in CTAs using individual managed accounts. Investors can also access the managed futures industry by investing through a commodity pool that resembles a mutual fund. Investments from several investors are pooled together and then invested in futures either directly by the pool operator or through one or more commodity trading advisor. CPOs may be either public or private. Currently several noninvestable as well as investable manager based CTA indices are available.

EXHIBIT 7.7 CISDM Hedge Fund Strategy Correlations (2001–2008)

	Equity Market Neutral	Fixed Income Arbitrage	Convertible Arbitrage	Distressed Securities	Event Driven Multi-Strategy	Merger Arbitrage	Emerging Markets	Equity Long/Short	Global Macro
CISDM Equity Market Neutral	1.00	0.39	0.45	0.54	0.68	0.61	0.65	0.76	0.57
CISDM Fixed Income Arbitrage	0.39	1.00	0.78	0.80	0.73	0.50	0.74	0.53	0.12
CISDM Convertible Arbitrage	0.45	0.78	1.00	0.79	0.71	0.56	0.69	0.53	0.24
CISDM Distressed Securities	0.54	0.80	0.79	1.00	0.90	0.68	0.83	0.75	0.36
CISDM Event Driven Multi-Strategy	0.68	0.73	0.71	0.90	1.00	0.82	0.86	0.89	0.47
CISDM Merger Arbitrage	0.61	0.50	0.56	0.68	0.82	1.00	0.65	0.79	0.45
CISDM Emerging Markets	0.65	0.74	0.69	0.83	0.86	0.65	1.00	0.83	0.47
CISDM Equity Long/Short	0.76	0.53	0.53	0.75	0.89	0.79	0.83	1.00	0.60
CISDM Global Macro	0.57	0.12	0.24	0.36	0.47	0.45	0.47	0.60	1.00

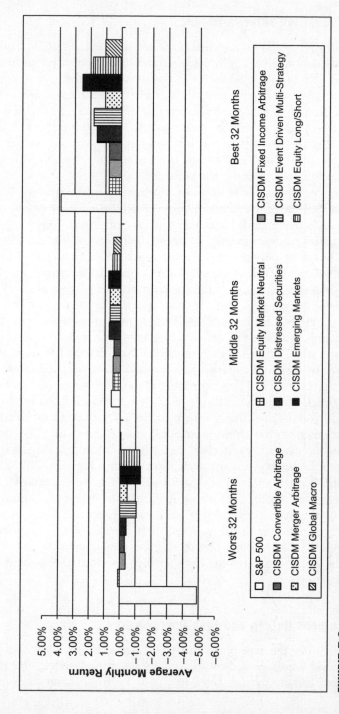

EXHIBIT 7.8 CISDM Hedge Fund Strategy Returns Ranked by S&P 500 (2001–2008)

Sources of Managed Futures Return

The sources of return to managed futures are uniquely different from traditional stocks, bonds, or even hedge funds. For instance, futures and options contracts can provide direct exposure to underlying financial and commodity markets. Therefore, while actively traded futures and options may provide similar returns to the underlying assets, but often with greater liquidity and less market impact, they may also easily take short positions or actively allocate assets between long and short positions. In addition, options traders may also directly trade market/security characteristics, such as price volatility, that underlie the contract.

As for hedge funds, the sources of managed futures returns have also been described as being based on the unique skill or strategy of the trader. Because CTAs actively trade, manager skill is important. Many managed futures strategies trade primarily in futures markets, which are zero-sum games. If CTAs were only trading against other CTAs, then it may be concluded that an individual managed futures program's returns are based solely on manager skill. However some spot market players are willing to sell or hedge positions even if they expect spot prices to rise or fall in their favor (e.g., currency and interest rate futures may trend over time due to government policy to smooth price movements). Since academic research (Schneeweis et al., 1998), has demonstrated that managed futures returns may be driven by systematic market factors such as changes in interest rates, exchange rates, or market volatility, rather than exclusively by an individual manager's alpha, we can also think of CTA returns as a combination of manager skill and an underlying return to the CTA strategy or investment style itself. Similar to the equity and bond markets, passive CTA security based indices have been created that are designed to capture the underlying return to the CTA strategy (Schneeweis, Kazemi, and Karavas, 2003; Jaeger and Wagner, 2005). If a manager's performance is measured relative to the systematic passive CTA index, for example, then the differential return may be viewed as the manager's "alpha" (return in excess of a non-manager based strategy similar replicate portfolio). If a manager's performance is measured relative to an index of other active managers, then the relative performance simply measures the over- or underperformance to that index of manager returns.

Managed Futures Return and Risk Performance

Exhibit 7.9 shows the risk and return performance of CTAs, traditional U.S. stocks and bonds, hedge funds, real estate, commodities, and private equity indices for the period 2001 to 2008. Portfolio combinations that

EXHIBIT 7.9 CTA and Comparison Benchmark Performance (2001–2008)

	S&P 500	BarCap US Agg	CISDM CTA EW
Annualized Total Return	−2.9%	5.7%	9.2%
Annualized Standard Deviation	15.0%	4.0%	8.7%
Information Ratio	−0.19	1.44	1.05
Maximum Drawdown	−40.7%	−3.8%	−8.7%
Correlation with CTA	−0.26	0.17	1.00

	S&P GSCI	CISDM EW Hedge Funds	FTSE NAREIT All	Private Equity
Annualized Total Return	−0.5%	5.6%	6.4%	−3.7%
Annualized Standard Deviation	25.6%	6.6%	20.9%	26.4%
Information Ratio	−0.02	0.84	0.31	−0.14
Maximum Drawdown	−62.2%	−21.1%	−58.8%	−70.3%
Correlation with CTA	0.22	0.02	−0.12	−0.14

include traditional and alternative investments for the most recent eight year period 2001 to 2008 are also reviewed in Exhibit 7.10. Over the period of analysis, managed futures reported a higher annualized return and lower volatility than the S&P 500. Compared to the returns of the Barclays Capital U.S. Aggregate Bond Index, managed futures again reported higher rates of return albeit with higher volatility. Compared to the private equity and real estate and commodities, managed futures reported a higher return with significantly lower volatilities. Finally, compared to hedge funds, managed futures reported higher returns but higher volatilities. It can be observed from Exhibit 7.10 that the information ratios for portfolios that include at least a 10% investment in CTAs dominate those portfolios which do not contain an investment in CTAs.

CTA strategies provide a broadly diverse mix of opportunities. Some CTAs trade in a more systematic fashion using an array of algorithmic based trading strategies often based on historical pricing patterns. Other CTAs trade a more discretionary style based on a wider range of economic and manager based trading systems. In addition, certain CTAs may concentrate on shorter- or longer-term models to dominate their trading focus. As a result, CTAs may be separated into a range of various strategy and market focus groupings including currency, financial, diversified CTAs, as

EXHIBIT 7.10 Multi-Asset Portfolio Performance (2001–2008)

Portfolio	A	B	C	D
Annualized Returns	1.7%	2.5%	2.2%	2.9%
Standard Deviation	7.5%	6.6%	8.8%	7.8%
Information Ratio	0.22	0.37	0.25	0.37
Maximum Drawdown	−21.0%	−17.3%	−27.8%	−23.6%
Correlation with CTA	(0.22)		(0.14)	
Portfolio A	Equal Weights S&P 500 and BarCap US Aggregate			
Portfolio B	90% Portfolio A and 10% CTAs			
Portfolio C	75% Portfolio A and 25% HF/Commodities/Private Equity/Real Estate			
Portfolio D	90% Portfolio C and 10% CTAs			

well as systematic and discretionary CTAs. As indicated in Exhibit 7.11, the results show that with the exception of CTAs who trade primarily in equity futures, most CTA managers (market or strategy based) have a low correlation with most traditional stock and bond markets.

In Exhibit 7.12, the correlation of various CTA strategies are given. In general most CTAs trade using systematic trading models. As a result, results in Exhibit 7.12 show a high correlation between the CTA systematic index and other market based CTA strategies (financial). However, results in Exhibit 7.12 also show a low correlation between the CTA systematic index and the CTA discretionary index reflecting the differential trading styles.

Managed Futures Performance in Down and Up Equity Markets

Exhibit 7.13 depicts the performance over various CTA strategies in months in which the S&P 500 had its worst and best performance over the period 2001 to 2008. Results show that, relative to other CTAs, the various CTA strategies with the exception of the equity CTAs provided positive returns in the worst S&P 500 months but also provided positive returns in the best S&P 500 months.

PRIVATE EQUITY

Private equity is often viewed as ownership in private or non-publicly traded business. These ownership stakes may take various forms (proprietorship,

EXHIBIT 7.11 Performance of CISDM CTA Indices (2001–2008)

	Annualized Return	Standard Deviation	Correlation S&P 500	Correlation BarCap US Gov	Correlation BarCap US Corporate High-Yield
CISDM CTA EW Currency	5.9%	5.6%	0.10	0.10	-0.10
CISDM CTA EW Financials	7.8%	8.5%	-0.28	0.30	-0.22
CISDM CTA EW Diversified	10.7%	11.2%	-0.28	0.27	-0.22
CISDM CTA EW Equity	6.6%	7.9%	0.37	-0.07	0.41
CISDM CTA EW Physicals	8.3%	8.7%	-0.13	0.04	-0.10
CISDM CTA EW Systematic	9.0%	9.8%	-0.27	0.23	-0.21
CISDM CTA EW Discretionary	11.1%	6.4%	0.19	0.09	0.23
S&P 500	-2.9%	15.0%	1.00	-0.39	0.68
BarCap US Government	6.4%	4.7%	-0.39	1.00	-0.09
BarCap US Corporate High-Yield	3.2%	11.0%	0.68	-0.09	1.00

EXHIBIT 7.12 CISDM CTA Indices Correlation (2001–2008)

	Currency	Financials	Diversified	Equity	Physicals	Systematic	Discretionary
CISDM CTA EW Currency	1.00	0.61	0.62	-0.02	0.30	0.65	0.20
CISDM CTA EW Financials	0.61	1.00	0.88	0.04	0.49	0.91	0.27
CISDM CTA EW Diversified	0.62	0.88	1.00	0.01	0.64	0.97	0.35
CISDM CTA EW Equity	-0.02	0.04	0.01	1.00	0.01	0.03	0.64
CISDM CTA EW Physicals	0.30	0.49	0.64	0.01	1.00	0.62	0.40
CISDM CTA EW Systematic	0.65	0.91	0.97	0.03	0.62	1.00	0.29
CISDM CTA EW Discretionary	0.20	0.27	0.35	0.64	0.40	0.29	1.00

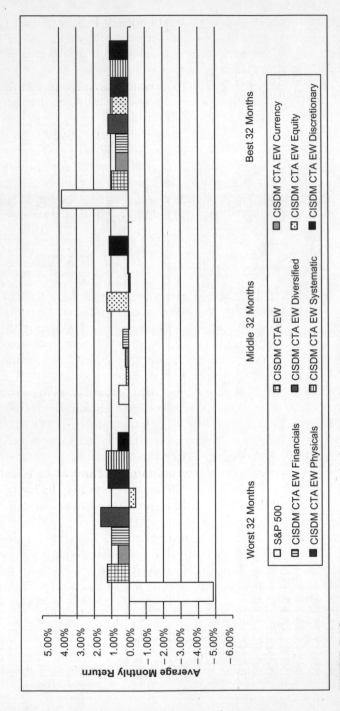

EXHIBIT 7.13 CISDM CTA Indices Ranked by S&P 500 (2001–2008)

partnership, and other corporate or legal entities). It is important to note that private equity is viewed by some as including the entire range of non-public investments from early stage through final stage investments. For others, private equity is limited to that section of the non-public investment process in which capital is raised via a private placement in contrast to a public offering. Often private equity is discussed within five distinct stages or forms of investment. These include angel investors (generally seed capital), venture capital (startup/first stage), leveraged buyouts, mezzanine investing, and distressed debt investing (later stage investing). The long-term goal of many private equity investments is to have the enterprise sold to other investors either through private sales, mergers, or initial public offerings. Investors in private equity should also be aware that the initial non-public nature of the private equity holdings makes valuation of the underlying shares difficult.

Sources of Private Equity Return

Private equity is generally regarded as an investment that offers investors the opportunity to achieve superior long-term returns compared to traditional public equity investment. The basis for returns to private equity is similar to that for traditional stock and bond investment, that is, a claim on long-term earnings, a return premium for providing capital to an illiquid and risky investment, and positive alpha generated from the value that private equity managers may create by their proactive influence on the invested companies' management and operations. However, it is difficult to determine the actual historical return to private equity investment. Private investment vehicles have a net asset value that is often determined as an internal appraisal value and not by a public market transaction. Thus actual returns are often measured as an internal rate of return or cash disbursements relative to capital investment. These cash flows may be lower at the initial stage than at later stages of the capital investment (known as the J-curve effect). However, in recent years, several forms of publicly traded private equity vehicles have come into existence. These include, among others, publicly listed investment companies, business development companies, and special purpose acquisition vehicles. These investment vehicles have provided a basis for measuring rates of return based on public market valuations.

Private Equity Return and Risk Performance

Exhibit 7.14 provides the risk and return characteristics of the private equity index, traditional U.S. equity and bond indices, and other alternative

EXHIBIT 7.14 Private Equity and Comparison Benchmark Performance (2001–2008)

Stock, Bond, and Commodity Performance	S&P 500	BarCap US Agg	Private Equity
Annualized Total Return	–2.9%	5.7%	–3.7%
Annualized Standard Deviation	15.0%	4.0%	26.4%
Information Ratio	(0.19)	1.44	(0.14)
Maximum Drawdown	–40.7%	–3.8%	–70.3%
Correlation with Private Equity	0.83	(0.06)	1.00

	CISDM EW Hedge Funds	CISDM CTA EW	S&P GSCI	FTSE NAREIT All REIT
Annualized Total Return	5.6%	9.2%	–0.5%	6.4%
Annualized Standard Deviation	6.6%	8.7%	25.6%	20.9%
Information Ratio	0.84	1.05	(0.02)	0.31
Maximum Drawdown	–21.1%	–8.7%	–62.2%	–58.8%
Correlation with Private Equity	0.80	(0.14)	0.29	0.62

investment indices for the period 2001 to 2008. Portfolio combinations that include traditional assets and alternative investments for the most recent eight-year period 2001 to 2008 are also reviewed. Over the period of analysis, the private equity index reported lower annualized return and higher risk (as measured by standard deviation) than the S&P 500, the Barclays Capital Aggregate Bond, CISDM hedge fund and CTA indices, real estate, and the commodities index.

The correlations between the private equity index and other equity sensitive assets such as real estate, hedge funds, and the S&P 500 are significant. However, the correlations of private equity with the other non-equity based indices are very low, suggesting that, over the most recent eight-year period, additional diversification benefits could have been achieved by adding private equity to a non-equity based portfolio, but that adding private equity to an equity biased portfolio may offer limited diversification. It can be observed from Exhibit 7.15 that the information ratios for portfolios that include at least a 10% investment in private equity hedge funds failed to dominate those portfolios that do not include an investment

EXHIBIT 7.15   Multiple Asset Class Portfolio Performance (2001–2008)

Portfolio	A	B	C	D
Annualized Returns	1.7%	1.34%	2.9%	2.4%
Standard Deviation	7.5%	9.0%	7.2%	8.9%
Information Ratio	0.22	0.15	0.39	0.27
Maximum Drawdown	−21.0%	−27.1%	−21.9%	−27.8%
Correlation with Real Estate	0.81		0.84	
Portfolio A	Equal Weights S&P 500 and BarCap US Aggregate			
Portfolio B	90% Portfolio A and 10% Private Equity			
Portfolio C	75% Portfolio A and 25% HF/CTA/Real Estate/Commodities			
Portfolio D	90% Portfolio C and 10% Private Equity			

in private equity. Investment in publicly traded private equity may therefore be based primarily on expected future returns rather than recent past performance.

Private Equity Performance in Down and Up Equity Markets

Private equity often refers to a wide range of potential pre-publicly traded investment opportunities. These opportunities are often grouped into angel investing (initial seed capital); venture capital (startup opportunities); mezzanine finance (bridge loans); and more mature private equity vehicles (mature or pre-IPO). These various opportunities can be broken down into specific areas of investment (e.g., biotech or computers) as well as geographical area of focus (e.g., U.S., Europe, or Asia). Each sub-area may have its own return and risk characteristics; however, as a general class, private equity remains more of an equity return enhancer than an equity diversifier. In Exhibit 7.16, the high correlation between publicly traded private equity vehicles and the S&P 500 is shown, with private equity performing poorly in down S&P 500 months and performing well in positive S&P 500 months.

REAL ESTATE

Real estate investment has generally been regarded as a primary part of individual and institutional investors' portfolios. Over the recent years,

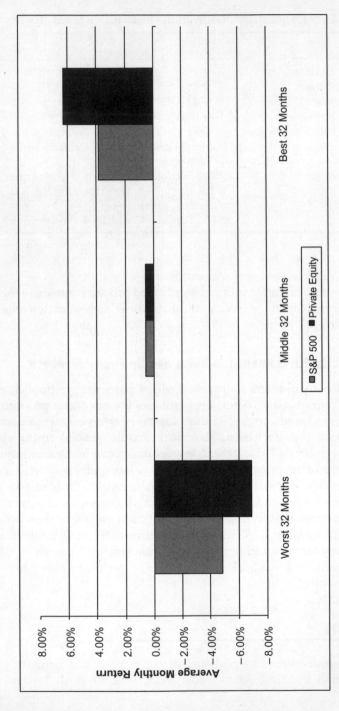

EXHIBIT 7.16 Private Equity Returns Ranked by S&P 500 (2001–2008)

however, the sector itself has undergone a dramatic transformation. In the past, the physical real estate market has been characterized by a relative lack of liquidity, high transaction costs, high management costs, high information costs, and low transparency. However, some of the costs of investing in real estate have been reduced in recent years, since initiatives to enhance liquidity and transparency in the property markets have been put forth. Despite these changes, real estate investments are still substantially different from country to country, region to region, and property type to property type. As real estate investment opportunities differ widely, traditional real estate may be better viewed as return enhancement vehicles to equity based as well as fixed income investments. This is due, in part, to the impact of interest rates on the present value of fixed cash flows often generated by real estate and the fact that dramatic changes in global economic conditions may impact both the financing of real estate as well as the demand. Moreover, many investors access real estate investment through equity based investment vehicles (e.g., real estate investment trusts). These investment firms often have investment characteristics associated with the general equity market in addition to their more specific real estate characteristics. While traditional real estate may provide diversification and return benefits, their co-movements with existing stock and bond investments as well as to certain alternative (hedge funds, private equity) portfolios must be considered carefully.

In addition, the relative performance characteristics are dependent in part on the business model of the investment firm and the characteristics of the underlying real estate (e.g., commercial, housing). Public investment involves buying shares of real estate investment companies (REITs) or other forms of indirect financial investment (e.g., futures or ETFs based on real estate). The real estate market is composed of several segments that include housing or residential real estate properties, commercial real estate properties, farmland, and timberland. Until recently, the advent of securitization has broadened investor access to include a wider range of real estate investment. The impact of recent market events on the future securitization of real estate investments depends both on future economic developments and regulatory constraints and oversight of these products.

Sources of Real Estate Return

Real estate prices are determined by a myriad of factors. Among those that have been mentioned in the literature, we can list the following (Case and Shiller 2003, and Sabal 2005):

- Long-term population growth, which is in turn determined by birth rates and migration flows.
- Uniqueness of the property. Since real estate is a heterogeneous asset, prices between two properties are not perfectly comparable. For example, new homes are priced differently than those in the secondary market, smaller properties are more expensive by the square foot, some homes respond better to customer needs and are thus more expensive, and so on.
- Government planning and regulations on the use of land have a crucial role in the real estate market through the influence these actions may have on real estate supply.
- Disposable income, which is closely related to unemployment and economic growth, and availability of financing are key determinants of property prices.

Real Estate Return and Risk Performance

Exhibit 7.17 shows the risk and return performance of real estate investment trusts, traditional U.S. stocks and bonds, hedge funds, CTAs, commodities, and private equity indices for the period 2001 to 2008. Exhibit 7.18 shows portfolio combinations that include traditional assets and alternative investments and real estate for the most recent eight-year period 2001 to 2008. Over the period of analysis, the real estate index reported a higher annualized return and a slightly higher volatility than the S&P 500. Compared to the returns of the Barclays Capital U.S. Aggregate Bond Index, real estate investments again reported significantly higher rates of return albeit with higher volatility. In addition, when compared to the hedge funds, the real estate index reported a higher return but with higher risk. When compared to the CTAs, the real estate index reported a higher return but with higher risk. Finally, the real estate index reported higher returns than private equity and commodity investments but with lower risk levels.

We can again observe moderate correlations between the real estate index and traditional asset classes and the other alternative investments (hedge funds, private equity) with equity exposure. This again suggests that, over the most recent eight year period, the additional diversification benefits that exist by adding real estate to an already diversified equity biased portfolio may come primarily from return enhancement in contrast to risk reduction. Exhibit 7.18 shows, however, that the information ratios for portfolios that include at least a 10% investment dominate those portfolios which do not contain an investment in real estate.

EXHIBIT 7.17 Real Estate and Comparison Benchmark Performance (2001–2008)

	S&P 500	BarCap US Agg	FTSE NAREIT All REIT
Annualized Total Return	−2.9%	5.7%	6.4%
Annualized Standard Deviation	15.0%	4.0%	20.9%
Information Ratio	(0.19)	1.44	0.31
Maximum Drawdown	−40.7%	−3.8%	−58.8%
Correlation with FTSE NAREIT All REIT	0.58	0.13	1.00

	CISDM EW Hedge Funds	CISDM CTA EW	S&P GSCI	Private Equity
Annualized Total Return	5.6%	9.2%	−0.5%	−3.7%
Annualized Standard Deviation	6.6%	8.7%	25.6%	26.4%
Information Ratio	.843	1.048	−.018	−.139
Maximum Drawdown	−21.1%	−8.7%	−62.2%	−70.3%
Correlation with FTSE NAREIT All REIT	.517	−.124	.159	.623

EXHIBIT 7.18 Multi-Asset Portfolio Performance (2001–2008)

	A	B	C	D
Annualized Returns	1.7%	2.3%	2.3%	2.8%
Standard Deviation	7.5%	8.2%	7.8%	8.5%
Information Ratio	0.22	0.28	0.29	0.33
Maximum Drawdown	−21.0%	−24.5%	−23.5%	−26.7%
Correlation with Real Estate	0.61		0.62	

Portfolio A	Equal Weights S&P 500 and BarCap US Aggregate
Portfolio B	90% Portfolio A and 10% Real Estate
Portfolio C	75% Portfolio A and 25% HF/CTA/Private Equity/ Commodities
Portfolio D	90% Portfolio C and 10% Real Estate

Similar to other alternatives, FTSE REIT securities cover a broad array of real estate concentrations. The performance characteristics and correlation of the primary FTSE REIT sectors are given in Exhibit 7.19 and Exhibit 7.20. The three primary sectors are:

1. **Equity REITs:** Equity REITs mostly own and operate income-producing real estate. They increasingly have become real estate operating companies engaged in a wide range of real estate activities, including leasing, maintenance, and development of real property and tenant services. One major distinction between REITs and other real estate companies is that a REIT must acquire and develop its properties primarily to operate them as part of its own portfolio rather than to resell them once they are developed.
2. **Mortgage REITs:** Mortgage REITs mostly lend money directly to real estate owners and operators or extend credit indirectly through the acquisition of loans or mortgage-backed securities. Today's mortgage REITs generally extend mortgage credit only on existing properties. Many mortgage REITs also manage their interest rate and credit risks using securitized mortgage investments, dynamic hedging techniques, and other accepted derivative strategies.
3. **Hybrid REITs:** As the name suggests, a hybrid REIT both owns properties and makes loans to real estate owners and operators. Of the various FTSE REIT sectors, those that concentrate on ownership of properties (equity REITs) have had the best performance relative to those such as mortgage and hybrid, which also include direct loans as a primary part of their portfolio.

Real Estate Performance in Down and Up Equity Markets

As with other alternative asset classes, real estate covers a wide range of potential investment opportunities. These opportunities are often grouped into retail and commercial investments. However, equity based investments in various real estate opportunities provide the most liquid and transparent of the various investment vehicles. Each sub-area may have its own return and risk characteristics; however, as a general class, when returns are ranked by the S&P 500, they provide negative returns in down S&P 500 markets and positive returns in up S&P 500 markets (see Exhibit 7.21). In short, public real estate vehicles also remain more of an equity return enhancer than an equity diversifier.

EXHIBIT 7.19 Performance of Real Estate Market Segment Indices (2001–2008)

	Annualized Return	Standard Deviation	Correlation S&P 500	Correlation BarCap US Government	Correlation BarCap US Corporate High-Yield
FTSE NAREIT All REITs	6.4%	20.9%	−0.10	−0.10	0.66
FTSE NAREIT Equity REITs	6.8%	21.6%	0.57	−0.10	0.66
FTSE NAREIT Mortgage REITs	5.8%	24.9%	0.33	0.03	0.37
FTSE NAREIT Hybrid REITs	−4.0%	30.2%	0.48	0.00	0.64
S&P 500	−2.9%	15.0%	1.00	−0.39	0.68
BarCap US Government	6.4%	4.7%	−0.39	1.00	−0.09
BarCap US Corporate High-Yield	3.2%	11.0%	0.68	−0.09	1.00

EXHIBIT 7.20   FTSE REITs Sector Correlations (2001–2008)

	All REITs	Equity REITs	Mortgage REITs	Hybrid REITs
FTSE NAREIT All REITs	1.00	1.00	0.51	0.66
FTSE NAREIT Equity REITs	1.00	1.00	0.45	0.62
FTSE NAREIT Mortgage REITs	0.51	0.45	1.00	0.63
FTSE NAREIT Hybrid REITs	0.66	0.62	0.63	1.00

COMMODITIES

Commodity indices attempt to replicate the returns available to holding long positions in agricultural, metal, energy, or livestock investments. Since returns on a fully invested futures contract reflect that of an investment in the underlying deliverable, commodity indices based on the returns of futures/forward contracts offer an efficient means to obtain commodity exposure. A number of commodities indices offer access to commodity investment. These indices may differ in a number of ways, such as the commodities included in the index, the weights of the individual commodities, as well as a number of operational trading issues (e.g., roll period or rebalancing).

Sources of Return for Commodities

Investor benefits of commodity or commodity based products lie primarily in their ability to offer risk/return tradeoffs that cannot be easily replicated through other investment alternatives. Academic research (Williams 1986), has examined the economic determinants of returns to commodity investment. As with any futures based investment, returns are determined by both the expected returns on the deliverable and the expected cost of carry returns, as well as other storage and deliverable options. For example, as expected, Fama and French (1988) and Schneeweis, Spurgin, and Georgiev (2000) identified a strong business cycle component in industrial metals based futures contracts, a finding that is consistent with the business cycle variation of spot and futures prices of industrial metals.[3] Commodity based index returns can also benefit from multiple sources of returns, many of which tend not to be correlated. These can include spot,[4] roll,[5] beta, momentum, rebalancing, and Treasury Bill, returns. However, each index has its own unique portfolio attribution characteristics and can be impacted by additional factors like diversification, commodity component weighting, and roll schedule.

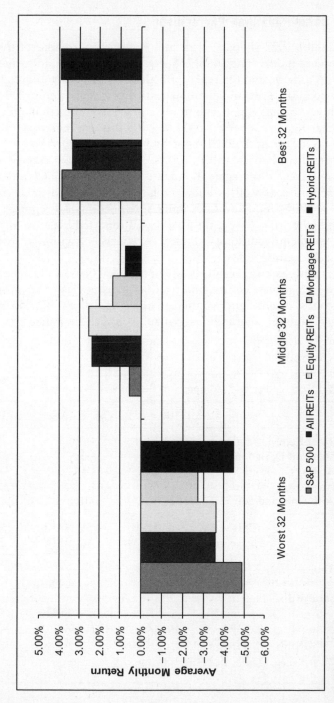

EXHIBIT 7.21 FTSE REIT Returns Ranked by S&P 500 (2001–2008)

Commodity Return and Risk Performance

Results in Exhibit 7.22 show the risk and return performance of the S&P GSCI commodity index, traditional U.S. equity and bond indices, the hedge fund and CTA indices, and the real estate and private equity indices for the period 2001 to 2008. Portfolio combinations that include traditional assets, alternative investments (e.g., hedge funds and CTAs), and commodities for the most recent eight-year period 2001 to 2008 are also reviewed. Over the period of analysis, the S&P GSCI reported higher annualized return as well as higher volatility than the S&P 500. Compared to the returns of the Barclays Capital U.S. Aggregate Bond index, the S&P GSCI reported a lower rate of return as well as higher volatility. Compared to the returns of the CISDM hedge fund and CTA indices, the S&P GSCI reported lower returns with higher risk. Lastly, the S&P GSCI reported higher returns and lower risk than the private equity and lower returns but with slightly higher risk than the real estate index.

In brief, the weak correlations between the S&P GSCI and hedge funds, CTAs, real estate, private equity, and traditional asset classes again suggest that over the most recent eight-year period additional diversification benefits can exist by adding commodities to an already diversified portfolio.

EXHIBIT 7.22   Commodity and Comparison Benchmark Performance

	S&P 500	BarCap US Agg	S&P GSCI
Annualized Total Return	−2.9%	5.7%	−0.5%
Annualized Standard Deviation	15.0%	4.0%	25.6%
Information Ratio	−0.19	1.44	−0.02
Maximum Drawdown	−40.7%	−3.8%	−62.2%
Correlation with Commodities	0.18	(0.02)	1.00

	CISDM EW Hedge Funds	CISDM CTA EW	FTSE NAREIT All REIT	Private Equity
Annualized Total Return	5.6%	9.2%	6.4%	−3.7%
Annualized Standard Deviation	6.6%	8.7%	20.9%	26.4%
Information Ratio	0.84	1.05	0.31	−0.14
Maximum Drawdown	−21.1%	−8.7%	−58.8%	−70.3%
Correlation with Commodities	0.4	0.2	0.2	0.3

EXHIBIT 7.23   Portfolio Performance (2001–2008)

Portfolios	A	B	C	D
Annualized Returns	1.7%	2.5%	2.6%	3.3%
Standard Deviation	7.5%	6.6%	.2%	7.3%
Information Ratio	0.22	0.37	0.32	0.46
Maximum Drawdown	−21.0%	−17.0%	−25.0%	−21.0%
Correlation with Commodity	0.21		0.27	
Portfolio A	Equal Weights S&P 500 and BarCap US Aggregate			
Portfolio B	90% Portfolio A and 10% Commodities			
Portfolio C	75% Portfolio A and 25% HF/CTA/Private Equity/Real Estate			
Portfolio D	90% Portfolio C and 10% Commodities			

As shown in Exhibit 7.23, information ratios for portfolios that include at least a 10% investment in commodities dominate those in portfolios which do not contain an investment in commodities.

Commodity investments cover a wide variety of sectors. The performance characteristics and correlation of the primary S&P GSCI commodity sectors with traditional market indices are given in Exhibit 7.24. As shown in Exhibit 7.25, over the period 2001 to 2008, the various commodity indices reflect a low correlation to traditional market indices as well as to other comparison commodity sub-indices.

Commodity Performance in Down and Up Equity Markets

Like other alternative investments, commodity investment is available through a number of product providers covering a wide range of alternative strategy emphasis (convenience yield, momentum patterns) as well as market emphasis (energy, livestock, precious and industrial metals, and agriculture). Each of these products has their own unique return and risk performance including their correlations with various market phenomena including inflation. While not the focus of this chapter, investors should be aware that the return and risk characteristics of any commodity product is impacted both by the commodities they trade (e.g., energy) and the form of the trading strategy (near- or far-term futures contracts). However, despite the differences between individual commodity sectors, results show in Exhibit 7.26 that none of the various commodity sectors showed a consistent return relationship with the S&P 500 in either down or up S&P 500 markets.

EXHIBIT 7.24 Performance of S&P GSCI Market Segment Indices (2001–2008)

	Annualized Return	Standard Deviation	Correlation S&P 500	Correlation BarCap US Govt	Correlation BarCap US Corporate High-Yield
S&P GSCI Agriculture	-3.2%	20.8%	0.05	0.05	0.26
S&P GSCI Energy	-1.1%	33.8%	0.12	-0.12	0.23
S&P GSCI Grains	-1.6%	23.8%	0.21	0.11	0.24
S&P GSCI Industrial Metal	5.8%	23.7%	0.48	-0.26	0.40
S&P GSCI Livestock	-4.3%	15.5%	0.08	-0.13	0.08
S&P GSCI Total Petroleum	5.9%	33.3%	0.14	-0.16	0.27
S&P 500	-2.9%	15.0%	1.00	-0.39	0.68
BarCap US Government	6.4%	4.7%	-0.39	1.00	-0.09
BarCap US Corporate High-Yield	3.2%	11.0%	0.68	-0.09	1.00

EXHIBIT 7.25 Commodity Sector Correlations (2001–2008)

	S&P GSCI Agriculture	S&P GSCI Energy	S&P GSCI Grains	S&P GSCI Industrial Metal	S&P GSCI Livestock	S&P GSCI non Livestock	S&P GSCI Petroleum
S&P GSCI Agriculture	1.00	0.17	0.96	0.37	0.05	0.31	0.17
S&P GSCI Energy	0.17	1.00	0.12	0.39	0.07	0.99	0.97
S&P GSCI Grains	0.96	0.12	1.00	0.28	0.07	0.25	0.11
S&P GSCI Industrial Metal	0.37	0.39	0.28	1.00	0.13	0.49	0.41
S&P GSCI Total Livestock	0.05	0.07	0.07	0.13	1.00	0.09	0.09
S&P GSCI Total Petroleum	0.17	0.97	0.11	0.41	0.09	0.96	1.00

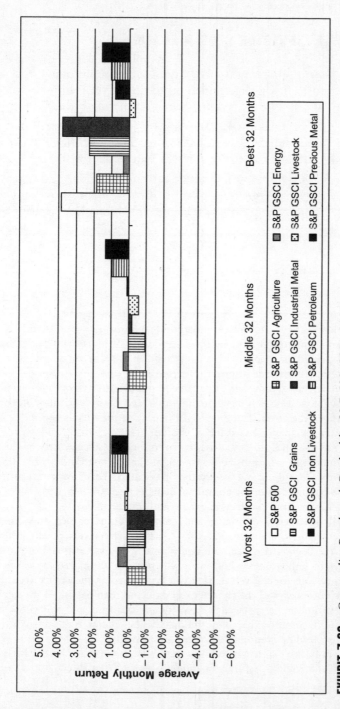

EXHIBIT 7.26 Commodity Benchmark Ranked by S&P 500 (2001–2008)

WHAT EVERY INVESTOR SHOULD REMEMBER

- The benefit of alternative assets addition to stand-alone stock and bond portfolios is determined primarily by their common or differential sensitivity to common market factors.
- Analysis of individual assets at the index level often fails to provide suitable evidence of the return and risk characteristics of unique strategies at the strategy or market sector level.
- Sources of return are time sensitive and dependant upon business models. Care should be taken in understanding how and why correlations change both at the index and individual security level.

NOTES

1. Modern alternatives also often incorporate unique risk and return solutions usually found in structured products. Structured products run the gamut from principal protection backed by a bank's balance sheet to quantitative driven models designed to trade at given inflection points.
2. These security based indices are available in tradable form from various platform providers. Public research has generally indicated that, depending on the hedge fund strategy, the correlation between the passive security based index and the active trading manager based index is often greater than .75. However, public research has also indicated that the return to such passive security based trading models often underperforms active trading manager based indices by 100 to 200 basis points, depending on the strategy replicated. This lower return must, of course, be balanced with the additional benefits to passive security based indices including greater transparency, capacity, and liquidity.
3. For a full discussion of pricing and modeling commodities and commodity derivatives returns, see Geman (2005). Lastly, Schneeweis et al. (2008) have explored the degree to which commodity prices follow various momentum patterns, for which their analysis provides evidence and summarizes research results.
4. Commodity spot for a given market can be defined as the return from holding the active contract until the contract roll date and then rolling to the next active contract. From the perspective of liquidity and transparency, this is the simplest way to hold commodities, and thus is the benchmark against which other methods of holding commodity futures are measured.
5. Roll return: Positive or negative roll returns, which are the profits or losses generated from the rolling of futures contracts, also have a direct impact on index performance.

CHAPTER 8

Return and Risk Differences among Similar Asset Class Benchmarks

The use of historical data to demonstrate what the performance of a portfolio could have been if certain investment decisions had been made has been termed "pro forma performance." Usually a manager will look at the return of certain published benchmark indices; conclude that these benchmarks reflect the strategy he would have invested in over some period; package them together; and then say to the potential investor: This would have been your performance had you invested with me. Needless to say, this type of performance data is ripe with hazards and the Securities and Exchange Commission (SEC) has strict rules regarding its distribution and marketing. Once you move beyond the obvious fact that there is a manifold difference between decision making where there is no risk and decision making where reputations and significant pools of money are at stake, there is the question of whether the indices or investment proxies actually reflect realistic investable returns or values. This chapter deals with the latter issue and leaves the moral hazards to the regulators and an investor's common sense.

One of the principal concerns in the application of multi-asset management is the degree to which the potential advantages shown in the asset allocation designed portfolio can be transferred to the investor. Where the design is based on investment benchmarks, the question is whether the benchmarks are investable in some meaningful manner or whether there is a suitable proxy. This can be a particularly thorny issue in dealing with alternatives such as private equity, commodities, hedge funds, or real estate where no commonly accepted single set of benchmarks exists. In contrast, a wide range of publicly available investment vehicles (that have been vetted over time) exist for equity and fixed income, which provide access to the returns reflected in their associated noninvestable benchmarks. This is simply not the case for alternatives, which is why this area requires a degree of hypervigilance. As we take this walk through our analysis, keep in mind that this is an ever-changing terrain and new developments occur almost daily.

In Chapter 8, we start with the obvious. Investment benchmark returns reflect portfolios of underlying assets. Similarly, investors wishing to invest in instruments that are reflective of the risks and returns of those benchmarks must also hold a portfolio of similar underlying assets or must hold an investable benchmark that has, as one of its goals, the return and risk properties of the related noninvestable surrogate. It should also be pointed out that the use of a particular benchmark index based on its historical return and risk properties assumes that the characteristics of the index have remained stable over time or that the changes in index construction have not dramatically changed its return and risk characteristics. *In short, for many indices, historical data may have little if any meaning relative to the current return and risk attributes of the benchmark.*

MAKING SENSE OUT OF TRADITIONAL STOCK AND BOND INDICES

Stock and bond indices and/or benchmarks have formed the basis for much of asset allocation research. In the 1960s the introduction of the Capital International Stock Indices provided a much needed basis for testing the potential benefits of international equity investment. In the 1960s, Salomon Brothers Bond Indices were commonly used to offer historical performance information on a range of fixed income benchmarks. The design of these indices provided data with a limited historical record. In the 1980s, additional series of U.S. and foreign stock and bond indices were developed, with data, in some cases, going back to the 1920s. This new data provided the ability to test the performance of primary stock and bond markets over a wide range of economic periods. While the availability of this data provided the groundwork for testing the potential benefits of various asset allocation processes, asset allocators failed to emphasize some of the problems in the use of these generic stock or bond benchmarks.

Over the years, improved data and research has shown that both equity and fixed income benchmarks, depending upon the provider and sector tracked, have unique portfolio characteristics. Indicative of the potential problems in the construction of any index is that for the period 2001 to 2008, the annualized return for the S&P 500 is –2.89% while the annualized return for the S&P equal weighted is considerably higher (.36%). Other examples of the potential problems in index creation are illustrated by other issues in the construction of the S&P 500. First, the S&P 500 is asset weighted and thus is really the S&P 50 stocks that we care about and 450 stocks that have very little impact on the value of the S&P 500. Second, if the larger asset weighted stocks have greater variability than other stocks, the index is even more biased to a small sample of securities. Third, if certain equity sub-sectors have risen and fallen in value over time, their influence on the performance of the S&P 500 index may also have risen and fallen such that the risk characteristics of today's S&P 500 may have little in common with the risk characteristics of the index 10 to 15 years prior. Finally, some argue that the firms with the largest market capitalization are more likely to be overvalued. In other words, the investors are more likely to have overestimated its future prospects and therefore cap weighted indices may perform poorly going forward. This has created a new industry under the name of "Fundamental Indices." Of course, whether sale, earning per share, or market cap is used to create indices, similar estimation biases are likely to be present. Therefore, investors should be skeptical of the pro-forma performances of new indices. Data mining and data snooping are likely to be big contributors to their pro forma performances.

The risk and return characteristics of any index over lengthy historical periods may provide evidence of current return and risk characteristics but may also represent performance attributes that no longer exist. For example, most asset allocation programs use dollar based international stock indices. Over various time intervals the returns to international stock indices may be dominated by currency returns and not the underlying returns (local returns) of each country. Even those international equity indices that are represented as fully hedged assume a perfect hedge (the future stock price can be hedged at today's forward rate—of course we do not know the future price to hedge so even here there is a potential bias). The need for accurate barometers that reflect the true source of returns of various asset and sub-asset classes have in part led to an entire industry of new investment products based on fundamental indices that attempt to capture more basic changes in market factors affecting stock prices.

The construction of bond indices reflect many of the same concerns related to equity benchmarking. For many years, bond indices were created not from actual market prices but from what is commonly referred to as benchmark prices (computer generated prices based on an assumed relative price movement to a benchmark bond). Second, many bond indices are based on maturity rather than duration. As a result, as coupon level changes, the underlying duration of some of the maturity based bond indices may change in such a manner that the sensitivity of the benchmark to yield changes may change over time. Finally, as the underlying bonds used to calculate the bond index change (e.g., industry component), the sensitivity of the portfolio to various changes in market sub-sectors may also change.

This chapter does not detail all the differences in the wide range of alternative stock and bond indices. Instead, in each of the following sections, we provide a brief review of commonly used alternative investment benchmarks. Where applicable we also provide performance comparisons between investable and noninvestable indices.

PRIVATE EQUITY

In research conducted on the asset allocation benefits of private equity, academics and practitioners have focused on a range of historical data series purporting to reflect the performance of various private equity opportunities. Private equity is often viewed as ownership in private or non-publicly traded business. These ownership stakes may take various forms (proprietorship, partnership, and other corporate or legal entities). It is important to note that private equity is viewed by some as including the entire range of non-public investments from early stage through final stage investment. For others, private equity is limited to that section of the non-public investment process in which capital is raised via a private placement in contrast to a public offering. There are as many approaches to valuation or performance reporting as there are business models. Often the basis for valuation is either accounting based (risk-adjusted cash flows) or various relative value assessments (comparisons to existing publicly traded firms). Within each approach the investment manager has a significant degree of discretion in pricing the underlying assets and in determining the associated fees and expenses. In addition, the level of investor control has direct impact on relative value among the various ownership interests. Research in the private equity area has often been based on non-market priced noninvestable internal rate of return based indices. Cambridge Associates and Thomson Financial publish benchmarks based on this approach. While these indices provide information on how private equity sectors are performing, because investors cannot directly invest in these indices this data is at best directional and cannot be used as a meaningful proxy for an investor's actual returns. The development of publicly traded firms specializing in the private equity has provided some reliable market data that enhances the use of some private equity indices as meaningful asset allocation tools, particularly those published by S&P and other large index providers.

The historical performance for popular private equity indices over the period 4/2004 to 2008 are displayed in Exhibit 8.1. All calculations utilize quarterly data. Results in Exhibit 8.1 indicate the impact of using public private equity returns versus accounting based returns for the construction of private equity indices. While the various private equity indices shown

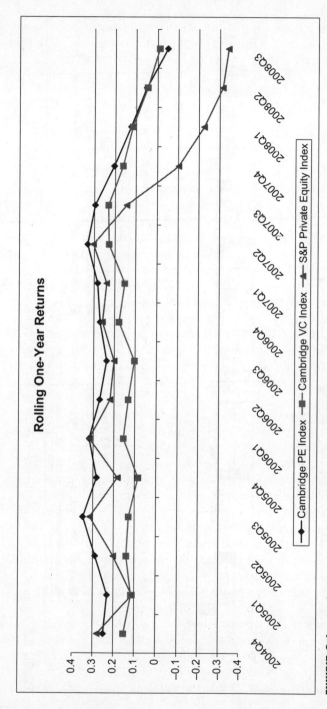

EXHIBIT 8.1 Performance of Private Equity Indices (4/2004–2008)

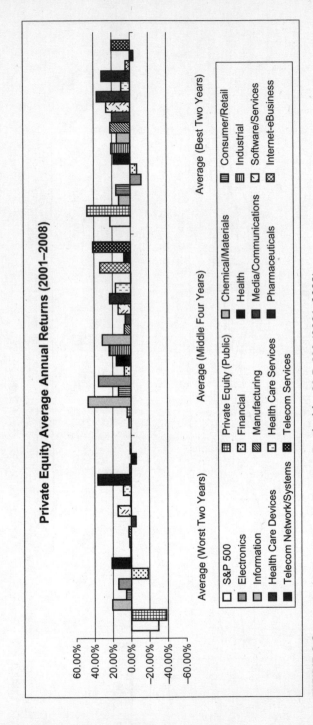

Private Equity Average Annual Returns (2001–2008)

Average (Worst Two Years) Average (Middle Four Years) Average (Best Two Years)

Legend:
- S&P 500
- Electronics
- Information
- Health Care Devices
- Telecom Network/Systems
- Private Equity (Public)
- Financial
- Manufacturing
- Health Care Services
- Telecom Services
- Chemical/Materials
- Health
- Media/Communications
- Pharmaceuticals
- Consumer/Retail
- Industrial
- Software/Services
- Internet-eBusiness

EXHIBIT 8.2 Annual Private Equity Returns Ranked by S&P 500 (2001–2008)

172

have similar return patterns for the first part of the data period, in the latter part of the investment period the accounting based (Cambridge Associates) index differs dramatically from the public private equity index.

As shown in exhibits 8.1 and 8.2, differences exist between returns based on public securities and those that are primarily accounting or investment manager based. In addition, as shown in Exhibit 8.2, private equity returns may differ widely depending on the area of investment emphasis. Results in Exhibit 8.2 indicate that the publicly traded private equity (private equity public) is impacted by general movements in the S&P 500 such that the public equity private equity index reports negative returns on average when the S&P 500 performs poorly and reports positive returns on average when the S&P 500 performs well. In contrast, performance varies among different private equity sectors which are measured by accounting rather than public equity returns. For example as shown in Exhibit 8.2 when the S&P 500 had its worst performance, results show a wide variation in the average return for private equity sectors when that performance is based on accounting based returns.

Even publicly traded indices may differ depending on the stage of the private equity investment or the regional area of concentration. In Exhibit 8.3 the relative performance of various public equity private equity indices is reported. Results show that the returns and risk for the LPX total return indices are similar to those for the comparison sub-indices. Similarly, the returns of the LPX Europe, America, and UK are similar (approximately −5%) for the period 2001 to 2008. However, from an international investor's perspective, it is important to focus on the potential currency impacts. Note that for a U.S. investor, the returns in USD are less negative than those in Euro. In short, the relative movement in the Dollar/Euro resulted in better returns noted in USD. Nevertheless, these USD returns may not reflect the true return to local markets. When reviewing global portfolios, investors should consider whether to use returns based in local country currencies or in the currency of the investor's home country.

REAL ESTATE

In this section, we analyze the performance characteristics of a range of real estate investment benchmarks. As for private equity, a range of investable and noninvestable real estate benchmarks exists. For a range of equity sectors, the FTSE NAREIT indices provide benchmarks based on public equity real estate investment trusts. For other areas, noninvestable indices dominate. For commercial real estate, NCREIF National Property Index (NPI) and the MIT Transactions-Based Index (TBI) are available as proxies

EXHIBIT 8.3   Private Equity Indices: 2001–2008

2001–2008	Currency	Annualized Return	Std Dev	Maximum Drawdown	Correlation S&P 500
S&P 500 Total Return Index	USD	−2.9%	15.0%	−40.7%	1.00
Private Equity Index	USD	−3.7%	26.4%	−70.3%	0.83
LPX50 Total Return	USD	−6.7%	24.3%	−71.6%	0.83
LPX Buyout Total Return	USD	−2.6%	22.7%	−74.0%	0.75
LPX Listed Private Equity Venture	USD	−9.6%	27.2%	−64.8%	0.78
LPX Direct Total Return	USD	−0.5%	23.2%	−69.9%	0.81
LPX Major Market Total Return	USD	−5.1%	23.7%	−72.2%	0.81
LPX Europe Total Return	USD	−5.4%	23.2%	−70.0%	0.81
LPX America Total Return	USD	−6.0%	27.1%	−74.3%	0.76
LPX UK Total Return	USD	−6.2%	23.1%	−75.3%	0.69
LPX50 Total Return	Euro	−11.2%	23.3%	−72.6%	0.81
LPX Buyout Total Return	Euro	−7.3%	21.5%	−74.8%	0.73
LPX Listed Private Equity Venture	Euro	−14.0%	26.1%	−73.6%	0.75
LPX Direct Total Return	Euro	−5.3%	22.1%	−71.0%	0.80
LPX Major Market Total Return	Euro	−9.7%	22.6%	−73.2%	0.79
LPX Europe Total Return	Euro	−10.0%	21.5%	−71.1%	0.81
LPX America Total Return	Euro	−10.6%	26.9%	−73.0%	0.71
LPX UK Total Return	Euro	−10.7%	21.9%	−76.2%	0.67

(Data for NCREIF NPI and MIT TBI indices are available from the NCREIF web site). For residential real estate, the S&P/Case-Shiller Home Price Indices are often used as a proxy. This index family consists of 23 indices: 20 metropolitan regional indices, two composite indices and a national index. One composite index consists of 10 regions, while the other consists of all 20 regions. In the following examples, we use the index that consists of 10 regions because it has historical data going back to 1990, while the composite 20 begins in 2000.

Summary statistics for various real estate indices displayed in Exhibit 8.4 are calculated from quarterly data. The annualized return over the period 1995 to 2008 for the FTSE NAREIT Composite Index was 9.6%, while those of commercial real estate indices MIT and the average of the NCREIF were 11.2% and 10.3%, respectively. For residential real estate, the annualized return, as measured by the S&P/Case-Shiller Composite 10 Index, was even lower at 5.7%. While the differences in reported returns reflect in part the different market sectors as well as the different forms of valuation, the differing forms of return calculation are most evident in volatility estimation. The volatilities of the NCREIF based indices, as well as the S&P/Case-Shiller Composite 10 Index, were far lower than that of the FTSE NAREIT Indices. The extremely low volatility of NCREIF returns is indicative of the volatility dampening problems associated with smoothing and lagging due to stale valuations often associated with non-exchange traded valuations. Similarly, the low volatility of the S&P/Case-Shiller or MIT TBI returns is indicative of the fact that even transaction based estimated real estate values may not result in a return series that fluctuates significantly from month to month.

Real estate investment, however, increasingly requires an international focus. In Exhibit 8.5 a performance comparison over the period also shows evidence of differential returns between real estate REITs with a U.S. focus (NAREIT All REIT) and REITs with an international focus. As shown in Exhibit 8.5, the return for the NAREIT All REIT index was higher than other indices that emphasized non-U.S. investment (FTSE EM/emerging markets, FTSE Euro, and FTSE AW Diversified). Similarly, the risk in terms of standard deviation of the NAREIT All REIT index was lower than other indices that emphasized non-U.S. investment (FTSE EM/emerging markets).

Real estate investments have often been promoted as offering investment diversification relative to traditional assets. However, as shown in Exhibit 8.6, for various independent periods (three-year period ending year cited), the correlations of the various real estate indices with the S&P 500 differ greatly. As important, benchmarks with the most liquid investment form (public equity REITS) have, in contrast to accounting based real estate

EXHIBIT 8.4 Performance of Alternative Real Estate Sector Indices, 1995–2008

	Annual Return	Standard Deviation	Information Ratio	Maximum Drawdown	Correlation		
					S&P 500	BarCap US Agg	FTSE NAREIT All REIT
HFRI Real Estate	6.9%	8.1%	0.86	−23.8%	0.52	−0.01	0.83
FTSE NAREIT HYB REIT	0.5%	26.8%	0.02	−84.0%	0.34	0.13	0.61
FTSE NAREIT MORT REIT	9.2%	26.5%	0.35	−64.4%	0.20	0.24	0.52
FTSE NAREIT COMPOSITE	9.6%	17.8%	0.54	−50.0%	0.48	−0.04	1.00
FTSE NAREIT EQTY REIT	10.1%	18.1%	0.56	−49.3%	0.47	−0.07	1.00
NCREIF Property Index Apartments	10.5%	3.6%	2.92	−8.7%	0.41	−0.11	0.54
NCREIF Property Index Office	11.0%	4.6%	2.41	−9.5%	0.41	−0.14	0.41
NCREIF Property Index Retail	10.2%	3.9%	2.61	−6.3%	0.31	−0.26	0.37
NCREIF Property Index Industrial	11.3%	3.8%	2.99	−8.0%	0.42	−0.11	0.51
TBI-Total Return Index	11.2%	8.0%	1.39	−17.7%	0.42	−0.08	0.49
TBI-Apartment	11.3%	8.8%	1.28	−14.3%	0.23	−0.25	0.33
TBI-Industrial	11.9%	10.4%	1.14	−19.8%	0.17	0.03	0.38
TBI-Office	12.1%	7.9%	1.52	−16.0%	0.34	−0.01	0.38
NACREIF Farmland	12.0%	7.5%	1.61	0.0%	0.09	−0.07	0.00
NACREIF Timber	9.7%	5.6%	1.73	−6.5%	0.13	0.12	−0.02
Case-Shiller 10	5.7%	5.5%	1.02	−26.6%	0.08	−0.07	0.30
FTSE NAREIT All REIT	9.6%	17.8%	0.54	−49.6%	0.47	−0.04	1.00
S&P 500 Total Return Index	8.2%	17.3%	0.47	−43.8%	1.00	−0.26	0.47
BarCap US Aggregate	6.8%	3.9%	1.73	−2.4%	−0.26	1.00	−0.04

EXHIBIT 8.5 International and U.S. FTSE Real Estate Returns

International Real Estate Index Performance 1994–2008	Annualized Return	Standard Deviation	Maximum Drawdown	Correlation S&P 500
FTSE AW Dev Ex US Real Estate USD	2.3%	22.8%	−60.5%	0.65
FTSE AW Dev Real Estate USD	1.6%	21.8%	−60.0%	0.66
FTSE AW Em Real Estate USD	−9.0%	35.5%	−87.9%	0.44
FTSE AW Eur Ex UK Real Estate USD	5.7%	19.3%	−69.2%	0.36
FTSE AW Eur Real Estate TR USD	4.8%	19.3%	−69.0%	0.41
FTSE AW Real Estate TR USD	1.1%	21.9%	−60.7%	0.66
FTSE NAREIT All REITs	7.7%	17.4%	−58.8%	0.46
S&P 500 Total Return Index	6.5%	15.0%	−44.7%	1.00
BarCap US Aggregate	6.2%	3.9%	−5.1%	0.07
BarCap US Corporate High-Yield	4.3%	8.8%	−33.3%	0.61

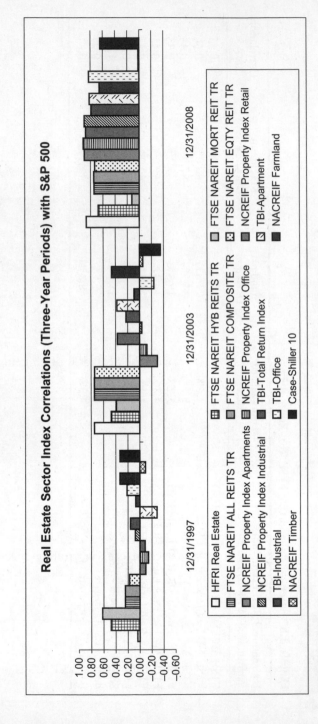

EXHIBIT 8.6 Real Estate Sector S&P 500 Correlation in Alternative Investment Periods

benchmarks, the highest correlation with the S&P 500. Lastly, in the most recent three-year period, with the exception of the NAREIT mortgage index and the accounting based timber and farmland indices, the correlation between the various real estate indices and the S&P 500 are well above .50.

ALTERNATIVE REIT INVESTMENTS INDICES

In early 2006, FTSE assumed the responsibility for the calculation and dissemination of the NAREIT Domestic Real Estate Index Series. As a result by April 2006, a number of new index series were created. Each represented investment for a particular real estate sector such as real estate used for health care or self-storage. It is interesting to note that as illustrated in Exhibit 8.7, with the exception of health care, the average returns of all the indices since inception of the sub-indices (April 2006) are negative (see Exhibit 8.7). The results are indicative of the fact that most sectors are affected by similar economic conditions, even though certain real estate sectors, for example self-storage, may provide positive return opportunities while other more general sectors, such as retail, exhibit negative returns. This common impact of economic conditions across various real estate sectors and sub-sectors is also illustrated in Exhibit 8.8 with the correlation of the various sectors and sub-sectors with the S&P 500 often being above .70. While this relatively high correlation may reflect the results of the recent subprime crisis, it is indicative of the necessity to determine the relative source of returns of each sector and its expected diversification value.

COMMODITY INVESTMENT

The number of commodity indices available to investors has multiplied over the past few years. There are now more than 10 publicly available commodity indices. All indices offer diversified exposure to commodity markets through the use of commodity futures contracts. The indices differ in terms of index composition, commodity selection criteria, rolling mechanism, rebalancing strategy, and weighting scheme. In this analysis, we have concentrated on the use of the S&P GSCI index. The index was created in the early 1990s and was created to reflect the relative production weights among the available commodities for which futures contracts existed. For the S&P GSCI, however, changes in asset weights among the primary commodity sectors has changed dramatically since the initial inception of the product (today energy comprises almost 70% of the S&P GSCI index in contrast to about 30% weight in the initial construction).

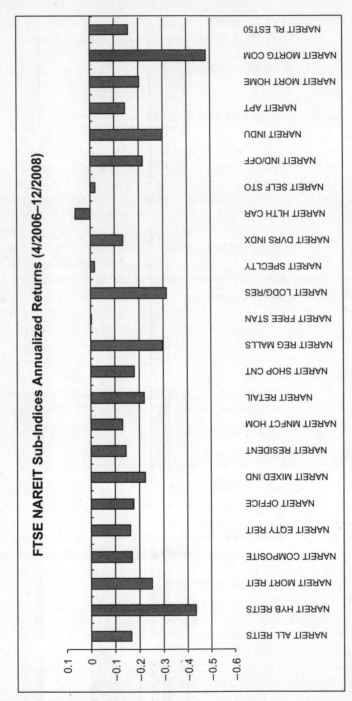

EXHIBIT 8.7 FTSE NAREIT Sub-Indices Annualized Returns (April 2006 to December 2008)

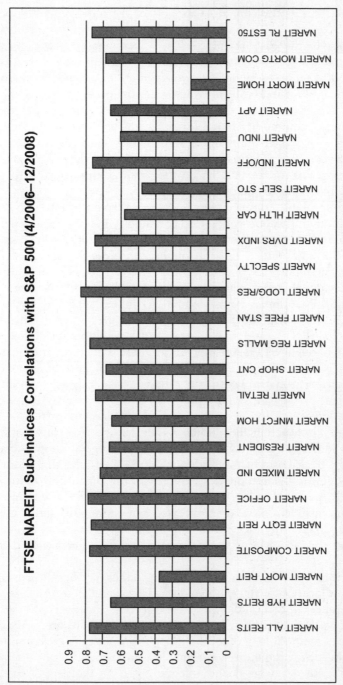

EXHIBIT 8.8 Alternative FTSE NAREIT Real Estate Indices Correlation with S&P 500 (4/2006–2008)

As important as the change in weights of the index, the index return and risk performance is impacted by the relative volatility of the various commodities. In the case of the S&P GSCI, as energy has increased in importance it has also increased in terms of weight in the index. The fact that energy also reports a higher relative volatility makes energy the primary driver of the current index. In previous years the performance of the S&P GSCI may in fact have been driven by other commodities. In short, when investing in any commodity index (or other indices), one is also investing in the process by which the index is constructed. Thus, commodity index performance can be a function of the methodology of the index, combined with the impact of market factors on the index components. As a result, commodity index performance can vary across indices.

Broadly speaking, commodity indices can be separated into two groups: first-generation and second-generation commodity indices. First-generation commodity indices were modeled on successful equity indices such as the S&P 500 stock index. In each of these indices, the weight assigned to a given commodity is free to evolve over a year before being reset during the annual rebalancing window. Members of this first group include the S&P Goldman Sachs Commodity Index (S&P GSCI), the Dow Jones-UBS Commodity Index (DJ-UBS), the Rogers International Commodity Index (RICI), and the Merrill Lynch Commodity Index eXtra (MLCX). Although based on the same basic structure and generally holding the same basket of commodities, there can be significant differences in their performance because of different weighting schemes and roll methodologies.

The second generation of commodity indices shares many features with the first group, but each includes some unique features that truly distinguish it from the indices in the first group. Major second-generation indices are the Deutsche Bank Liquid Commodity Index (DBLCI), the UBS Bloomberg Constant Maturity Commodity Index (CMCI), the Diapason Commodities Index (DCI), and the Bache Commodity Index (BCI). These commodity indices often include a more dynamic aspect of commodity index creation (e.g., Bache Commodity index uses daily rebalancing based on momentum pricing, and the UBS Maturity Commodity Indices often target different futures maturity).

The primary determinant of commodity index performance in recent years is the allocation to the energy sector. This single factor explains most of the differences in commodity index returns that are observed over short time horizons. However, over longer time horizons there are other differences in index methodology that influence performance. These components, which follow, define the indices in terms of composition, performance, and inflation and down-market hedge potential.

- **Index Constituents:** The number of commodity markets in major indices ranges from 6 to 24. Some commodity indices are designed to hold all liquid markets, while others exclude essentially similar commodity pairs such as Gold/Platinum and WTI Crude Oil/Brent Crude Oil, unless there is sufficient liquidity to support both commodities as well as sufficient diversification benefit for doing so. Other indices avoid "double-counting" input commodities that are used in the production of other commodities. An example of this is holding Soybeans but not Soybean Oil, or Soybean Meal, which is produced from soybeans.
- **Selection Criteria:** Commodity indices use different component selection criteria. These can include importance to the global economy, liquidity and trading history, location of the commodity exchange, or the currency of the contracts. For many commodity indices, the final component selection is set by a committee.
- **Value Based versus Quantity Based Weighting:** A value based index has fixed component weights. The number of futures contracts in the index changes dynamically to maintain constant weights. A quantity based index holds a fixed quantity of each commodity, so that the index weights change each day. For example, the S&P 500 stock index is quantity based since the number of shares of each company in the index only changes when the index constituents are changed. A benchmark that consists of 60% stocks and 40% bonds is value based.
- **Roll Schedule:** The frequency and timing of rolls differ for each index. Across the major indices, and even within indices, commodity contracts can follow different roll schedules due to the liquidity or seasonality of the underlying commodity. The schedule used to roll commodity futures as they approach expiry can have a great impact on index performance. Larger roll windows can mean that contracts do not have to be rolled under negative trading circumstances. This flexibility can be an important source of performance.
- **Average Maturity:** The weighted average maturity of the component contracts can also vary for each commodity index. This is also an important factor in fixed income indices. Equity indices, due to the infinite life of corporate stock, do not have an average maturity.
- **Energy Allocation:** Since energy markets are highly volatile and highly correlated, energy is the dominant factor that drives the returns of commodity indices.

In Exhibit 8.9, the performance statistics for the BCI, S&P GSCI, and DJ-UBS commodity indeces and commodity sector indices for the period 1991 to 2008 are given. The return and volatility of the various commodity indices often differ within each commodity sector but the correlation of the

EXHIBIT 8.9 Performance Comparison of Alternative Commodity Indices (1991–2008)

	Annualized Return	Standard Deviation	Information Ratio	Maximum Drawdown	Correlation		
					S&P 500	BarCap US Aggrgate	SPGSCI Sector Index
Bache Index (BCI)	10.3%	12.8%	0.80	−31.4%	0.09	0.01	0.94
Dow Jones–UBS Index	4.9%	14.5%	0.34	−49.4%	0.19	0.05	0.90
S&P GSCI Index	2.8%	21.0%	0.13	−62.2%	0.12	0.03	1.00
Bache Agriculture	5.2%	9.7%	0.54	−27.2%	0.15	−0.01	0.86
Dow Jones–UBS Agriculture	0.8%	16.8%	0.05	−53.2%	0.21	0.05	0.95
S&P GSCI Agriculture	−1.1%	17.1%	−0.06	−63.9%	0.20	0.07	1.00
Bache Energy	13.1%	23.0%	0.57	−39.9%	0.02	0.02	0.95
Dow Jones–UBS Energy	5.8%	31.2%	0.19	−69.4%	0.06	0.04	0.97
S&P GSCI Energy	3.3%	31.3%	0.11	−68.8%	0.07	0.03	1.00
Bache Industrial Metals	10.8%	18.1%	0.59	−33.5%	0.24	−0.10	0.85
Dow Jones–UBS Industrial Metals	3.8%	20.1%	0.19	−60.0%	0.31	−0.10	0.99
S&P GSCI Industrial Metal	2.6%	19.3%	0.14	−59.6%	0.29	−0.12	1.00
Bache Precious Metals	3.8%	11.4%	0.33	−27.1%	−0.04	0.14	0.95
Dow Jones–UBS Precious Metal	5.2%	16.3%	0.32	−34.4%	0.02	0.10	0.98
S&P GSCI Precious Metal	5.4%	15.1%	0.36	−30.3%	−0.01	0.13	1.00
Bache Livestock	6.1%	9.8%	0.62	−24.6%	0.04	−0.01	0.93
Dow Jones–UBS Livestock	−1.1%	14.4%	−0.08	−49.1%	0.06	0.04	0.99
S&P GSCI Livestock	−0.9%	14.1%	−0.06	−43.8%	0.06	0.01	1.00
Bache Grains	4.8%	14.1%	0.34	−35.6%	0.11	0.06	0.94
Dow Jones–UBS Grains	0.1%	20.6%	0.00	−56.1%	0.20	0.09	0.95
S&P GSCI Grains	−1.8%	20.8%	−0.09	−73.7%	0.18	0.09	1.00

non-S&P GSCI indices show a high correlation with the S&P GSCI index within each commodity sector. As noted in Exhibit 8.9, the BCI index generally had the lowest volatility (due primarily to its ability to rebalance intra-month to various contracts as well as to cash), and the S&P GSCI had the highest volatility primarily due to its overweight in energy. Lastly, most of the listed commodity indices are available through various investable vehicles including ETF, futures, or mutual funds. However, the fees for each investment vehicle may differ such that the return performance shown in Exhibit 8.10 is only indicative of the actual investor returns.

HEDGE FUNDS

The performance characteristics of the major hedge fund indices are given in Exhibit 8.10 for the period 2001 to 2008. In addition, correlations with S&P 500, Barclays Capital U.S. Bond Aggregate, and the CISDM Hedge Fund indices for each strategy are also shown in Exhibit 8.10. While not shown in the following exhibits, the differences in reported return and risk may dramatically impact the inclusion or exclusion of hedge funds in any asset allocation model. It is worth noting that, while the various return and risk characteristics of the indices are similar by strategy, differences do exist (note the CSFB EMN reported a much lower annual return (.04%) than that reported by CSDM (5.6%), HFR (3.3%), or Barclays (4.1%)). This is in part due to the different approaches to index construction (e.g., at the hedge fund strategy level the CSFB is asset-weighted, HFRI is fund-weighted, and CISDM is median).

INVESTABLE MANAGER BASED HEDGE FUND INDICES

The growth in hedge fund investment has encouraged a number of firms to offer manager based investable hedge fund index products. These manager based investable hedge fund indices differ in many ways. As a result, seemingly similar hedge fund indices may have different return and risk performance over similar time periods. However, previous studies (Schneeweis et al., 2006) show that despite differences in risk and return, the various hedge fund indices (investable and noninvestable) generally report similar correlations to each other as well as to major market factors such as stock and bond indexes.

Exhibit 8.11 emphasizes the relationships between noninvestable CISDM hedge fund indices and the investable Hedge Fund Research (HFRX)

EXHIBIT 8.10 Performance of Alternative Hedge Fund Indices (2001–2008)

	Annualized Return	Standard Deviation
Barclays Hedge Fund Index	5.1%	6.6%
CISDM Equal Weighted Hedge Fund Index	5.6%	6.6%
CSFB/Tremont Hedge Fund Index	5.4%	5.6%
HFRI Fund Weighted Composite Index	5.0%	6.4%
Barclays Equity Market Neutral	4.1%	3.1%
CISDM Equity Market Neutral	5.6%	2.0%
CSFB/Tremont Equity Market Neutral	0.4%	14.7%
HFRI Equity Market Neutral	3.3%	2.9%
Barclays Fixed Income Arbitrage	1.3%	6.4%
CISDM Fixed Income Arbitrage	3.6%	4.8%
CSFB/Tremont Fixed Income Arbitrage	0.8%	7.1%
Barclays Hedge Convertible Arbitrage	1.7%	7.5%
CISDM Convertible Arbitrage	3.3%	6.2%
CSFB/Tremont Convertible Arbitrage	1.2%	7.9%
HFRI Convertible Arbitrage	0.7%	8.2%
Barclays Event Driven	6.6%	6.3%
CISDM Event Driven Multi-Strategy	5.6%	6.3%
CSFB/Tremont Event Driven	7.6%	5.6%
HFRI Event Driven	6.0%	7.1%
Barclays Merger Arbitrage	5.7%	3.8%
CISDM Merger Arbitrage	4.8%	3.4%
CSFB/Tremont Risk Arbitrage	4.1%	3.9%
HFRI Merger Arbitrage	4.3%	3.7%
Barclays Distressed Securities	6.6%	7.3%
CISDM Distressed Securities	7.6%	6.0%
CSFB/Tremont Distressed	8.5%	6.1%
HFRI Distressed Securities	7.7%	6.6%
Barclays Equity Long Short	4.8%	5.4%
CISDM Equity Long/Short	4.4%	6.0%
CSFB/Tremont Long/Short Equity	4.5%	7.2%
HFRI Equity Hedge	2.8%	8.2%
Barclays Global Macro	7.7%	5.2%
CISDM Global Macro	6.4%	3.3%
CSFB/Tremont Global Macro	11.6%	5.5%
HFRI Macro	8.8%	5.1%
Barclays Emerging Markets	9.7%	12.6%
CISDM Emerging Markets	7.9%	10.5%
CSFB/Tremont Emerging Markets	8.7%	10.3%

			Correlation	
Information Ratio	Maximum Drawdown	S&P 500	BarCap US Aggregate	CISDM HF Strategy Index
0.78	−23.1%	0.78	0.01	0.99
0.84	−21.1%	0.79	0.00	1.00
0.97	−19.7%	0.62	0.05	0.91
0.78	−20.5%	0.80	−0.03	0.99
1.34	−6.1%	−0.13	−0.03	0.57
2.84	−2.8%	0.44	0.00	1.00
0.03	−42.7%	0.21	−0.22	0.07
1.16	−8.3%	0.02	−0.07	0.59
0.20	−28.6%	0.50	0.11	0.85
0.74	−19.3%	0.56	0.11	1.00
0.11	−29.0%	0.44	0.19	0.89
0.23	−31.5%	0.48	0.25	0.97
0.53	−22.5%	0.46	0.32	1.00
0.15	−32.9%	0.45	0.21	0.93
0.08	−35.3%	0.49	0.26	0.97
1.05	−19.6%	0.72	−0.08	0.94
0.90	−20.2%	0.76	0.00	1.00
1.36	−18.9%	0.62	−0.04	0.92
0.85	−23.9%	0.77	−0.04	0.96
1.50	−7.2%	0.62	0.06	0.86
1.43	−5.7%	0.66	0.05	1.00
1.04	−8.2%	0.56	0.14	0.67
1.16	−8.1%	0.66	0.06	0.90
0.91	−34.3%	0.58	−0.02	0.87
1.26	−21.2%	0.65	0.10	1.00
1.40	−21.5%	0.58	−0.07	0.83
1.18	−26.9%	0.58	−0.01	0.91
0.89	−14.0%	0.77	−0.11	0.98
0.73	−17.0%	0.77	−0.10	1.00
0.62	−21.6%	0.68	0.04	0.91
0.34	−28.5%	0.81	−0.07	0.96
1.47	−6.4%	0.30	0.12	0.81
1.93	−2.6%	0.30	0.11	1.00
2.10	−14.9%	0.21	0.30	0.45
1.71	−4.9%	0.13	0.12	0.76
0.77	−40.1%	0.75	0.05	0.98
0.75	−35.3%	0.69	0.09	1.00
0.84	−30.9%	0.69	0.10	0.95

EXHIBIT 8.11 Comparison on Noninvestable and Investable Indices (2004–2008)

Performance and Correlations 2004–2008	Annualized Return	Standard Deviation	Information Ratio	Maximum Drawdown	Correlation			
					CISDM Strategy Index	S&P 500	BarCap US Aggregate	BarCap US Corporate High-Yield
CISDM Equal Weighted Hedge Fund Index	3.8%	7.2%	0.53	−21.1%	1.00	0.82	0.12	0.74
HFRX Equal Weighted Strategies Index	−1.7%	6.6%	(0.25)	−23.6%	0.93	0.80	0.12	0.75
CISDM Equity Market Neutral	.3%	2.2%	2.45	−2.8%	1.00	0.49	0.06	0.37
HFRX Equity Market Neutral	1.4%	3.4%	0.42	−6.0%	0.29	0.05	−0.24	−0.11
CISDM Convertible Arbitrage	−0.9%	7.4%	(0.12)	−22.5%	1.00	0.69	0.37	0.80
HFRX Convertible Arbitrage	−15.7%	18.2%	(0.86)	−60.4%	0.88	0.75	0.19	0.80
CISDM Distressed Securities	4.2%	6.8%	0.62	−21.2%	1.00	0.82	0.11	0.81
HFRX Distressed Securities	−2.7%	8.2%	(0.33)	−31.8%	0.80	0.61	−0.11	0.54
CISDM Event Driven Multi-Strategy	3.3%	6.9%	0.48	−20.2%	1.00	0.87	0.05	0.76
HFRX Event Driven	−0.2%	7.3%	(0.03)	−25.8%	0.96	0.86	0.04	0.71
CISDM Merger Arbitrage	5.4%	3.8%	1.43	−5.7%	1.00	0.77	0.10	0.63
HFRX Merger Arbitrage	5.1%	3.8%	1.35	−3.4%	0.83	0.55	0.28	0.47
CISDM Equity Long/Short	4.1%	6.3%	0.65	−17.0%	1.00	0.77	0.03	0.60
HFRX Equity Hedge	−2.2%	8.6%	(0.26)	−28.5%	0.91	0.83	0.06	0.70

indices over the period 2004 to 2008.[1] The HFRX indices are based on a set of managers that provide daily transparency and follow a set of selection rules (e.g., size, years since inception) that are typically demanded by large institutional investors. Results show that the various investable indices have at least moderate correlations to their noninvestable counterparts. For example, with the exception of equity market neutral (for which no central driving market factor exists), the correlation between the investable and noninvestable indices is above 0.50. Likewise, the correlations between the noninvestable CISDM hedge fund indices with market factors and the corresponding investable HFRX indices with market factors are generally similar. For example, the correlations of the CISDM Distressed Securities with the S&P 500 (.82), BarCap US Aggregate (.11), and BarCap US Corporate High-Yield index (.81) are similar to that for the HFRX Distressed Securities correlation with the S&P 500 (.61), BarCap US Aggregate (–.11), and BarCap US Corporate High-Yield (.54).

CTA INVESTMENT

The growth in CTA investment has encouraged a number of firms to offer manager based CTA index products. Each of these CTA indexes differs in unique ways. As a result, seemingly similar manager based CTA indexes may have different return and risk performance over common time frames. The return and risk characteristics of the various noninvestable CTA indices are given in Exhibit 8.12. The return and volatility of the various CTA indices often differ within each strategy or trading sector but the correlation of the non-CISDM indices show a high correlation with the CISDM indices within each CTA strategy sector.

INDEX VERSUS FUND INVESTMENT:
A HEDGE FUND EXAMPLE

Most of the results presented in previous chapters emphasized the use of asset class benchmark or indices in various asset allocation procedures. As discussed previously, these benchmarks or indices may reflect particular security holdings or are often portfolios of managers based on the unique selection and methodology of the benchmark or index providers. Investors should be aware of the degree to which index performance may not reflect the performance of an individual manager or security.

This is especially true in areas of investment such as hedge funds and managed futures where discretion may play a larger role in the investment

EXHIBIT 8.12 Performance of Comparison CTA Indices (2001–2008)

	Annualized Return	Standard Deviation	Information Ratio	Maximum Drawdown	Correlation		
					S&P 500	BarCap US Aggregate	CISDM CTA EW Strategy Index
CISDM CTA Asset Weighted Index	8.87%	8.29%	1.07	−8.25%	−0.19	0.14	0.94
CISDM CTA Equal Weighted Index	9.17%	8.75%	1.05	−8.75%	−0.26	0.17	1.00
Barclays Trader Index CTA	6.43%	7.54%	0.85	−7.74%	−0.25	0.22	0.98
CISDM CTA Asset Weighted Currency	4.56%	6.44%	0.71	−9.74%	0.15	0.05	0.64
CISDM CTA Equal Weighted Currency	5.92%	5.56%	1.06	−7.37%	−0.10	0.07	1.00
Barclays Currency	3.33%	5.35%	0.62	−6.61%	−0.04	0.14	0.92
CISDM CTA Asset Weighted Discretionary Index	10.64%	6.71%	1.58	−5.04%	0.10	0.13	0.69
CISDM CTA Equal Weighted Discretionary	11.12%	6.43%	1.73	−10.11%	0.19	0.18	1.00
Barclays Discretionary	7.29%	4.15%	1.76	−3.29%	0.00	−0.04	0.48
CISDM CTA Asset Weighted Diversified	8.61%	9.35%	0.92	−11.36%	−0.19	0.13	0.95
CISDM CTA Equal Weighted Diversified	10.73%	11.21%	0.96	−11.37%	−0.28	0.16	1.00
Barclays Diversified	8.82%	11.33%	0.78	−11.96%	−0.30	0.18	0.99
CISDM CTA Asset Weighted Financials	11.27%	9.91%	1.14	−10.25%	−0.23	0.14	0.86
CISDM CTA Equal Weighted Financials	7.84%	8.46%	0.93	−8.69%	−0.28	0.20	1.00
CISDM CTA Asset Weighted Physicals	2.71%	13.02%	0.21	−20.84%	0.07	−0.08	0.50
CISDM CTA Equal Weighted Physicals	8.28%	8.74%	0.95	−13.19%	−0.13	−0.01	1.00
CISDM CTA Asset Weighted Systematic	8.07%	8.08%	1.00	−6.96%	−0.15	0.12	0.90
CISDM CTA Equal Weighted Systematic	8.98%	9.76%	0.92	−9.91%	−0.27	0.13	1.00
Barclays Systematic	6.62%	9.15%	0.72	−10.13%	−0.30	0.22	0.96
CISDM CTA Asset Weighted Equity Index	10.86%	9.42%	1.15	−10.08%	0.16	0.14	0.67
CISDM CTA Equal Weighted Equity Index	6.65%	7.90%	0.84	−14.09%	0.37	0.06	1.00
S&P 500	−2.89%	15.05%	−0.19	−40.68%	1.00	−0.14	0.37
BarCap US Aggregate	5.74%	3.99%	1.44	−3.83%	−0.14	1.00	0.06
BarCap US Corporate High-Yield	3.19%	10.96%	0.29	−33.31%	0.68	0.22	0.41

process.[2] In this section we emphasize the degree to which hedge fund indices track the performance of hedge funds reporting as that strategy. It is important to realize that results at the individual fund level may not reflect the results of the relevant index to the degree that the fund does not represent the underlying performance of the index (e.g., portfolio) strategy. Previous research has shown that a portfolio of four to five funds is required for the portfolio to reflect that of the strategy index (Schneeweis et al., 2003). It was also shown that the relationships between individual funds and the underlying hedge fund strategy or the market factors that drive those strategies are impacted by the level of strategy or market returns. Research (Schneeweis et al., 2002, 2003) has shown that, when strategy returns or market returns are at their historical high or low, the percentage of individual funds with similar directional return movement is high (often above 80%). At the same time, when index returns or market returns are near zero, individual hedge fund returns are as likely to be positive as negative (Schneeweis et al., 2002). In brief, individual funds may show little correlation with their underlying index or market factors, when index or market factor returns are near zero, but are highly correlated with their underlying index or market factors, when those returns are either highly positive or highly negative.

In addition, individual funds that represent returns to specific asset strategies may differ across a wide range of qualitative factors and quantitative factors. Funds may differ by asset size, leverage, years since inception, level of incentive fees, management fees, lockups, investment structure (e.g., partnership or corporate entity), currency, as well as a number of other factors. Research has indicated that some of these characteristics have little impact on fund performance (e.g., size) but other factors do seem to impact expected return and risk (e.g., lockups, years since inception). Investors should also be aware that a single database does not represent all funds across the industry and that multiple databases often are required to represent adequately the investment strategy universe.

As important, investors should be aware that the performance of funds currently reporting to major databases often do not reflect the average returns of funds that existed in the past, but no longer report in the current database. The often higher historical returns to funds listed in the current database are often reported to be due to several biases (Fung and Hsieh, 2006) in database construction such as (1) backfill bias/incubation bias (the historical returns of new funds reporting to the database are included in the database. Since, in most cases, only funds with superior historical returns report their returns to databases, the returns before their database entry date may be biased upward relative to all those funds that do not report) and (2) survivorship bias: Funds that used to exist historically in the database are removed from it when they stop reporting. Often these funds stop reporting because of poor returns. The often lower returns of these funds are not contained in the live portion of most databases and one must ask for the dead fund databases in order to measure the actual returns to investment in funds that may have existed in the past.

Other biases may also exist in any single database, such as selection bias (databases differ on their requirements for reporting) and reporting bias (managers may be in one strategy but report as in another). The extent of these biases may differ by strategy, time period, and database. Thus, proper due diligence must be used in understanding the actual performance characteristics of a fund before considering investment. For example, research (Fung and Hsieh, 2006) has shown that, if the first year or so of performance is removed from a fund reporting to a database, the impact of backfill bias is removed dramatically. Similarly, most hedge fund indices do not contain survivorship bias or backfill bias, as managers reporting to the database at any one time are used. Historical index returns are not changed when these managers are removed from the database and therefore do not reflect survivorship bias. Likewise, as new managers are added to the database, the historical index returns are not changed in order to reflect those new managers and corresponding historical index returns. Hence, no backfill bias is contained in the many indices.[3]

The impact of survivorship bias and backfill bias, as well as the impact of the use of hedge fund indices to reflect the performance of individual hedge funds, is shown in Exhibit 8.13 for Equity Long/Short hedge funds (other strategies are not shown in this report but results for other strategies are similar and are available from the authors). A portfolio of equal-weighted ELS funds, for which complete CISDM data from 2000 to 2008 are available, is compared to the CISDM ELS Index, which includes all ELS funds regardless of the completeness of their data for this period. Results show that the equal-weighted portfolio of ELS hedge funds reports a higher return (7.8%) than that of the CISDM ELS index (4.9%) over the same period. This is consistent with both backfill and survivorship bias. (Note that the correlations with the S&P 500, BarCap US Government and Corporate High-Yield indices and the CISDM ELS index are similar at the portfolio level.) Of greater importance is that the average of the standard deviations of the individual ELS (15.9%) funds is higher than the standard deviation of the ELS EW Portfolio (9.0%) or of the CISDM ELS Index (6.6%). In addition, while the average return of the individual funds is the same as the portfolio mean, the average standard deviation of returns around the average return for individual ELS funds (5.5%) indicates that a wide variation in returns exists among the reporting ELS with complete information. Similar wide variations in standard deviations as well as correlations with the S&P

EXHIBIT 8.13 Performance Comparison of CISDM ELS Index and Individual ELS Funds (2000–2008)

| | | | | Correlation | | |
		Average Return	Standard Deviation	S&P 500	BarCap US Government	BarCap US Corporate High-Yield	CISDM Equity Long Short (ELS) Index
CISDM ELS Index	Index	4.9%	6.6%	0.72	−0.21	0.57	1.00
CISDM ELS Funds	EW Portfolio	7.8%	9.0%	0.72	−0.25	0.66	0.94
CISDM ELS Funds	Average	7.8%	15.9%	0.39	−0.13	0.36	0.52
CISDM ELS Funds*	Std Dev of Sample	5.5%	9.1%	0.28	0.13	0.22	0.27

* Equity Long Short Funds with full data for period. From CISDM database.

500, Barclays Capital US Government, and Barclays Capital US Corporate High-Yield indices are also reported. In short, individual ELS managers on average may reflect the benefits illustrated in an ELS index or portfolio, but wide variations exist among individual ELS managers.

It is important to point out that the results in Exhibit 8.13 are indicative of similar potential problems in the use of individual funds to provide access to the returns of any particular asset class. In short, as indicated previously, style pure peer groups of funds must be constructed if one expects the results at the fund level to represent the returns at the asset class level.

WHAT EVERY INVESTOR SHOULD REMEMBER

- Asset allocation results are sensitive to the benchmark used in analysis.
- Each benchmark has unique return and risk characteristics that flow from their underlying structure and composition.
- The investability of a benchmark is essential in its use in asset allocation.
- Benchmarks are corporate products and therefore reflect business models that may or may not be apparent to the investor.

NOTES

1. HFRX investable indices have various inception dates between 2003 and 2005 and thus the comparison here is for the past five years.
2. Asset benchmarks form the basis for much of asset allocation analysis; considerable research has focused on desired benchmark characteristics. Academics have also addressed various aspects of concern including the degree to which various benchmarks may overestimate actual historical returns due to failure of the indices/benchmarks to correct for backfill bias (historical benchmark data includes current reporting managers); survival bias (managers who leave, generally due to poor performance, leave the database and the index is recalculated). Most indices, including most hedge fund and managed futures indices, are not recalculated when current managers leave or new managers enter (begin reporting to the data base) In brief, individuals should be aware of the actual construction issues relating to the return calculation for each benchmark used in the asset allocation process.
3. Note that the period before the data inception of an index may contain survivorship and backfill bias. For instance, if an index was started in 2002, returns pre-2002 would contain backfill bias and survivorship bias.

CHAPTER 9

Risk Budgeting and Asset Allocation

Asset allocation and risk management are about finding the right balance of risk and return. In this chapter, we focus on several practical techniques that can be used to measure, monitor, and manage the risk of a portfolio. What we want readers to take from this chapter is that asset allocation is the same as risk allocation and that the road to a portfolio which meets an investor's investment goals through time comes from actively monitoring and managing the risk of the portfolio.

The concept of risk-adjusted returns is not easy to explain because there is no consensus on how the "true" risk of a portfolio should be measured and because, as was discussed in previous chapters, risk cannot be measured in isolation—it depends on other assets and liabilities of the investor. While an investor's interest is on the total return generated by a portfolio, good returns are difficult to achieve. The fact that markets are efficient most of the time means that high returns will typically come at the cost of higher risk. The good news is that while managing a portfolio to earn a high rate of return is difficult, managing the risk profile of a portfolio is relatively easy.

PROCESS OF RISK MANAGEMENT: MULTI-FACTOR APPROACH

Risk management is a process that involves several steps. When it comes to risk management of multi-asset portfolios, the first step is to understand the investor. What are her attitudes toward risk, what are her liabilities, and what does she hope to achieve with help of the portfolio? Once this first step is completed, our attention must turn to the portfolio. In this context, first, we need to find out what the sources of portfolio risks are.

Next, we must use quantitative and qualitative tools to measure the exposure of the portfolio to these sources of risk. This is important because, in the long run, the major determinants of a portfolio's total return are its exposures to various sources of risk. At this stage, we need to define various sources of risk. These may include:

- **Market risk:** This is the risk associated with unexpected changes in broad asset classes or economic variables. Let's look at some of the major sources of risk that come under market risk:
  - Equity risk: This is the most well known and best understood source of risk. It results from unexpected changes in global economic prices. Since equity prices are expected have a positive return in the long run, higher exposure to this risk should lead to higher return.
  - Interest risk: This is also a fairly well understood source of risk and it mostly affects fixed income instruments and equity prices of financial institutions.
  - Currency risk: Positions denominated in foreign currencies have direct exposure to this source of risk. However, currency risk is not one of those risks that should contribute to a higher return on a portfolio. This means that if the hedging cost is zero, one may consider eliminating this risk.
  - Commodity risk: Investment in commodities has become an increasingly important asset class in recent years. A portfolio may have exposure to unexpected changes in commodity prices even if it does not have direct investment in commodities; e.g., an unexpected increase in oil price may significantly affect several sectors of the economy.
  - Inflation risk: This risk will manifest itself through changes in interest rates and commodity prices. Further, this is a larger risk for those portfolios where the total return is supposed to fund operations of an entity, cover the cost of living of a family, or pay for the replacement of real assets.
  - Others: Risks associated with various economic sectors, small capitalization firms, emerging markets, and so on.
- **Credit and counterparty risk:** This risk is caused by the failure of a counterparty or a debtor to meet its legal obligations. It can also be caused by changes in the credit rating of a credit instrument. Counterparty risks arise whenever positions are established in over-the-counter instruments such as credit derivatives, interest swaps, or forward contracts. Higher exposure to credit risk may not always lead to higher return on the portfolio. This is especially correct for counterparty risk, where higher return may come at too high a cost. The reason

is that most instruments that are exposed to counterparty risk are purchased for risk management purposes rather than return enhancement. The cost of not having the anticipated protection when it is needed could be quite high.

- **Liquidity risk:** This arises when an investment cannot be converted into cash quickly without paying a significant penalty. For exchange traded instruments, this risk can be measured using the bid-ask spread. For alternative investments, liquidity risk is difficult to measure. Recent experience with hedge funds imposing restrictions on redemptions shows that liquidity risk is not constant and could arise exactly when liquidity is most valued. Liquidity can be a major source of return for some alternative asset classes (e.g., private equity and some hedge fund strategies). A major difficulty in this area is measuring liquidity risk. Quantitative methods to measure this risk are lacking and therefore common sense and qualitative due diligence should be used to supplement the analysis.

- **Volatility risk:** This risk arises when there are unexpected increases in volatility. This source of risk can be further expanded by looking at volatility of specific segments of the market (e.g., equity, interest rate, commodity prices, and so forth). This risk is particularly important if the portfolio has instruments with non-linear payoffs (e.g., options) or the portfolio manager is using dynamic trading strategies to replicate the payoff to such instruments. There is some controversy with regard to this risk; that is, do investments that have positive exposure to this risk earn a premium (positive or negative) for exposure to volatility? Available empirical evidence seems to indicate that the market price of risk for volatility is actually negative. This means that those instruments that are positively correlated to changes in volatility offer lower rate of return.

- **Operational risk:** This risk generally arises if the portfolio has allocation to active managers. System failures, lack of adequate control, and fraud are examples of operational risk that could affect a portfolio's performance. As discussed later, there are generally no rewards for exposure to operational risk and therefore it pays to avoid it.

- **Others:** There are several other sources of risk that could affect a portfolio's return. For instance, political risk may be important for a portfolio that has allocation to emerging economies. Changes in regulatory environment and tax codes represent additional sources of risk.

In general, the higher the total risk of a portfolio, the higher its long-term rate of return. This statement is correct in the long-run and during normal periods. However, during periods of market stress, higher risk is typically associated with lower return. The reason is that investors begin to reassess their risk exposures and start selling risky assets during such periods. As a result, higher risk is associated with lower return during periods of market stress. Further, even in the long-run not every risk exposure is going to translate into higher return, or a marginal higher return could come at the cost of much higher risk. Two examples may demonstrate this. First, suppose a portfolio manager is considering allocation to both AAA and BBB rated corporate bonds. In this case, any increased allocation to the BBB rated bond index should increase the long-term return of the portfolio while increasing the portfolio's exposure to credit risk. So depending on the current risk profile of the portfolio and the investor's attitude toward risk, one may decide to increase the allocation to BBB rated bond index in order to generate a higher return over time. Second, consider a portfolio manager who is considering allocation to two hedge funds. One has a state-of–the-art enterprise risk management system and therefore will expose the portfolio manager to very little operational risk. The other manager runs a rather small fund and cannot afford to have all risk management tools in place. In this case, there is no reward to bearing the operational risk of the second manager.

Once the relevant sources of risk are identified, next comes the more difficult task of measuring a portfolio's exposure. The most common approach to measure exposure is to use a multivariate linear regression. These multi-factor models can be quite effective as long as one can find a factor that has pure exposure to the desired source of risk. Some risk factors can be identified quite easily while others have to be constructed through a careful process, and some risk factors may be impossible to identify (e.g., liquidity risk factor).

The general form of a multi-factor is:

$$R_{it} - R_f = \alpha_i + \beta_{i1}F_{1t} + \beta_{i2}F_{2t} + \ldots + \beta_{iK}F_{Kt} + \varepsilon_{it}$$

where

R_{it} = Total return on asset class i in time period t,
R_f = Riskless rate
α_i = Intercept
β_{i1} = Exposure of the investment to factor 1
ε_{it} = Unexplained part of return
F_{kt} = Factor representing the source of risk

The factors must be selected carefully so that they unambiguously represent a unique source of risk. For example, credit risk can be expressed as the difference between the return on a high-yield bond index and the return on a Treasury Bond index with the same duration, or interest rate risk can be measured as the return differential between an index of medium-term Treasuries and short-term Treasuries. Generally, as you can see, one should attempt to represent the factors as excess returns on portfolios.

The goal of risk management in the context of portfolio management is not to eliminate every risk, but to find the right combination of risks that is consistent with the investor's risk preference and at the same time not to expose the portfolio to risks that do not contribute to its long-term performance. Thus, in the next step of the risk management process, the portfolio manager has to decide on the potential reward from various sources of risk. The issues related to estimating risk premiums associated with various factors were discussed in previous chapters. Briefly, for those risk factors that are represented by returns on traded assets, the risk premium associated with risk factors can be estimated by examining the excess return on the corresponding asset. For instance, the mean of the return differential between a high-yield bond index and Treasury index of the same duration is a reasonable estimate of the price of credit risk. If no such an asset can be identified, then the procedure discussed in Chapter 2 should be followed; that is, create a portfolio with high exposure to the factor and a portfolio with low exposure to the same factor. The mean of the return differential between the two portfolios is a reasonable estimate of the risk premium associated with that factor. For instance, if the mean return for a portfolio with positive exposure to inflation is not different from the mean return on a portfolio with negative exposure to inflation, then inflation risk is not priced by markets. This means that having exposure to inflation is not likely to contribute to the portfolio's performance and therefore should be eliminated, assuming the cost of doing so is zero. However, eliminating exposure to inflation without affecting the entire risk-return profile of a portfolio is a difficult task.

Once market prices of various factors are estimated, and considering the investor's tolerance for risk and her liabilities, the portfolio manager has to decide how much exposure to each risk the portfolio should have. For instance, if the only relevant risk factor were equity risk, then risk management would require the portfolio manager to establish the right equity beta for the portfolio, and then adjust the portfolio's allocation to equity through time to maintain the targeted beta. As stated, the portfolio should have exposures to those sources of risk that contribute to the portfolio's performance, and the exposure should be relatively low for those sources of risk that do not provide a large benefit.

The final step is to construct the portfolio with the appropriate risk attributes and then monitor changes in those risk exposures through time to ensure that the portfolio remains within the parameters set forth in the investment policy statement. Given the factor model that was expressed in the previous equation, the expected return on the portfolio is given by

$$E[R_{it}] - R_f = \alpha_i + \beta_{i1} \times E[F_{1t}] + \beta_{i2} \times E[F_{2t}] + \ldots + \beta_{iK} \times E[F_{Kt}]$$

Therefore, the expected total return on the portfolio is primarily determined by its exposure to various sources of risk. Since the beta of the portfolio with respect to each risk factor is just the weighted average of the risk exposures of the components of the portfolio, the weights should be selected to manage the portfolio's risk exposures. The following quantitative approach can be used to construct the portfolio:

$$\min_w \quad Var[R_p] \quad \text{Subject to}$$
$$w_i \geq 0$$
$$\sum_{i=1}^{N} w_i \beta_{i1} = \text{Exposure}_1$$
$$\ldots$$
$$\sum_{i=1}^{N} w_i \beta_{iK} = \text{Exposure}_K$$

This means the portfolio is constructed to have minimum volatility subject to various constraints on the portfolio's exposure. This problem can be solved using standard optimization packages such as Microsoft Excel's Solver. Note that one can eliminate the usual constraint that weights should add up to one by using returns in excess of a riskless asset.

Typically, the above analysis is performed using available equity, fixed income, and alternative asset indices. Once the optimal allocations are determined, the portfolio manager has to find the investment products that have the same characteristics as those indices. This task is relatively straightforward for equity and fixed income investments. However, when it comes to alternative asset classes and especially those for which manager skill is rather important, it may be impossible to find managers who have the same exposures as the indices. In some cases, the portfolio manager may need to revise the equity and fixed income exposures of the portfolio in order to rebalance the overall exposure of the portfolio. For instance, if the equity exposures of the hedge fund managers who are selected are higher than the equity exposure of the hedge fund index used in the analysis, the portfolio manager may need to reduce the fund's exposure to equity using the liquid portion of the portfolio.

PROCESS OF RISK MANAGEMENT: VOLATILITY TARGET

A simple and yet effective application of what was discussed above is to adjust a portfolio's overall exposure to markets by adjusting its volatility.

Though we have argued in this and previous chapters that risk is multi-dimensional and that volatility should not be used as a portfolio's only measure of risk, monitoring a fund's volatility and making appropriate adjustments to the portfolio mix can significantly improve a portfolio's risk-return profile. The procedure described here is rather simple and inexpensive to implement. Therefore, unless the portfolio manager has implemented a more sophisticated risk management model (e.g., a multi-factor model), portfolio rebalancing through volatility balancing is a sensible risk management method.

Here, we present this method through an example. Exhibit 9.1 provides one sample portfolio allocation across multiple asset classes. Consider the case of a family business, which currently has an investment of $200 million in a well diversified portfolio of traditional global equity and fixed income assets as well as alternative investments.

The five-year historical volatility on the portfolio's pro-forma return has been 10%, while during the same period the average implied volatility of U.S. equity market has been around 18%. This means that the portfolio's volatility has been about 55% of VIX. Once the portfolio is constructed, the portfolio manager will need to monitor the VIX. If there is a significant increase in VIX, the portfolio manager will use index futures to hedge out some of the portfolio's volatility such that its expected volatility remains close to the target. For instance if VIX increases to 24%, the expected volatility of the portfolio will be 55% × 24% = 13.2%. Using a relatively small short position in S&P 500 futures, the portfolio manager would be able to bring back the portfolio's expected volatility close to the target. Consider the expression on the following page for the volatility of portfolio plus a position in the futures contract.

EXHIBIT 9.1   Sample Portfolio Allocations

Broad Asset Classes	Allocations
Global Short-Term Fixed Income	5%
Global Long-Term Fixed Income	35%
Developed Markets Equity	20%
Emerging Markets Equity	10%
Funds of Hedge Funds & CTAs	10%
Private Equity	5%
Commodities	5%
Real Estate	10%
Total	100%

$$Target = \sqrt{\sigma_P^2 + w^2 VIX^2 + 2w VIX^2 \beta_P}$$

where

σ_p = Standard deviation of the portfolio (13.2% in this case)

w = Size of futures position relative to the size of the portfolio

β_p = Beta of the portfolio with respect to S&P 500 futures (e.g., 0.5 in this case)

Calculation will show that a short position of about 8.5% of the portfolio will reduce the expected volatility back to 10%. The rebalancing can take place on a regular basis (e.g., monthly) or whenever the expected volatility of the portfolio moves outside a narrow band. This strategy will reduce the portfolio's risk exposure when there is a spike in VIX because of market stress, while it will slowly increase the portfolio's exposure as markets calm down, because changes in VIX are not symmetric; that is, increases in VIX tend to be dramatic when there is market stress, but declines in VIX tend to be gradual as the market returns to normal.

RISK DECOMPOSITION OF PORTFOLIO

As we have tried to emphasize throughout this book, asset allocation is the process of creating a portfolio with a proper risk-return balance. Further, as we have also argued, the performance of a diversified portfolio is mostly determined by its exposures to various sources of risk. In this section, we use value at risk (VaR) to measure a portfolio's overall risk. Then we show how the VaR of a portfolio can be decomposed so one could know how allocation to each asset class contributes to the total risk of the portfolio. In this way, the portfolio manager can balance the potential return from each allocation by the contribution of the allocation to the total risk of the portfolio.

As was pointed out in Chapter 2, the VaR of a portfolio measures its potential losses due to market risks. In particular, the daily VaR of a portfolio at the confidence level of α states that the portfolio will not suffer a loss greater than VaR with probability of α. Let $Var(R_p)$ denote the per-period VaR of a portfolio. Then this measure of total risk can be decomposed as follows:

$$VaR(R_p) = MVaR(R_1) \times w_1 + MVaR(R_2) \times w_2 + \ldots + MVaR(R_N) \times w_N$$

where $MVaR(R_i)$ is the marginal VaR of asset class i and it measures the contribution of one unit of asset class i to the total VaR of the portfolio.

The marginal VaR of investment i is calculated using the following expression:

$$MVaR(R_i) = VaR(R_p) \times \beta_i$$

where β_i is the beta of asset class i with respect to the portfolio. This result indicates that an asset class that has a high beta with respect to the portfolio makes a relatively large contribution to the total risk of the portfolio. It is essential that a portfolio manager be fully aware of how much risk each asset class contributes to the total risk of the portfolio. For a portfolio that is properly balanced in terms of risk and return, the expected return from each asset class should be directly related to the marginal contribution of that asset class to the risk of the portfolio. Therefore, if the contribution of an asset class to the total risk of a portfolio, as measured by $MVaR(R_i) \times w_i$, is twice as high as the marginal contribution of another asset, then the expected contribution of the first asset to the portfolio's performance should be about twice as high as that of the second asset.

RISK MANAGEMENT USING FUTURES

It is well known that futures provide a means to directly track underlying investment markets as well as to provide risk reduction opportunities. Since futures markets permit individuals to buy or sell financial assets for future delivery at a price set today, futures contracts offer a means to hedge the risk of unexpected price changes. For instance, a commodity, foreign currency, equity, or fixed income hedge is usually caused by buying (selling) a futures contract to initiate a futures position and closing out (offsetting) the position at a later date by selling (buying) the contract in the futures market rather than taking delivery. The hedger benefits to the extent that a gain in the futures position offsets a loss in the spot position. An investor purchasing long-term bonds in September may wish to reduce the risk of interest rate variability by simultaneously selling a December T-Bond futures contract. If interest rates rise during the holding period, the losses in the spot market are reduced by gains in the futures market. Likewise, the foreign currency futures market offers similar protection against unanticipated currency price changes. A U.S. exporter selling goods to a French customer on March 1 but not expecting delivery (payment) until June in euros may wish to sell a June euro futures contract. If the value of the euro falls in the interim, the loss in the spot market is balanced by the gain in the futures position.

It is important to note that opposite price movements result in similar final values as a rise in the value of the euro results in gains on the spot market but losses in the futures market. There is, of course, no guarantee that the spot market gain or loss will be perfectly offset by the futures trade. Since price changes of the cash security and futures contract are often not of the same magnitude, the success of the hedging strategy depends on determining the proper hedge ratio. For many, the proper hedge ratio is determined simply by the relative sensitivity of the return on the spot asset to the return on the futures contract (e.g., beta for stocks, duration for bonds). The actual number of contracts held is determined by the proper hedge ratio times the relative cash value of the spot position times the relative value of the futures contract.[1]

For equities, the minimum risk hedge ratio (X_f^*) is equivalent to the negative of the slope coefficient of regression of cash price changes on futures contract price changes. The higher the correlation between cash and futures price changes, the higher the expected effectiveness of the futures market for hedging purposes. The implementation of this model requires a portfolio manager to regress time series data of historical price changes of the cash instrument to be hedged (ΔP_c) against the price changes of the futures contract (ΔP_f). The optimal hedge ratio (HR) is simply the slope coefficient of:

$$\Delta P_{ct} = \alpha + HR\Delta P_{ft}$$

If an individual holds a \$1 million position in a stock index futures market, for an HR = 0.90, a \$900,000 principal position $(0.9 \times \$1$ million$)$ would be taken in the stock index futures market. For stock index futures, the contract value depends on the level of the index. For example, if the S&P futures price is 1,006.90, the face value of the futures contract is \$251,725 $(1,006.90 \times \$250)$. This would translate into four S&P futures contracts (e.g., \$1 million ÷ \$251,725 × 0.9 = 4). The regression based model, however, assumes that historical relationships between price changes of the cash security and price changes in the futures contract are stable. However, for fixed income securities, price changes are a function of duration that changes through time. The following duration model attempts to explicitly account for these duration estimates.

For fixed income securities, the minimum risk hedge ratio is often based on the relative durations of the security and the futures contract:

$$HR = \frac{D_i R_i P_i}{D_f R_f P_f}$$

where

R_f = Expected change in yield on the instrument underlying futures contract f

R_i = Expected change in yield on bond i

P_f = Price agreed upon the futures contract f to be paid upon maturity of the futures contract for title to the instrument underlying P_f

P_i = Price of bond i expected to prevail on (1) the planned termination date of the hedge for an anticipatory hedge and (2) today's date for cash hedge

D_i = Duration of bond i expected to prevail on (1) the planned termination date of the hedge for an anticipatory hedge and (2) today's date for cash hedge

D_f = Duration of the instrument underlying futures contract f at the delivery date

The duration of a 3-3/8 percent coupon T-Note with a 9-year 11 months maturity yielding 3.44 percent (price = 99.46) is 8.49 years. The duration of the 7-1/2 percent coupon, 6 year 11month T-Note yielding 2.83 percent (price = 129.21) underlying the futures contract is 5.70 years. Assume that the relative yield change of the two bonds is the same (i.e., $R_i = R_f$). Using this information, the HR is

$$HR = \frac{(\$99.46)(8.49)}{(\$129.21)(5.70)} = 1.14$$

This means that 1.48 T-Bond contracts should be traded for each $100,000 face value of the cash bond held. If the manager holds $1 million in bonds, he should sell approximately 11 T-Bond futures contracts ($1 million ÷ 100,000 × 1.14). The duration model makes some assumptions about the kind of interest rate changes that will occur. Different models exist for alternative forecasts of yield shifts. The model therefore requires certain assumptions on relative yield curve shifts. Moreover, duration theory itself has been criticized as not adequately measuring bond price movement. The duration model also requires certain forecasts of expected relative yield volatilities. Historical estimates may be used; however, the stability of past yield relationships is often questionable.

There are a multitude of considerations and approaches involved in futures trading or the use of futures in risk and return management. There are also various means to determine the proper hedge ratio and for many assets no direct futures based contracts exist. Notwithstanding the foregoing, futures contracts have been used to both reduce risk exposure and to increase exposure to particular market factors. For instance, futures have been used to create various portable alpha programs in which the market risks of a particular strategy are hedged away, leaving the excess return. Futures have also been used to create benchmark-plus type programs in which futures contracts are added to an existing portfolio in order to create a new portfolio with a correlation closer to the benchmark portfolio and with hopefully a higher return than the benchmark portfolio.

RISK MANAGEMENT USING OPTIONS

Options can be used to implement drastic changes in the risk-return profile of an investment. Traditional long only assets offer investors a limited set of choices in terms of directly managing the risk of the underlying spot positions. As discussed earlier, futures contracts offer the ability to reduce or increase the underlying variability of an asset, but futures do not permit one to fundamentally change the risk structure of the asset (e.g., create a skewed distribution). Options (when available) provide the means to purchase (call) or sell (put) a security in the future for a price determined today. Unlike with a futures contract, the purchaser of an option has the right but not the obligation to make or accept delivery. Below we discuss two examples involving using options to manage the risk profile of an investment.

COVERED CALL

A covered call writing strategy (often referred to as a buy-write) typically entails the writing (selling) of a call on an equity index against a long position in the same underlying equity index. However, the strategy may be implemented on individual equities or other indices that have options written on them. In essence, the sale of the call sacrifices a portion of the upside return distribution of the underlying index in exchange for the collection of a fixed premium. The extent of upside participation depends on the initial moneyness of the written call. The further out-of-the-money the call is when written, the less of the upside that will potentially be sacrificed. On the other hand, the further out-of-the-money the call is when written, the smaller the premium that will be collected. The other factor that must be considered in the choice of calls is the initial time to expiration. Since an option's time value decay rate increases as the option approaches expiration, short term options tend to decay in value quicker than long-term options, all things being equal. For this reason, many researchers use one-month calls when considering buy-write strategies.

The interest in the use of buy-write strategies for investment purposes has grown significantly in recent years. In light of the growing investment interest, the CBOE has recently introduced a number of buy-write indices based on a variety of equity indices such as the S&P 500, the Dow Jones

Industrial Average, the NASDAQ 100 and the Russell 2000. In addition, a number of funds based on a buy-write strategy have been introduced over the last five years.[2] As illustrated in Kapadia and Szado (2007), the excess risk-adjusted performance of the passive buy-write strategy is primarily derived from selling calls at an implied volatility that exceeds the subsequently realized volatility. In fact, they find that if the calls were sold at the Black-Scholes price corresponding with the realized volatility, the buy-write strategy would underperform the underlying index. In this sense, the buy-write is providing something more than a simple return distribution truncation; it is also providing an additional source of returns—the option volatility risk premium. While Kapadia and Szado (2007) consider a variety of implementations of a buy-write strategy on the Russell 2000, Exhibit 9.2 provides summary statistics for the one-month call buy-write for their period of analysis.

Over this 10-year period, the buy-write strategy provided similar returns to the underlying Russell 2000 at far lower standard deviations and drawdowns. In addition, they break the 10-year period into two periods, one that is decidedly unfavorable for the buy-write (relative to a buy-and-hold strategy on the underlying) as well as a favorable period. Since the buy-write sacrifices potential upside for guaranteed premium collection and the size of premiums are based on expected volatility levels, one would expect the buy-write to perform poorly relative to the underlying in sustained low volatility markets with strong upward trends. Kapadia and Szado (2007) chose the sub-period from February 20, 2003, to November 16, 2006, to represent such an unfavorable market environment.[3] Interestingly, the results suggest that even in this unfavorable market environment, the buy-write strategy achieved over two-thirds of the return of the index at about half its volatility. Not surprisingly, in the earlier (favorable) period of January 1996 to February 2003, the buy-write strategy had a higher annualized return than the index (5.06%, versus the 3.84%).

EXHIBIT 9.2 Performance Statistics for Comparison Spot and Buy-Write: Summary Statistics for the One-Month to Expiration Russell 2000 Buy-Write (Jan 18, 1996–Nov 16, 2006)

	Russell 2000	2% OTM	ATM	2% ITM
Annualized Return	10.7%	10.6%	9.2%	9.6%
Annualized Standard Deviation	20.5%	14.9%	13.4%	11.9%
Maximum Drawdown	−34.7%	−27.2%	−17.5%	21.3%

Source: Kapadia and Szado (2007).

It is interesting to note that this higher return was achieved at a significantly lower volatility of 15.41% compared with the index volatility of 22.69%.

The results of the study certainly suggest that the buy-write strategy is capable of enhancing return and providing some loss mitigation if applied in the right market environment. While the buy-write strategy is often referred to in the literature as a hedging or downside protection strategy, it would be more accurate to think of it as a return enhancing strategy. The small returns typically generated month to month from the option volatility risk premium tend to provide a cushion in market down moves and a return enhancement in sideways markets.

LONG COLLAR

One of the limiting factors of the use of the buy-write is that, while it typically provides a return enhancement that can help cushion losses, it leaves one exposed to the full downside of the underlying's return distribution. The collar strategy can address this shortcoming. The long collar essentially combines a buy-write strategy with a protective put. In general, a long collar strategy involves the purchase of a put against a long position in the underlying, combined with the writing of a call on the same underlying. The purpose of the put is to provide protection against a downside move of the long underlying position.

The call is written to at least partially cover the cost of the purchase of the put, at the expense of limiting the strategy's participation in upside moves of the underlying. A collar strategy is particularly appealing for investors who are seeking some protection from a potential downside move, or a reduction in the market exposure of their portfolio. Ultimately, the collar strategy is expected to offer investors an opportunity to significantly reduce the volatility of their returns, relative to a long position in the underlying index. This is due to the fact that the payoff of the long put reduces the losses of the long index position in downward market moves, while the short call reduces the gains of the long index position in upward market moves.[4] The long collar provides a great deal of flexibility. At one extreme, a very wide collar using far out-of-the-money options is essentially equivalent to a long position in the underlying, with no protection from downside market moves, and full participation in upside moves. At the other extreme, an at-the-money collar is essentially equivalent to a cash or money market position, insulated from market movements when held to expiration. Relative to a long position in the underlying index, the collar strategy has the highest advantage when the market experiences a strong downward trend and has the highest relative disadvantage during sustained strong upward trends.

To take advantage of the faster decay of short term options, the collar can be implemented using 6-month puts and 1-month calls. In this way, the long six-month put decays relatively slowly, while each sequential one-month short call decays quickly. Exhibit 9.3 provides results that suggest that a one-month call/six-month put 2% OTM collar strategies on the QQQ (NASDAQ 100 ETF) significantly outperformed the underlying QQQ in the period from April 1999 to May 2009. The returns for the collar were far higher at about 1/3 the volatility.

EXHIBIT 9.3 Performance Statistics for Underlying and Long Collar April 1999–May 2009

April 1999–May 2009	QQQ TR	QQQ 2% OTM Collar 1 Mo. Put/1 Mo. Call.	QQQ 2% OTM Collar 6 Mo. Put/1 Mo. Call.
Annualized Return	−3.6%	−0.3%	9.3%
Annualized Std Dev	30.4%	6.3%	11.0%
Stutzer Index	−0.07	−0.50	0.59
Maximum Drawdown	−81.1%	−22.9%	−17.9%
April 1999–Sept 2002			
Annualized Return	−23.3%	−3.5%	21.2%
Annualized Std Dev	42.4%	6.4%	13.7%
Stutzer Index	−0.51	−1.18	1.21
Maximum Drawdown	−81.1%	−22.7%	−7.5%
Sept 2002–Sept 2007			
Annualized Return	20.4%	3.5%	5.2%
Annualized Std Dev	17.5%	5.8%	7.9%
Stutzer Index	1.01	0.14	0.32
Maximum Drawdown	−12.4%	−6.7%	−14.0%
Sept 2007–May 2009			
Annualized Return	−19.8%	−4.7%	−1.4%
Annualized Std Dev	29.2%	7.2%	11.6%
Stutzer Index	−0.67	−0.85	−0.20
Maximum Drawdown	−49.7%	−14.4%	−17.9%

Source: Szado and Schneeweis (2009).

Ultimately, the risk of the collar strategy relative to holding the underlying is an opportunity cost risk. This risk is common to any hedging program. If the underlying performs extremely well, then a portion of the potential returns will be lost on the short call position (which is written to fund the purchase of the put's downside protection). Likewise, the ultimate relative benefit of the collar is equivalent to the protection provided by a standard insurance contract or hedge; that is, if the market experiences a significant downward move, losses are largely eliminated.

WHAT EVERY INVESTOR SHOULD REMEMBER

- Application of risk management tools in the context of portfolio management does not mean elimination of risks. It means that the portfolio has the right balance of risk and return from the viewpoint of the investor.

- Risk management requires that a portfolio's exposures to various risks be measured and monitored over time.

- Only those risks that contribute to the performance of the portfolio should be assumed and the others should be eliminated, assuming the cost of doing so is close to zero.

- Decomposition of total risk as measured by VaR enables the portfolio manager to understand the contribution of each asset class to the total risk of a portfolio.

- Risk contribution of an asset class should be closely related to the contribution of that asset class to the performance of the portfolio.

- Futures and options provide direct means both to reduce or enhance an asset's standard deviation (futures) or to fundamentally change the characteristics of the distribution (options).

- Dynamically managing the exposure of an asset relative to various measures of volatility may help limit an assets drawdown in periods of extreme negative market returns.

NOTES

1. For more detail on the use of financial futures as a risk management tool, see www.cmegroup.com.
2. Academic and industry research papers have consistently found that the buy-write strategy on major equity indices such as the Russell 2000 and the S&P 500

typically outperform the underlying indices on a risk-adjusted basis. For example, see Kapadia, Nikunj, and Szado (2007), and Hill, Balasubramanian, Gregory, and Tierens (2006, 29–46).

3. The favorable and unfavorable periods refer to the performance of the buy-write strategy in comparisons to a buy and hold Russell 2000 investment. The annualized return for the Russell in the unfavorable period (February 20, 2003, to November 16, 2006) and favorable periods (January 1996 to February 2003) was 24.82% and 3.84%, respectively. The volatility in the unfavorable period was 15.34% compared with 22.69% for the favorable period.

4. As discussed in Chapter 10, Madoff's investment strategy was primarily a long collar strategy.

Myths of Asset Allocation

From time to time, we have to challenge our strongly held beliefs. This is a difficult endeavor because it may very well be that mistakes were made that upon reflection could have been prevented. The financial disturbances of 2007 and 2008 have forced the discipline of asset allocation and those who profess to practice it to enter into this new reality phase. However, what we know from experience is that if this reality check suggests additional oversight and the possible loss of investor allure (as well as the corresponding fees), many asset allocators will simply turn a blind eye and hope the markets right their mistakes so that they can return to the days when they were viewed as magicians or wizards. It is not a coincidence that most asset allocation programs are linked to investment vehicles that "offer return opportunities not easily found in other investment vehicles." Who would want an asset allocation program that offers return opportunities easily found in other investment vehicles or other investment firms? For the most part, asset allocation services have been turned into a mere stalking horse for a firm's investment products and are offered as essentially a free service. In the wake of recent events, investors are discovering that these "free asset allocation service models" contain a significant and at times hidden price.

In contrast, asset allocation looks beyond particular products and instead focuses on the asset strategies or opportunities presented within the overall investment world in which each strategy or opportunity makes money in certain markets or environments and is less likely to make money in others. This strategy matrix recognizes that while there are different sources of returns and risks associated with each unique asset class and opportunity, there are conditions in which most, if not all, will lose money in the same market environment.

The truth and one that is not commonly associated with the marketing of asset allocation is that asset allocation should not be viewed primarily as a method that ensures that positive returns can be obtained in any market environment. Investors must fundamentally understand that if an asset allocation process suggests that it can produce positive returns in any economic environment, the return it offers should be the risk-free rate. Rather, at its core, asset allocation is a risk management tool that permits a meaningful discussion of the risk and return tradeoffs within a portfolio.

How do we travel from the well-marketed myth of asset allocation as a method to provide positive returns (or at least minimal losses) across almost any market environment to the reality of asset allocation as a risk management tool? Some might say—with difficulty. We know that the human condition is a constant tradeoff between the comfort of constancy and the necessity for change. It is this tension that often creates innovation. One of the major challenges facing an educator or manager is how to get others to change or revise heartfelt views that may have once proved useful but no longer fit reality. This is particularly true in a world of rapid innovation based on new technologies, new regulation, and new investment opportunities. Most of us have a natural and well-earned series of beliefs that help us sort out events. Myths may be regarded as the "collected beliefs" that serve to help one understand the past or to exist in the present. Unfortunately, as noted earlier, not all beliefs are true; and the natural corollary of this statement is that not all beliefs are based on fact. Even so, individuals work and make decisions within their traditional belief systems.

Change is a common part of the investment world as well as academic research. Research in the areas of stock and bond investment, as well as other asset classes, evolves. New theories and information come into existence that better explain past relationships. Any delay in understanding these market forces often results in a delay in an investors' appreciation of change. In short, as markets change, so do myths; some just change more slowly than others. Having dealt with the core myth of asset allocation, that is, the myth that asset allocation provides positive returns in almost any market environment, the remainder of this chapter follows some of the additional myths that have become working beliefs within this discipline.[1]

INVESTOR ATTITUDES, NOT ECONOMIC INFORMATION, DRIVE ASSET VALUES

Some investors may believe that sentiment and not fundamental information drive market prices. Academic theory suggests and empirical results support the conclusion that investments should offer an expected return that is consistent with their underlying risk. What investors must realize, however, is that an asset's own volatility or its correlation with a market portfolio is not by itself the source of return but is reflective of the risks driving the volatility of asset prices. An asset volatility or market correlation merely reflects the asset's sensitivity (movement) to new information entering the market. This new information impacts not only the individual security's price movement but the price movement of other assets as well. Thus a security's expected return is conditional on the expected information and investors' assessment of the risks surrounding that expected information. In general, past research shows that the sharpest gains and losses on various investments happen on days in which there is a release of information that changes attitudes toward expected information or informational risk and thus required returns (academic event day methodology is based on measuring the impact of informational release). For instance, empirical results show that if informational uncertainty increases expected volatility, stock and bond prices often fall in order to offer new investors an expected return consistent with the new perceived greater risk of holding the asset. In short, asset returns simply reflect changes in an investor's reaction to their new perception of risky information. Unfortunately, it's difficult to forecast informational change or an investor's attitude toward those changes in information.

Academic research has shown that while a large number of investors acting on faulty beliefs may in the short term affect market prices, in the longer term assets will move to valuations that reflect the market consensus. For instance, in academic theory, the Arbitrage Pricing Model suggests and empirical results support that two assets that respond similarly to the same set of economic information will have similar levels of expected return. While behavioral implications on stock and bond movement remain a principal focus of some recent research, empirical research has shown that stock and bond market value remains linked to market based risk estimates and required rates of return (e.g., risk premia).

DIVERSIFICATION ACROSS DOMESTIC OR INTERNATIONAL EQUITY SECURITIES IS SUFFICIENT

Modern Portfolio Theory advanced originally by Markowitz in the 1950s centers on the correlation relationships and risk reduction opportunities of adding together securities that respond differently to changing economic conditions. In short, by combining securities that react differently to changes in information one can reduce a portfolio's expected variance. Empirical research, however, now shows that especially during periods of negative informational change, such as an unexpected global credit crisis which may have a negative impact on domestic and global stock markets, domestic or international equity diversification may not reduce volatility significantly. As a result, diversification into alternative investments that respond to different market factors than equity markets is required to benefit most from asset diversification.

HISTORICAL SECURITY AND INDEX PERFORMANCE PROVIDES A SIMPLE MEANS TO FORECAST FUTURE EXCESS RISK-ADJUSTED RETURNS

Because firms change financial structure, because security based indices change composition, and because the future risk environment may differ from today's, simple use of historical data may not provide the means to forecast alpha returns in the near future. Investors should be aware that one can get "free" historical price data from a data supplier that is only five minutes old. One must ask why a "for profit" company would give away historical price data if it had any value.

RECENT MANAGER FUND RETURN PERFORMANCE PROVIDES THE BEST FORECAST OF FUTURE RETURN

Unfortunately, while empirical research has shown that historical fund performance is the primary factor in investor money flows and that there is hard evidence that investors tend to chase yesterday's performance as if yesterday will repeat itself, there is little evidence that recent return performance is the best forecast of future performance. Similarly, there is little indication that past "best" performing managers will be the best future performing managers even in market conditions conducive to that strategy. Given the competition for information, this is as expected. However, empirical research has shown that while it is difficult to use the past performance of the best managers to determine future performance, a manager's poor past performance may be an indicator of future increased volatility. Poor performing managers have a tendency to increase volatility by "going for the gold" in order to obtain "high performance." In short, past return data may be related to future returns only to the degree that one can forecast the underlying risk of the fund and the fund's future risk premia associated with the future risk environment.

SUPERIOR MANAGERS OR SUPERIOR INVESTMENT IDEAS DO NOT EXIST

Yes, unicorns do exist. There is the rare occasion where a manager has an insight that is not currently shared by the market and the execution of that insight results in outsized returns (e.g., those managers that shorted the ABX Index in 2007 and 2008 or managers such as Barton Biggs and Madav Dhar who exploited the new opportunities in emerging markets in the late 1980s and 1990s). There is also the rare circumstance where a manager creates a legitimate informational advantage and acts on it prior to the market knowing its value (e.g., finding information within SEC filings that has been overlooked or not digested by the market). The fact that past manager performance alone does not provide a means to obtain superior future performance does not mean that superior performance does not exist, only that if a manager has consistent superior gross performance they most likely will charge a fee for their services such that the net return across competitive funds would be similar.

PERFORMANCE ANALYTICS PROVIDE A COMPLETE MEANS TO DETERMINE BETTER PERFORMING MANAGERS

No investment package is complete without the inclusion of Sharpe ratios, information ratios, beta comparisons, and so on. However, while the analytical comparison of like managers forms the basis of manager selection, one must be reminded that for comparison purposes, an asset's Sharpe ratio tells us little as to the marginal risk that an asset adds to a portfolio, and beta estimation is fraught with error (e.g., which index to use, index composition changes constantly). In sum, there is currently no all-inclusive quantitative package available that will provide a means to determine conclusively the better performing manager. Further, investors should be extremely wary of any purely quantitative approach to the selection of managers.

Among other things, a manager's investment process and philosophy should be reviewed as well as all operational aspects associated with the day-to-day management of the portfolios and their valuation. In the market collapse of 2007 and 2008, we saw a great deal of investor money lost to the reliance on quantitative models and dated information as to a manager's actual investment process and philosophy. As a rule of thumb, investors rarely question outsized returns. In fact, this scenario should serve to provide as much light on changed investment strategies and risks as underperformance. For example, Amaranth lost over $6 billion of its clients' monies. From all indications there was no fraud in their approach or disclosures. They simply went from being a solid convertible arbitrage manager to an energy trader without the requisite risk management for such a program.

TRADITIONAL ASSETS REFLECT "ACTUAL VALUES" BETTER THAN ALTERNATIVE INVESTMENTS

While the best efforts are made to have current stock and bond prices reflect current trade prices, one must remember that illiquid stocks and bonds have similar problems in valuation as other illiquid assets. Prices may be several days old, some bond prices are computer generated (benchmark based), and some assets (e.g., real estate) are appraisal based. In short, traditional assets may have pricing issues similar to that existing in some alternative assets and often worse than alternative investments that concentrate on exchange traded derivatives. A quick historical example: Early on, equity derivatives were called more risky than the stocks they were based on because the futures contract reported higher historical volatility. The reason, we later discovered, was that individuals just traded in the derivatives markets because derivatives had lower transaction costs. Moreover, because of the lower transaction costs, the futures price would move even if the underlying stock index did not trade because of its higher transaction cost. No real difference in price, no difference in risk; it just looked so to the less educated observer.

STOCK AND BOND INVESTMENT MEANS INVESTORS HAVE NO DERIVATIVES EXPOSURE

Simply not true in today's market. In fact, almost every investment into a firm's equity or bond is also, if indirectly, an investment into derivatives. Almost every firm uses derivatives (e.g. currency futures/forwards, stock and bond futures and options) in the management of their daily operations (treasury operations, pension fund investment decisions). Many firms (e.g., oil exploration and refinery, gold and other precious metal mining companies, airlines, bottling companies, or food processing or manufacturing companies) use derivatives to offset fundamental risks in their business.

STOCK AND BOND INVESTMENT REMOVES INVESTOR CONCERNS AS TO LEVERAGE

Academic research has shown that for many alternative assets many investment strategies use no leverage (e.g., distressed debt) and those that do so use leverage to control risk levels and not to enhance returns. In contrast, many financial and corporate firms have equal or greater leverage exposure than many alternative investment strategies. Banks, for instance, often are levered 5 to 8 times equity, and from a historical perspective investment banks were levered as much as 30 times equity. As a result, highly levered firms may try to reduce total risk by investing in less volatile products or ideas. The raw conclusion is that leverage is used in almost every investment in some way. Investors must simply be aware of the leverage impact on the asset's sensitivity to informational change.

GIVEN THE EFFICIENCY OF THE STOCK AND BOND MARKETS, MANAGERS PROVIDE NO USEFUL SERVICE

Not true. While the inability of managers to consistently outperform passive indices reflecting their underlying strategy may result in questions about the benefits of manager based security selection, managers do provide many investor services (accounting, tax reporting). In addition, when an investor purchases an index, he simply rides the index up and down. Managers provide an asset allocation function in that they can rebalance in markets or securities which trend. Managers who provide such skills result in a type of downside risk protection similar to put protection. In short, the fees paid to a manager also should be considered in part as an alternative to a simple put or option protection. The real question to be considered is "How free is that option?" given that a manager based investment does not provide a guaranteed constraint on investment loss similar to stand-alone put protection.

INVESTORS CAN RELY ON ACADEMICS AND INVESTMENT PROFESSIONALS TO PROVIDE CURRENT INVESTMENT MODELS AND THEORIES

Investors must realize that if information is costless, it is almost certainly worthless. Academic textbooks take two years to write using two-year-old studies with data that is even older. The result is that academic articles and textbooks generally are three to five years out of date upon initial publication. Even investment professionals do not generally have unique access to stock and bond information and those who have some special insight are not going to give it to you first and are certainly not going to provide information that does not help their agenda.

This is not to say that analyzing information has no value. However, in markets where large amounts of information are cheaply available to large numbers of people, an investor should only expect to receive the market expected return. There are genuinely no free lunches in the market and those who expect them are usually doomed to disappointment. One final point, however, is that while meaningful information is generally not free, sometimes an insight is drawn from the readily apparent and it is not so much as what is said, but how it is repackaged, that leads to innovation and the "obvious" opportunity. The best opportunities in terms of excess return should be in those investment areas in which "costly to know" subtle issues exist and which are not known by the general investor.

ALTERNATIVE ASSETS ARE RISKIER THAN EQUITY AND FIXED INCOME SECURITIES

For many, private equity and real estate are by their very nature often riskier than most equity or fixed income securities; however, other alternative investments (hedge funds) report dramatically lower price variability. As noted earlier in this chapter as well as throughout the preceding chapters of this book, the existence and validation of information is crucial to determining an investment's underlying risk. Certainly, private equity and real estate firms tend to disclose as little information as possible regarding their business. This is one of the reasons they are typically structured as partnerships rather than as corporations that are required to provide information under governing securities laws. The information dislocation between these asset classes and stocks and bonds creates the risk that investors should be concerned about—not the market tools used to reach return objectives. While few investors would question whether stocks were riskier than bonds (although in certain market environments such as high interest rate volatility, some bonds are expected to be riskier than some stocks), the question remains whether investments in these asset classes are by nature riskier than an investment in a portfolio of alternative investments.

In fact, in some ways equity ownership in a corporation is not that dissimilar from equity claims on a portfolio of various alternative investments such as hedge funds. First, similar to hedge funds, corporations take both long and short positions to manage both product and financial risk. Second, similar to private equity, their research and development arms invest in ideas or products that do not currently exist or for which there is no immediate market (e.g., Sun Microsystems, General Electric, or Apple). Similar to various arbitrage firms, they take global and hedge currency positions against expected revenue and tax obligations (e.g., Coca Cola, Microsoft, or Sony). As for real estate firms, some corporations have significant exposure to real estate (Wal-Mart, Starbucks, or Target). Moreover, similar to many non-transparent alternative investments, individuals who purchase stocks and bonds are, for the most part, unaware of the actual current and expected business activities of the firm outside of its corporate image. Is Wal-Mart a great retail company that has managed to meet consumer demand or is it a great transportation and distribution company that uses these strengths to create a commanding presence in the retail market? Frankly, in most instances investors have little or no understanding of the financial exposures and complexities associated with a modern corporation.

Ask yourself this question: What would you call a non-transparent entity that invests in private equity, real estate, and financial claims (pension fund), takes long and short positions, uses leverage, and often has asymmetric compensation plans for its chief executives? Answer (A) Hedge Fund or (B) General Electric.

ALTERNATIVE ASSETS SUCH AS HEDGE FUNDS ARE ABSOLUTE RETURN VEHICLES

Yes and no, with the truth lying somewhere in the middle. For example, the sources of hedge fund returns and managed futures are often described as being based on the unique skill or strategy of the trader. Because hedge funds and managed futures are actively managed, manager skill is important. However, academic research demonstrates that hedge fund returns and managed futures are also driven systematically by market factors such as changes in credit spreads or market volatility, rather than exclusively by an individual manager's alpha. Therefore, one can think of hedge fund and managed futures returns as a combination of manager skill and an underlying return to the hedge fund strategy or investment style itself. Similar to the equity and bond markets, passive investable security based indices have been created that are designed to capture the underlying return to the hedge fund and managed futures strategy (Amenc et al., 2008; Jaeger and Wagner, 2005).[2] The performance of an individual manager can be measured relative to that "strategy" return. If a manager's performance is measured relative to the passive algorithmic based hedge fund/managed futures index/benchmark, then the differential return may be viewed as the manager's "alpha" (return in excess of a similar non-manager based replicate portfolio). If a manager's performance is measured relative to an index of other active managers, then the relative performance simply measures the over- or underperformance to that index of manager returns.

ALTERNATIVE INVESTMENTS SUCH AS HEDGE FUNDS ARE UNIQUE IN THEIR INVESTMENT STRATEGIES

One of the essential questions raised with various alternative investments is the degree to which they may be regarded as a separate asset class. We know that the modern hedge fund had its genesis on the trading floors of investment banks. In trading its proprietary money, the investment banks permitted traders to go short as well as use leverage. The short positions as well as strategic positions that were inapposite to the interests of some of the investment banks' major clients caused some consternation, and the traders were permitted to leave with the backing of their firms.

Probably the most pronounced backing came in the form of the growth of Prime Brokerage units within the investment banks where they provided capital for trading as well as client introductions to secure an additional as well as meaningful revenue stream for the investment banks. It is no accident that there is a direct correlation between the rise of the Prime Brokerage business on Wall Street and the rise of hedge funds as money managers in the institutional trade. As indicated above, hedge funds can be viewed as the privatization of the trading floor of investment banks. In sum, these strategies are not new, and insurance companies, endowments and other institutional investors have employed their services for decades with observable results.

What is new is the introduction of these strategies into the mainstream, and one has to question whether individual investors have the ability to effectively monitor and understand the information quotient attached to these approaches. In fact, given recent events it is even questionable as to whether regulators and large institutions such as rating agencies have the knowledge and tools to effectively monitor this market. Unquestionably, this is an area that has and can continue to add value to a portfolio. The immediate question is whether a responsible regulatory paradigm can be established and not whether hedge funds should be treated as a distinct asset class.

HEDGE FUNDS ARE BLACK BOX TRADING
SYSTEMS UNINTELLIGIBLE TO INVESTORS

Hedge funds are not black boxes. Two of the authors conceived and built a "managed account" firm with over USD 4 billion under management based on the premise that all strategies have an innate source of return and that there are concrete market variables that account for a strategy's behavior. For the initiated who are willing to study the source of their returns, hedge funds are not only understandable, but predictable. For the most part, hedge funds protect their internal trading techniques from public scrutiny, but the same is true for mutual funds. Academic research (Harris, 2003) has shown that pre-trade transparency may have negative impacts on investor returns as well as market efficiency. Post-trade transparency, however, may provide investors with an understanding of the source of returns to various strategies. In fact, today hedge funds' trading approaches and sources of returns are well known. High-level risk management tools are available to track the risk of individual hedge funds. Many investors have access to daily positions through managed accounts. For the most part, hedge funds are not black boxes any more than traditional mutual funds or corporate firms are. One may not know the particulars of each trade or product creation pre-trade, but how and why they perform post-trade is well known within the industry.

HEDGE FUNDS ARE TRADERS,
NOT INVESTMENT MANAGERS

Generalizations are generally wrong. Of course hedge funds hedge—some more, some less, some not at all. Again, there are many different forms of hedge funds (a large percentage of hedge funds do not even trade equities). For those that do trade equities, many of them are not day traders in the traditional sense, moving quickly between long and short positions as the market whims take them. For instance, equity market neutral managers often attempt to match paired trades or at least structure their portfolio as a dollar long/dollar short approach in order to hedge away almost all equity market related movements. Do some traders concentrate on just shorting stocks they think will fall and buying those they think will rise without a direct emphasis on hedging? The answer is yes. But some hedge funds also provide a break on the decline in equity values during periods of equity decline by buying stock when individuals are "herd selling" and, in many instances, selling stock because they believe the stock market is "herd buying." Managers like Julian Robertson were not buyers of growth internet stocks during the tech bubble, but concentrated on buy and hold/ value based equities, that is, buying out-of-favor undervalued stocks that investors wished to sell.

ALTERNATIVE INVESTMENT STRATEGIES ARE SO UNIQUE THAT THEY CANNOT BE REPLICATED

The growth in alternative investment has encouraged a number of firms to offer a series of products called replication indices/benchmark products. These products have the goal of providing returns that capture the underlying return of basic fund strategies. In brief, to the extent that the strategies' core return is related to market factors and tradable vehicles exist that capture those market factors, investable indices can be and have been created that offer transparent and liquid investment alternatives to a wide range of alternative investments.

IT MAKES LITTLE DIFFERENCE WHICH TRADITIONAL OR ALTERNATIVE INDICES ARE USED IN AN ASSET ALLOCATION MODEL

Various indices even within the same asset class arc often structured differently and often report widely different historical return and risk performance. As a result, the index used to represent the return of a particular asset class can have major impact on recommended asset allocations. While we have warned against generalizations, this statement is true of all indices and sub-indices irrespective of the asset class. Moreover, investors should be aware that if they already hold a particular asset class portfolio they may wish to use an index which reflect the return movement of their portfolio. Finally, if their portfolio is not currently constructed, for the indices to be of value for asset allocation the portfolio should be constructed to track the index in question.

MODERN PORTFOLIO THEORY IS TOO SIMPLISTIC TO DEAL WITH PRIVATE EQUITY, REAL ESTATE, AND HEDGE FUNDS

MPT often focused on maximizing return while minimizing risk where risk is often measured by standard deviation. Additional distribution moments such as skewness and kurtosis are often not considered. Normality is often based on historical data. However, historical return distributions may be affected by funds, for example, changing leverage, which by itself may result in leptokurtic distributions if one uses long time periods to obtain distribution (leverage changes increases likelihood of outliers and therefore leptokurtic or skewed distributions when in fact for that single investment period the expected distribution is normal but with changing mean and expected variance). In short, a strategy's distribution may not be normal even if the historical data says it is and it may be normal even if the data says it is not. Generally, Modern Portfolio Theory has a number of issues in providing a basis for forecasting expected risk and return relationships. Primary among these are:

- Return estimates dominate results—where do you get them from
- Most programs are based on mean and variance—if assets are non-normal or if an investor has different risk concerns (liquidity) results may not reflect investor needs
- The number of assets in a portfolio—MPT optimization often results in just four or five assets in a portfolio—in short, diversifiable risk remains and parameter estimates may be poor

WHAT EVERY INVESTOR SHOULD REMEMBER

- The financial disturbances of 2007 and 2008 have forced the discipline of asset allocation and those who profess to practice it to enter into this new reality phase. However, what we know from experience is that if this reality check suggests additional oversight and the possible loss of investor allure (as well as the corresponding fees), many asset allocators will simply turn a blind eye and hope the markets right their mistakes so that they can return to the days when they were viewed as magicians or wizards.

- Finally, the truth—and one that is not commonly associated with the marketing of asset allocation—is that asset allocation should not be viewed primarily as a method that ensures that positive returns can be obtained in any market environment. Investors must fundamentally understand that if an asset allocation process suggests it can produce positive returns in any economic environment, the return it offers should be the risk-free rate. In short, asset allocation should not be viewed as merely low cost insurance. If it is, then, like any other low cost insurance, it will fail to meet the needs of the investor at the most critical times. Rather, at its core, asset allocation is a risk management tool that permits a meaningful discussion of the risk and return tradeoffs within a portfolio.

- We know that the human condition is a constant tradeoff between the comfort of constancy and the necessity for change. One of the major challenges facing an educator or manager is how to get others to change or revise heartfelt views that may have once proved useful but no longer fit reality.

NOTES

1. For additional commentary on Myths of Managed Futures and Myths of Hedge Funds, see Frequently Asked Questions (INGARM, 2009).
2. These security based indices are available in tradable form from various platform providers. Public research has generally indicated that, depending on the hedge fund strategy, the correlation between the passive investible security based index and the active trading manager based index is often greater than .75. However, public research has also indicated that the return to such passive security based trading models often underperforms active trading manager based indices by 100 to 200 basis points, depending on the strategy replicated. This lower return must, of course, be balanced with the additional benefits of passive security based indices, including greater transparency, capacity, and liquidity.

CHAPTER 11

The Importance of Discretion in Asset Allocation Decisions

Asset allocation is a discipline of judgments and decisions. This requires discretion, in the models we choose and in the decisions we make. However, more and more asset allocation is being presented as a mathematical science. Somewhere, we seem to have lost the capacity or willingness to make or take responsibility for these discretionary decisions; instead, we rely on systematic, algorithmic-driven models. If one is to increase the importance of discretionary based decisions in asset allocation decisions, what is the place and the value of discretion in the asset allocation modeling process? Is not "discretion" simply another way of saying that judgment and not models must be the deciding factor in a portfolio's design and implementation? However, if we permit the introduction of judgment, at what point do we lose the value of the quantitative model?

Asset allocation is not a simple science. There are a number of risks involved in its use. In Chapter 11 we discuss the benefits and costs of various asset allocation approaches from more algorithmic to more discretionary. What is the role of practitioners, academics, and regulators in this discussion?[1] As shown throughout the book, asset allocation models have logical stopping points, and without the oversight of discretion, unpredictable and unmanaged consequences will occur. While two of the authors of this book are practicing academics, this is an area where common sense instead of academic rigor should prevail. Discretion is inherent in the creation and implementation of all asset allocation programs, everywhere from model selection to choosing the underlying assets or managers.

THE WHY AND WHEREFORE OF ASSET ALLOCATION MODELS

The theory and implementation of asset allocation across investments or asset classes has long been a continuous focus of practitioners, academics, and regulators. Each, we believe, brings certain well-intentioned guiding principles to this discussion. However, in so doing, they also bring the "business models" of their professions. There is no doubt that practitioners understand the need for asset allocation as an investment tool. The better ones understand its importance as a risk management program that will assist their clients in making difficult decisions. Yet, for all their good intentions, they have to confront two institutional problems.

First, in a large investment bank there may be as many as 20,000 client service representatives calling on individuals and institutions to present the bank's asset allocation view of the world. These people are of differing educational backgrounds, intellect, and abilities. As a consequence, the bank must design services that can be used and explained and then implemented by this diverse team. Also, the bank's senior management must always be aware that the bank operates in a world where regulators and plaintiff lawyers stand as a brooding omnipresence, questioning the integrity of the advice given as well as its place within applicable securities laws and regulations.

Second, a significant part of the bank's client base, while perhaps understanding the necessity and value of asset allocation, believe that this advice should be a part of the service provided and are not willing to pay a separate premium. After all, the Internet will readily provide over seven million different sites, most for free, that purport to assist with the asset allocation decision.

Given that banks are in the business of making profits, the practical solution from their standpoint is to create a suite of asset allocation products based on quantitative standards that can be used by the entire sales force, assign each of these products a risk profile (e.g., highly conservative, conservative, or aggressive), ensure that the clients sign a document stating that they belong to a particular grouping so as to offset any potential liability, and—again, because the banks are in the business of making profits—insert their own investment products into the asset allocation mix as a proxy for the returns of each asset class. This ensures that the cost associated with the asset allocation process is offset by the profits of the investment products. Within this practical construct, asset allocation is reduced to a product to be used and understood by the lowest common denominator; on the surface, providing no discretion and therefore diluting the risk of litigation; and simultaneously, providing a workable margin for the banks to pay for this service. More important, because all competitors essentially have the same time and regulatory proven models, the asset allocation decision has become so enwrapped with the investment decision that it is presented as a way of enhancing returns (as compared to competitors) and not as an effective risk management tool.

Academics, for the most part, have a different starting point on discussions of asset allocation and work within a different model. They agree with practitioners that asset allocation is the single most important decision that is to be made in the management of a portfolio. Depending upon the study cited they will concur that this decision alone will account for a major portion of a given portfolio's return. Where they part with the practitioner is in the willingness to subject the asset allocation decision to:

- An evolutionary discussion based on new and changing information
- A challenge of past ideas as well as the development of postulates that account for past behavior and perhaps predict that of the future
- A meaningful discussion of discretion as ideas are pushed to their optimal limits (and sometimes beyond)

It is fair to say that every theory or idea has its logical stopping point. To go beyond that point is to either enter the world of the absurd or court unintended consequences without preparation. In Chapter 3, we speak to this point as we examine certain theories that provide very real value within their parameters, but have been misused or are not allowed to die a proper death because they serve an unintended and sometimes misguided purpose.

We have also seen this phenomenon at work in the current market. The Collateralized Debt Obligation (CDOs) is first and foremost an asset allocation product and was first designed by JP Morgan to assist its clients in securitizing certain obligations. In designing this program, the bank also designed risk control features that assured a workable understanding of the bank's obligations as well as those of its clients. We have witnessed the awful destruction of wealth tied to this asset allocation product when discretion and proper risk controls are removed from its design. At its collapse in 2008 the CDO market was in excess of USD 2 trillion (nominal without the inclusion of synthetic products based on the returns of each basic product—also, while the dollar amount associated with the synthetics remain an unknown variable it is safe to point out that AIG, Lehman Brothers, and Bear Stearns each fell victim to this unknown), and most market participants could not identify or value their underlying assets. Similarly, the subprime market started as a reasoned approach to provide housing for the middle class within the United States and was fully supported by the Bush administration and the United States Congress. The subprime portfolios were asset allocation decisions on the purchase of home loans from participating lenders that were subsequently packaged as both real and synthetic bonds. Each issuer based decisions on its proprietary quantitative model. The base premise of each model was the belief that by diversifying home loans among and between homeowners living in differing geographic areas with differing risk profiles, the risk of the bonds or their corresponding synthetic obligations would be significantly reduced. What was not seen and not intended was that in delinking the lending decision (discretion) from liability, a free option would be created and exploited by vast numbers of special interests (e.g., local banks, mortgage brokers, homeowners, investment banks, rating agencies, and insurance companies) without regard for a homeowner's ability to pay. Further, because each issuer created the bonds within its proprietary model, there was no universal means of collecting and understanding the data or the supporting economics of this market.

Unfortunately, in both the CDO and subprime scenarios their inclusion in many asset allocation models was seen as costless, and little, if any, additional information as to the additional risks of the investments had to be shared with an independent party. We are left to speculate on the actual cost of similar free asset allocation services. In such a world we are left to ask what are the roles of the regulators and the impact of the regulators' business models. Here, in a world of extreme complexity, how does one protect individual investors while protecting the financial system as a whole? In this regard, the regulators' job is to fashion a set of rules that reflect and support market practice as well as regulatory goals which are fundamentally fair, provide notice, and can simultaneously be monitored and enforced. That said, they are not neutral agents in this discussion. They must adapt and respond to a changing political constituency as elected leaders and financial paradigms come and go. They must modify technology and recruiting efforts (personnel) to meet changing markets and the crisis of tomorrow. For example, the United States Securities and Exchange Commission (SEC) is composed primarily of lawyers working with technology designed to ferret out and prosecute insider trading. Not surprisingly, they do an incredibly good job at this given its legislative mandate was/is to ensure fair and open markets without manipulation; and, that this mandate evolved out of the stock manipulation schemes that facilitated the market collapse of 1929. The current problem is that new and unpredictable fronts have opened as markets have become more complex, and the agency must search for rules and the resources to meet this challenge.

How do we reconcile these differing business models in making the case for discretion within asset allocation? Fortunately, this question is a straw man. The critical path for each group is not whether discretion should be an integral dimension of the asset allocation process. Each understands that asset allocation without discretion is rather like the fruit of the medlar tree—rotten before it is ripe. The seminal issue is how to create a rule based approach that is capable of some sort of universal application. As noted, the diversity of the constituents' demands that such an approach is understandable as a common denominator and is based on some reasoned standard with general application.

While earlier we eschewed the cost of the asset allocation service as a primary driver in reaching an optimal result, it is clear to us that any workable solution must take this variable into consideration. From our perspective this is simply an acknowledgement of two separate markets. The first is a set of investors who believe the asset allocation decision to be important but view it as part of the service. The second is a set of investors who believe the asset allocation decision is too important to be an imbedded service. Thus any meaningful approach must protect both while permitting the latter to purchase the additional insurance of a dedicated asset allocator.

VALUE OF MANAGER DISCRETION

For many of the reasons stated above, asset allocation has had an increasing reliance on quantitative models that provide one-size–fits-all solutions to complex problems. If finance theory has provided any perspective on the investment world, it is that expected return is a function of risk (i.e., there are few solutions without a return/risk impact), and one can fundamentally adjust the return and risk profile only through the use of options or their synthetic alternatives. As a result, discretion in the asset allocation process should exist. Discretion in asset allocation is an additional factor in the asset allocation process. For much of this book, we have centered our discussions on the concept of risk management (e.g., a process for determining the probabilistic impacts of various investor choices). However, we also emphasized very early in our discussions that in fact most of our actions exist not in the world of risk but in the galaxy of uncertainty. The use of discretion adds an evolutionary control variable to the asset allocation process as well as adding an additional risk factor reflecting the uncertainty in the discretionary process and results.

What is the value of discretion? It is very difficult if not impossible to put a unique value on manager discretion. First, if the source of value is the manager's skill in forecasting risks and returns, the fair value of that skill will depend on the amount of risk that the investor is willing to assume and the nature of the markets where the manager can apply his skills. For example, for a highly risk averse investor who wants to diversify in emerging markets, a manager with skill in predicting and managing the risk could be of significant value. Let's perform a simple exercise. Suppose we have an investment with 10% expected annual return and 12% expected annual standard deviation. If a manager can help us avoid the four worst months over a five-year period, the average annual performance of the portfolio is expected to increase by 1.5%. This manager will deserve a 1% fee. This may appear to be a rather small fee; but note that we assumed the manager has no skill in predicting returns and can only avoid one bad outcome per year. In this context, it is clear that if we increase the volatility of the investment, the value of discretion would increase. This could explain why managers who manage riskier asset classes (e.g., small cap stocks) tend to charge higher fees. Of course, markets for riskier asset classes are also more likely to be inefficient and therefore an active manager is more likely to find opportunities in those markets.

Academic research has addressed option theory as a means to represent the potential benefits of managers' ability to actively asset allocate between stocks and cash (Merton and Hendrickson, 1981). This approach will allow an investor to model a manager's skill using option pricing theory and therefore estimate the value of discretion. In this and other models of performance valuation, the key issue is that ex ante we have very limited tools in measuring the true skills of the manager. For example, managers may not have enough of a track record; they may not wish to disclose enough information about their set of skills; the alleged skills may have already been discovered by other managers; changing economic conditions may make the skill valueless, and so on.

This is not to say that financial theory on options has no place in the asset allocation space or in determining the value of managerial discretion.[2] It does reflect the hope that a manager would, could, or should be able to move positions freely such that his returns may reflect the ability to capture the best of all possible worlds. If the manager did not charge for this service and if there was no risk in his making an incorrect decision, it would be a "Free Lunch."[3]

In reality, the story can become even more complex. Let's explore this concept further, again, in hedge funds. If the individual buying a product is forced to pay for the implicit cost of funds that meet new regulatory rules, the first question might be can we manage these risks more cheaply through other means (e.g., out-of-the-money equity options)? If we are paying for insurance protection for individuals who refuse to educate themselves, they are the ones getting the free lunch, not us. In short, the costs are spread over individuals who do not share in the benefits. For that purpose, as an educated hedge fund investor, one may favor government efforts to protect hedge fund investors from ex post errors of hedge funds through greater regulation but only if these costs are covered by individuals who cannot or will not invest in hedge funds. This is in our world the real "free lunch," that is, someone we do not know or even care to know picking up the tab for our lunch with no desire or requirement that we ever do the same for them.

The additional benefit of managers making discretionary choices is that the manager may concentrate on also holding a set of relatively low cost options (e.g., real asset theory), that may have value in some future market environment. The investor continues to pay for these options even if they are not acted upon. Differential return between two managers in the same investment space may simply reflect differences in the number of low cost potential investment opportunities held by one manager in contrast to another. How to include the value of these potential investments in comparing two managers remains an area of future research. One of the primary problems of discretionary choice is that not all decisions are good, and in the opposite vein, often there is no way of knowing whether a bad decision was avoided. While we have been involved in active management platforms for over 20 years and believe that there are active managers and organizations endowed with extraordinary insight at given moments, we cannot think of one that would actually articulate an ability to see the future—but we have witnessed a number of managers who maintain that they hold a number of low cost investment alternatives that have high potential return in certain future market environments.

Finally, some argue that even in the absence of skill, discretion may still have some value because in the case of extremely poor performance, the investor could use the threat of legal action to recoup some of the loss. This is less cynical than it may first sound. If a manager claims to have skill he does not have and collects fees based on this claim, then the manager should be prepared to potentially give up most of the fees collected when investors suffer significant losses. The possibility of using legal means to recover some of the large losses from a manager may be modeled as an option as well; that is, through time the investor pays premiums to the manager in the form of fees, knowing that the investor will have the option to use legal means to recoup some losses.

MANAGER EVALUATION AND REVIEW: THE DUE DILIGENCE PROCESS

As discussed in Chapter 6, once we move beyond the more passive instruments in the core asset allocation decision process and choose to invest in unique managers or products to provide the diversification of judgment necessary within a particular asset class, the question becomes how to best use quantitative as well as qualitative information in identifying the best performing manager. There are a number of books that attempt to summarize the manager/product selection process. In sum, these books purport to remove discretion from the discretion process. Each uses the normal "storytelling" buzzwords of "thoroughly, rigorously, fully" as if one would profess to conduct such a process partially and halfheartedly. We briefly summarize the normal or accepted manager/product selection due diligence process below.

The process of evaluating and monitoring investment product selection begins with an extensive study (what other kind of study would one conduct?) of the manager's performance history and a number of other factors, both qualitative and quantitative. There are at least three parties that would play an important role in determining what kind of manager an investor selects:

- Consultant: Some investors do not perform enough due diligence on the consultant, while the consultant has strong influence over the choice of the manager. Investors must learn about the consultant's background, the experiences of current and previous clients, potential sources of conflict, and areas of expertise.
- Portfolio manager: This is where investors spend most of their time performing due diligence. The investor should examine risk-return characteristics of current and past portfolios of the manager. Perhaps the most important thing is that the investor should carefully examine the source of value in the strategy that the manager follows and use common sense to decide if the claims made by the manager could be a source of competitive advantage in the current economic and financial environment.
- Risk manager: This is another area where investors tend not to spend enough resources performing due diligence. The data sources, statistical methodologies, metrics, and technologies employed have to be carefully evaluated.

No matter how an investor arrives at the managers and/or vehicles that are chosen for implementation, monitoring the strategy over time is key. Just as market fluctuations will gradually move the initial asset allocation decision, any number of the above concerns regarding the manager and due diligence may also undergo changes. Thus due diligence on manager and/or product goals and objectives should be periodically reviewed.

MADOFF: DUE DILIGENCE GONE WRONG OR NEVER CONDUCTED

Investors can learn a great deal from what goes right in manager/product selection but perhaps even more from where it goes terribly wrong. Beyond fundamental due diligence such as visiting the office of Madoff's accountants or ensuring that assets were held at an independent administrator, a seminal question in regard to the recent Madoff scandal is whether there was any reasonable way that an investor could have determined that the various feeder funds offering the investment vehicle were in fact not offering what they claimed to be offering. In other words, was it possible for investors to determine that the reported returns could not have been generated by the split strike conversion strategy that Madoff was supposed to follow?

The split strike conversion strategy is well known in investment circles. Basically, it calls for selling an out-of-the-money call, using the proceeds to purchase an out-of-the-money put and placing the actual invested dollars in an equity investment. The collar (sold call and purchased put) limits upside return but also reduces exposure to downside price movements. The dynamics of this strategy are explored in greater detail by Schneeweis and Spurgin (2001). In this article they created a collar strategy (index plus 2% out-of-the money collar). While the strategy replication was systematic in nature and thus would differ slightly from a more active management of the process, the results showed that the annual returns for the active program (Gateway fund) and the model were almost identical (10.1% and 10%) for the period of analysis (January 1987 to December 1999) with a volatility for the active program a bit higher than the replication model (5.3% vs. 4.6%). Moreover, the analysis shows that in periods of market decline, the returns from the split strike collar provide similar returns to that of the comparison mutual fund (e.g., Gateway). In short, while not necessarily a strict replicate of Madoff's process, public data was available from funds that had similar strategy processes and expected return and risk profiles.

As an alternative to the use of a simple fund comparison, Markov (2008) has shown that the Fairfield Sentry return series (one of the Madoff feeder funds) was not well explained by the very factors (e.g., equity index puts and calls and long equity) that should have been the primary determinants of the underlying split strike conversion strategy. Of course an investor could create scenarios in which Madoff's stock picking skills were so extraordinary that his returns could have produced a return series somewhat dissimilar to that of a simple split strike conversion. However, other authors (Clauss, Roncalli, and Weisang, 2009) have provided additional examples of split strike conversion programs that would have indicated that the return stream from Madoff feeder funds with a split strike conversion program would have required a consistent excess return to the S&P of nearly 8.5% per year (for the period starting 1994 and ending in 2008), but even then the volatility of this program was higher than that reported by Fairfield Sentry.

Most investors, however, are limited to a simple analysis of the return properties for Madoff feeder funds for whom public return data is available. In the majority of public hedge fund data sets, the various Madoff feeder funds were described as market neutral. Exhibit 11.1 provides a simple year to year comparison of the annual returns of the average of three Madoff feeder funds with the CISDM Equity Market Neutral index. An investor may have rightfully questioned why the average of the annual returns of the Madoff feeder funds were often superior to a well known market neutral hedge fund index.

If investors were concerned about the differences in the performance characteristics and factor sensitivities of the feeder funds and the relevant hedge fund index, they could take the analysis to the next level. Exhibit 11.2 shows that differences in the performance and market sensitivities of feeder funds and an equity market neutral index (CISDM Equity Market Neutral) exist across a wide range of descriptive factors. The average of the Madoff feeder funds has a higher return, higher information ratio, lower maximum drawdown, different correlations with S&P 500, Barclays Government Bond Index, and Barclays High-Yield Bond Index, a higher percentage of winning months a lower percentage of losing months and a low correlation to the CISDM Equity Market Neutral index.

One answer could be that Madoff's split strike conversion strategy was dramatically different from other equity market neutral managers. Exhibit 11.3 presents the average (moving) correlation of three Madoff feeder funds with a split strike conversion (collar) strategy (QQQ (NASDAQ) plus 2% out-of-the money collar similar to that presented in Chapter 9. While this replication is not simple for most investors, the fact that the Madoff feeder funds are not highly correlated with an investment process which purports to follow a similar strategy indicates that the returns to the Madoff feeder funds were not based on this approach.

The results clearly show that a typical non-institutional investor could have determined that the various investment vehicles by which investors accessed Madoff were in fact not offering what they claimed to be. The potential problem was there in the footprint of the returns, but unfortunately the footprints were well hidden. Admittedly, this type of analysis requires some skill. As a consequence, the stand-alone investor was at a disadvantage. But what of the investor who relied on consultants and advisors in making the investment decision? Should this not be the type of analysis provided? Again, we have more questions than answers. However, the underlying theme continues to echo clearly. The due diligence process, as the asset allocation decision, is not free. There are substantial hidden economic costs in not properly reviewing and analyzing information.

Annual Returns: CISDM Equity Market Neutral and Average of Feeder Funds

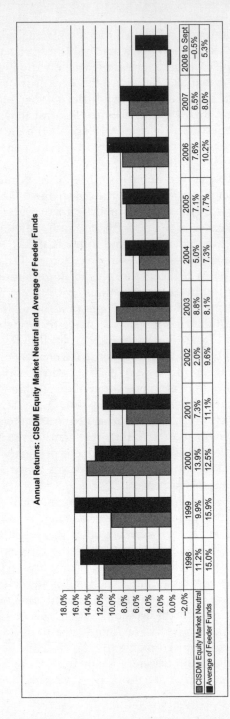

	1998	1999	2000	2001	2002	2003	2004	2005	2006	2007	2008 to Sept
CISDM Equity Market Neutral	11.2%	9.9%	13.9%	7.3%	2.0%	8.8%	5.0%	7.1%	7.6%	6.5%	−0.5%
Average of Feeder Funds	15.0%	15.9%	12.5%	11.1%	9.6%	8.1%	7.3%	7.7%	10.2%	8.0%	5.3%

EXHIBIT 11.1   Performance—CISDM EMN Hedge Fund Index and Average of Feeder Funds

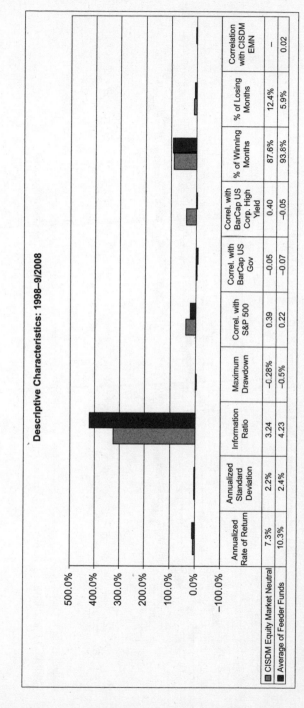

Descriptive Characteristics: 1998–9/2008

	Annualized Rate of Return	Annualized Standard Deviation	Information Ratio	Maximum Drawdown	Correl. with S&P 500	Correl. with BarCap US Gov	Correl. with BarCap US Corp. High Yield	% of Winning Months	% of Losing Months	Correlation with CISDM EMN
CISDM Equity Market Neutral	7.3%	2.2%	3.24	-0.28%	0.39	-0.05	0.40	87.6%	12.4%	-
Average of Feeder Funds	10.3%	2.4%	4.23	-0.5%	0.22	-0.07	-0.05	93.8%	5.9%	0.02

EXHIBIT 11.2 Descriptive Statistics: CISDM EMN Hedge Fund Index and Average of Feeder Funds

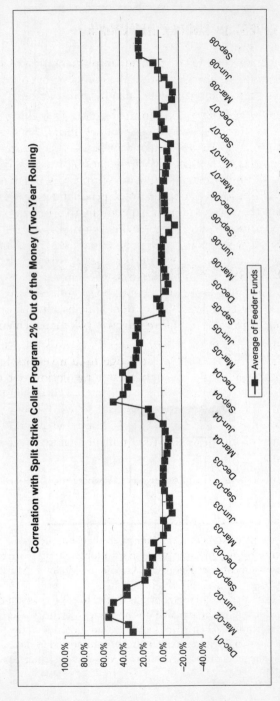

EXHIBIT 11.3 Rolling Two-Year Correlation: Passive Collar, Gateway, Average of Two Feeder Funds

WHAT EVERY INVESTOR SHOULD REMEMBER

- Discretion is inherent in the creation and implementation of all asset allocation programs—whether within the model or in choosing the underlying assets or managers (who also have discretion).

- Because the investment banks are in the business of making profits, they often insert their own investment products into the asset allocation mix as a proxy for the returns of each asset class, thus ensuring that the cost associated with the asset allocation process is offset by the profits of the investment products. Within this practical construct, asset allocation is reduced to a product to be used and understood by the lowest common denominator; on the surface, providing no discretion and therefore diluting the risk of litigation; and simultaneously, providing a workable margin for the banks to pay for this service. More important, because all competitors essentially have the same time and regulatory proven models, the asset allocation decision has become so enwrapped with the investment decision that it is presented as a way of enhancing returns (as compared to competitors) and not as an effective risk management tool.

- For that purpose, as an educated hedge fund investor, one may favor government efforts to protect hedge fund investors from ex post errors of hedge funds through greater regulation but only if these costs are covered by individuals who cannot or will not invest in hedge funds. This is in our world the real "free lunch," that is, someone we do not know or even care to know picking up the tab for our lunch with no desire or requirement that we ever do the same for them.

NOTES

1. There are a wide range of stakeholders each with their unique list of regulatory and market constraints. For an example of asset allocation alternatives within a Pension Fund Environment, see Dempster, Germano, Medova, Murphy, Ryan, and Sandrini (2009).
2. In fact, Kritzman and Page (2002) used options theory to price asset allocation skill and security selection skill in their article on the value of security selection versus the value of asset allocation. Their results emphasized the value of the probability of increased dispersion on the potential benefits of trading and in this context supported the potential benefits of security selection versus asset allocation.
3. See Fung and Hsieh (2006).

CHAPTER 12

Asset Allocation: Where Is It Headed?

As a matter of full disclosure, the authors have managed clients' monies over the last 20 years. In so doing, our starting and ending point has always been transparency as to the basis for and direction of our investment platforms and the ideas supporting them. Throughout this book we have attempted to give the reader the same transparency as to the source of our approaches and positions. Here, our starting and end points are that there is risk in the discipline of asset allocation and that this risk is inherent both in the models that we use and in the discretion that we apply in using them.

Historical examples exist where asset allocation has been, in part, sidetracked by myths, greed, and irresponsible behavior on the part of various market participants—including investors themselves who often search for that "free" portal that offers a "free" option on the accumulation of wealth. Free is so seductive. As we have shown, the cost of asset allocation is not free. The hidden charges can be and have been the horrendous destruction of wealth as individuals became focused at times on the most recent "asset allocation fad." It's easy to make the argument that the regulators failed to protect or that investment practitioners failed to be moral. Each of these statements is true. But the defining truth is that investors also have a responsibility for both their decisions and their belief systems.

For the sake of argument, let's eliminate the small investor from this discussion on the basis that he does not have the resources to independently test and monitor investment processes and must rightly rely on government oversight and regulation of the investment function. Institutions, however, cannot be given this pass. Rather than directly pay for asset allocation and accumulate the necessary information to access risk, they blindly trusted a "brand"—a rating agency, an investment bank, or a friend to protect their interests acting as if they did not know who these people actually worked for. We suspect that a new reality will emerge from the recent circumstances. Time and events will tell. The question remains of where we go from here in regard to the current market and regulatory issues facing the investment management industry.

AN UNCERTAIN FUTURE

Irrespective of how we got here, the current arguments as to the proper form of financial regulation to oversee the financial system is indicative of the lack of agreement on a long-term workable solution. This is not a doomsday scenario; this is simply a statement of fact. There is no doubt that changes will be discussed, solutions agreed upon, and modern finance will not come to a standstill. Our concern is that the solutions will not be lasting because the stakes are so high and fear so intense that the arguments have taken on the type of religious overtones (e.g., moral order, market order, government order) that are inapposite to a fundamental change in belief systems. If a god is the guarantor of your beliefs—why change? So where do we go from here?

Given the number of financial pundits, there is no lack of theories on what financial markets may look like in the future as well as the role of asset allocation. However, be careful not to be taken in by storytellers. Sometimes a good story is just that and nothing more—a good story. Unfortunately, most of us want something more than just a good story; we want the story to be true. In fact, it is often said that most Americans will forgive almost anything but the ultimate sin—that of being boring. So then, taken to the extreme, a lie well told is worth much more than the truth poorly spoken. Even the concept of truth is hard to keep up with. For many of us, knowledge comes from constant re-education. Unfortunately, most investment books (including this one) even with a current copyright were written several years ago, using articles written several years before that and based on data several years before that. In short, much of our belief system as well as the regulatory system (e.g., exams, oversight reviews) are based in part on ideas or data that are by their very nature dated by the time the report is read or the exam taken.

As discussed in the previous chapters, confronting and managing the vagaries of change may be the biggest challenge facing the discipline of asset allocation. Asset allocation has entered into a new era that we call the reality phase. Once the favorite toy in the investment room, traditional asset allocation between and among cash, stocks, and bonds must now be extended to include the many competing alternative opportunities for investors. If being made "real" means additional oversight and the loss of investor allure, many asset allocators would simply hope to return to the days when they were viewed as magicians or wizards. Going forward, an asset allocation decision must include investment vehicles offering return opportunities not easily found in other traditional investment vehicles. These additional investments do not offer returns without risk but with return opportunities that hopefully offset the corresponding risks. In this new world, asset classes comprise a set of investment strategies offering returns consistent with the risks underlying the markets in which they trade (e.g., distressed securities based hedge funds prosper in markets in which credit spreads decline, equity long/short based hedge funds prosper in markets in which corporate stocks generally rise).

Today most investors have at least some working idea of investment strategies and how they perform. This new reality will not change the view of those who continue to hold to the belief that wizards exist and that superior above market returns will be found in what are often described as "absolute return" vehicles. Perhaps the most disturbing facet of the Madoff scandal is the extent to which a very large number of wealthy individuals and institutions placed all of their investable assets with one man—a wizard who promised and gave surreal returns for well over two decades. Most investors, hopefully, view each investment strategy and asset class as part of the overall investment world, in which each strategy/asset class makes money in certain markets and is less likely to make money in other market environments.

Hopefully, we have even advanced to the stage where, in both traditional and alternative investment markets, firms and individuals offering investment or asset allocation advice are honest as to their own and their competitors' real abilities. The growth of Internet and cable based information does have an upside—it's a lot more difficult to twist truths for someone who really wants to do the research. However, the problem remains: "Whom do you trust?" If behavioral finance has taught us anything, it is that want often trumps needs and wish often beats know. Given two individuals selling the same investment product and one forecasting 12% return with 10% standard deviation and the other suggesting that the product may return 10% with a 10% standard deviation, which do you choose? For most individuals, the answer is simple, that is, door number 1 (12% return and 10% standard deviation). Even if the first individual is puffing up the story, at worst the investor expects that one will be no worse off and perhaps better off if they go with door number 1. This is not to say that differences in products do not exist at the margin. Skill does exist. The question is how often promised excess returns are equated with skill rather than undisclosed or misunderstood risks. Simply put, products and product managers as well as those who use their services exist within a competitive investor, corporate, and government culture. As a result, there is an efficient market in ideas. Successful firms and products are more often the result of chance than the reflection of a well-executed strategic plan founded in a once-in-a-lifetime product—the right people at the right time with the right concept. Moreover, for the firm in the marketplace, the real economic foundations of the product are less important than how the product is presented and the degree to which the product is accepted by the market itself.

When we travel, it is common to pick up a map or travel book to gain comfort with the new destination. A constant tradeoff exists between the comfort of an old map and the necessity for a new one. This same tradeoff exists for new forms of financial products. Most people have a series of beliefs that help to sort out events. As discussed in Chapter 10, myths may be regarded as the "collected beliefs" that serve to help understand the past or to exist in the present. Unfortunately, these beliefs may not be based on facts, but we know individuals work within their belief systems. Thus if we are to make an impact in a dynamic world, how do we integrate changed facts into relatively constant belief systems? Just as important, how do we make belief systems take into account a wide range of new possibilities (risk) or probabilities (uncertainties)? The human mind is not like a computer. A computer comes across an unknown variable and embraces it—holding a space for this unknown until there is additional information. In contrast, the mind, while perhaps sending signals of fear or apprehension, discounts the value of the unknown and proceeds with business as usual.

WHAT IS THE DEFINITION OF ORDER?

The economic crisis of 2007 and 2008 and the associated global recession have reconfigured the financial landscape. Certain investment firms have gone out of existence. Others that survived have drastically changed in both form and substance. Governments in the United States, Europe, and Asia are holding a series of meetings designed to meet the new challenges of derivatives, alternative opportunities, and disclosure in the marketplace. While it is outside the scope of this book to detail all of the issues raised in these discussions, the primary question is: "In whom do you trust?"

Many of the new financial products have been marketed under various names and models, but for the most part they promised either superior returns or superior risk reduction. Many of these products promised, in short, to take the downside out of the risk equation. In this, their promises echoed that of previous products (e.g., portfolio insurance, target returns, and principal protection) that often, for promised much of what could not be delivered. In fact, many of these products did deliver their promises as long as the insurance company survived or markets remained supportive.

The problem with many of the products developed during the period from 2000 onward was that their success was based not only on design but on the organizational system backing up the product. Many firms refused to let their products fail and underwrote losses to protect their reputations; others underwrote the losses as they closed the product; and still others simply closed the products and hoped for the best. Today, a greater emphasis is being put on various forms of exchange based trading with the hope that centralized clearing may reduce some of the exposures previously hidden at the corporate level. Moreover, regulators and elected officials have acknowledged essentially, that industry self-regulation has failed and are fearful that a continued lack of transparency in over-the-counter products will further disrupt the financial markets as well as undermine the legitimacy of their banking and regulatory institutions. There has become an increased urgency to regulate or provide oversight to investment products that have escaped strict regulatory controls through the use of private partnerships that bypass several existing securities laws and regulations.

These discussions provide an interesting insight into the debate on the relative worth of government order, market order, and moral order; and have taken on religious overtones (which is almost always a guarantee that there is no common ground). The government expresses the concern that somehow, someway, someplace, there was someone doing something to somebody. They are not sure of exactly what, but obviously it was bad and correspondingly it is the government's duty to find those involved in this process and find ways to stop them. The respondents, a collection of practitioners, academics, and investors, attempt to respond in various ways to this charge but generally calling on the proven history of market and/or moral order. As expected, the practitioner's starting point is that regrettably mistakes have obviously happened; and, notwithstanding these mistakes, they operate within a systemic code of market order in which the actual trading of strategies and the traders themselves are forced by the trading environment to provide an honest product, backed by honest people, providing honest services to honest investors. Here, the invisible hand of the market actually ensures order and governments are overreacting.

Order means, of course, different things to different participants in the investment process. Those who promote government order are concerned that government order is required to ensure market order (e.g., systemic risk). Those concerned with market order express concerns that government regulation may lead to a government-based system that might in fact lessen the probability of market order. Restrictions on short sales, increased transparency, and forced liquidity might all reduce market stability under the guidance of promoting "government order." In fact, it is argued, increased government regulation might result in the demise of liquidity in the markets that government order is supposed to promote. If government supervision is a good thing, how much of a good thing can the market withstand? Practitioners argue that, as in most cases, when individuals are forced into being good at an extreme cost, they have a tendency to run away or find a means to reduce that cost. If the government forces a moral order through government order, many private funds will simply move to those geographic areas where "religion" is less costly or the sun is shining.

Today each side takes refuge as the seeming protector of the investor. Those invoking the market order argue that all investors deserve the right to make their own decisions and that the special privilege to invest in alternative funds, derivatives, and special opportunities should not be the right of only the wealthy. Those invoking government order respond that any religion (i.e., government order) is primarily responsible for protecting its flock. In short, there is a higher authority than the market; and the religion of government order would not be necessary if the participants in the market simply had some level of personal "moral order." Many of those individuals promoting market or personal morality as the solution have in the past, government officials persist, participated in some fairly immoral acts including false pricing and false marketing and outright deceit. Simply put, the government is not about to give the keys to the cash box of investors to the market order of product development. Nor is the government order willing to bet on the moral order of fund or product providers to ensure the safety of the investor.

At a recent research presentation on accounting information and security valuation, the speaker put a rather intimidating chart on the blackboard. He pointed out that from far away the chart looked benign enough, that is, clean and straightforward. Closer up, he pointed out, the line is not nearly as clean or consistent and spaces appear. He walked up and put his face within inches of the graph. "And from here," he pointed out, "this graph looks real ugly!" The same could be said for the process of investment and the market in which investment products exist. Moreover, the search costs of finding, monitoring, and assessing risk and return are extensive, continuous, and variable. Richard Feynman of physics fame (remember the O-ring and the Challenger story in which Feynman, instead of a lengthy discussion, simply put the rubber O-ring into a cold class of water, pulled it out, showed how inflexible it was when too cold, and thereby showed how cold temperature made it fail—end of story) has pointed out that what works at the "macro" may not work at the "micro" and that "things on a small scale behave nothing like things on a large scale." Advances in technology, regulation, and globalization have further increased the pace of change and the need to manage it. Increasing competition has also led to the necessity for individuals, firms, and countries to embrace the new means of asset management. Risk management, however, when it concentrates on the macro, may fail to understand the micro. In sum, no easy answers, but at least we should be aware of the players, where they come from, and what they want.

COSTS AND BENEFITS

It would be shortsighted not to admit that current market events have not come without cost to many. It is obvious that individual investors have in certain cases been taken advantage of by those marketing new products. What rules should we employ to protect the investor? It is difficult to imagine a system that could be created to protect individuals from bad decisions. In fact, if there is no risk of a bad decision, academic research has shown that people make more risky decisions. At issue is how to make the information set more accessible across decision makers. Information is costly and there must be some reward to obtaining it. Even if information is obtained, how is it distributed and how do we ensure that it is interpreted correctly? For example, today the risk sources and the return sources of most alternatives are well understood by some but not acted on by many. Few are aware of how markets really trade or how products are really created. If they do, they downplay this information or its significance if it is not well understood.

TODAY'S ISSUE

Simply put, economic and financial change is difficult for all of us. Moreover, the dynamics of the ultimate winners and losers is not an easy forecast. For much of the past, larger fund firms with all their financial resources would seem easily positioned to defeat smaller rivals; however, new technology and regulatory freedoms have permitted smaller "specialized" firms to compete directly with larger rivals. Technology, globalization in trade and investment, and the ease of knowledge transfer provides many smaller firms that offer specialized local "financial products" with a comparative advantage as they take advantage of global risk management tools. Just as this technology has arrived to permit a more level playing field, the worry is, of course, that government regulation will tilt the game back in favor of larger financial firms that can meet the cost and oversight needs of new regulatory concerns.

It would also be negligent of us not to point out that simple reliance on technology is not the answer. Governments order but markets rule. As mentioned earlier, a quick click on a web search engine for asset allocation brings up millions and millions of hits. A multitude of models exist, each with their own unique twist on pricing and risk management. Complex problems are not solved with simple solutions. Risk management models are mostly based on historical data that either do not reflect today's markets or fail to capture the probability of potential events. In any case, the dynamics have changed. Recent events in the United States have confirmed the failure of a "rule based" only approach to risk management. Even if it works in general, it may fail in the particular.

Is there a simple "one-size-fits-all" regulatory, technological, and financial framework that provides markets with both the financial needs and the competitive environment required for long-term market survival? This would have to protect the existing system from the impacts of that change while taking into consideration the competing interests of government, firms, and investors who are the partners and the players in the modern global world of financial change. Even more so, how we proceed with this change will certainly affect the outcome. Given the dynamics of the competing interests and competing economic reality, how best can investors deal with future uncertainty? For those who manage funds, the concepts of option pricing should be familiar. Firms or funds that succeed must be flexible enough to react to any new reality. Firms must hold, if possible, a number of costless "real" call options that may not provide them with success in this current economic environment, but that can be easily turned on in the next. It is the ability of funds to have the characteristics (costless real options) that allow them to mutate and enable firms or funds or countries to meet those changes. One need not spend too much time thinking of past examples of firms, funds, countries, or species that were dominant, only to fail as they were unable to adapt to new conditions and reality. Maybe the best thing we can learn from the past is that it is just that, the past. The future remains open to those who are prepared to meet the new realities of the present and are not constrained to constantly attempt to correct past shortcomings.

POSSIBLE GOVERNMENTAL AND PRIVATE FUND RESPONSES TO CURRENT MARKET CONCERNS

Investors always seem to be fighting the last war. Capital flowed to various global macro strategies in the early 1990s in response to the volatility in currency, commodity, and interest rates. In the mid 1990s, the growth of new trading technologies, emerging markets and market liquidity lead to a rise of various equity and fixed income trading and arbitrage strategies. The financial crisis of 1998 exposed the risks of these strategies in terms of liquidity and transparency. Soon after however, the internet boom triggered the flood of capital into equity based strategies, including private equity. The market decline after the technology bubble in the early 2000s brought a renewed interest in risk managed products. Unfortunately, it was these very structured products that eventually failed in the 2007 and 2008 credit crisis and have focused investor and government concerns on issues related to various structured products and the use of over-the -counter derivatives in various fund products. It seems unlikely that investors will suddenly overcome the urge to invest in last year's strategy. However, there are several things that can be said about what we have learned about fund managers and their investors in the past decade, and the likely response of the investment industry, its investors, and its regulators going forward.

Greater emphasis is being placed on risk management—both by financial intermediaries who trade with and lend to fund managers and by the investment managers themselves.[1] Recent discussions among various professionals have centered on attempting to create a common platform and standard for fund reporting and risk monitoring.

As in the traditional markets, where mutual fund families dominate the landscape, new organizational structures are being created to group together various funds in a single financial entity, providing for cross-marketing opportunities and more efficient management of back-office functions. New means of trading are being developed. Financial institutions are now acting as market-makers to particular sets of funds and offering them via their own trading platforms, thereby creating a liquid market in the underlying funds. Finally, managers are increasingly concerned about capacity constraints within their particular strategies. The need to ration manager capacity more efficiently is resulting in new product structures and product designs based on more liquid futures and option markets.

Whatever the future may hold, it will require investors and managers alike to adapt to the changing regulatory, technology, and market conditions. The ability to meet these changes will require the use and understanding of a wide range of quantitative approaches to asset allocation and risk management as well as the added discretion of when and how best to use them. Hopefully, managers and investors alike are up to the task.

WHAT EVERY INVESTOR SHOULD REMEMBER

- Here our starting and end points are that there is risk in the discipline of asset allocation and that this risk is inherent both in the models that we use and in the discretion that we apply in using them.

- The cost of asset allocation is not free. The hidden charges can be and have been the horrendous destruction of wealth as individuals became focused at times on the most recent "asset allocation fad." It's easy to make the argument that the regulators failed to protect or that investment practitioners failed to be moral. Each of these statements is true. But the defining truth is that investors also have a responsibility for both their decisions and their belief systems.

- The fundamental driver of rational decision making is information. Absent meaningful transparency at the model, product and portfolio level it is difficult to envision a market or regulatory solution that actually protects investors.

- There is likely to be an increase in compliance oversight driven by concern over the suitability of certain products for certain investors. The question remains, however, as to how best to ensure that those making the regulations, those creating the products, those selling the products, and those purchasing the products have any real level of financial knowledge. How to educate, how to inform, how to reeducate, and how to reinform is the struggle for the next decade.

NOTE

1. There is considerable research on alternative means of tracking and evaluating the potential volatility of existing fund strategies and overall portfolio risk. The generic term given to such analysis often falls under the classification of VaR (value at risk), which often offers a simplified forecast of the probability of losing more than x dollars of asset value. The entire area of monitoring and evaluating fund risk is constantly evolving, and readers are directed to articles in academic (*The Journal of Alternative Investments*) and practitioner press to track changes and advances in the field.

Risk and Return of Asset Classes and Risk Factors Through Business Cycles

This appendix presents graphs of risks and returns of major asset classes through time. The goal is to familiarize readers with the behavior of these variables as the economy goes through various stages of the business cycle. Our other goal is to show that return and, especially, risk characteristics of asset classes do change through time and some of these changes will be quite dramatic during periods of economic stress.

On the graphs that follow, periods of economic stress are highlighted with shading.

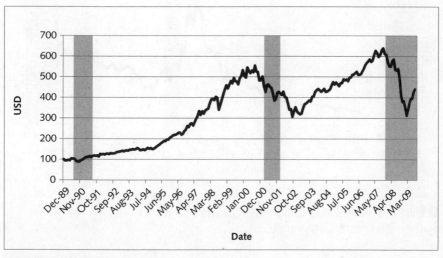

EXHIBIT A.1   S&P 500: Growth of $100
Source: Bloomberg Corporation

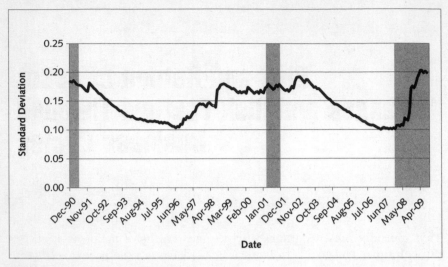

EXHIBIT A.2   S&P 500: Volatility
Source: Bloomberg Corporation.

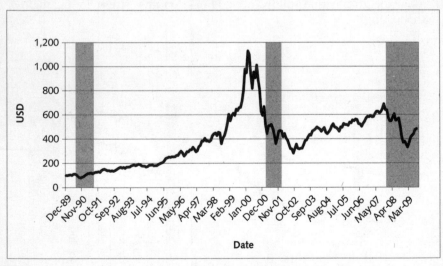

EXHIBIT A.3   NASDAQ Composite: Growth of $100
Source: Bloomberg Corporation.

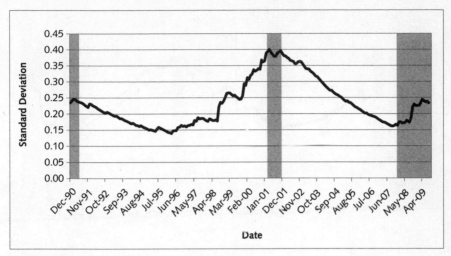

EXHIBIT A.4 NASDAQ Composite: Volatility
Source: Bloomberg Corporation.

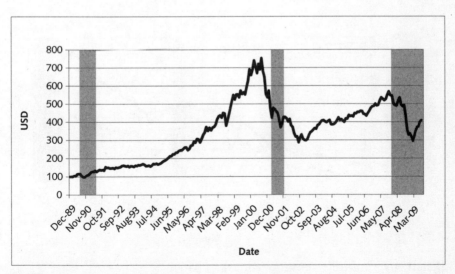

EXHIBIT A.5 Russell 1000 Growth: Growth of $100
Source: Bloomberg Corporation.

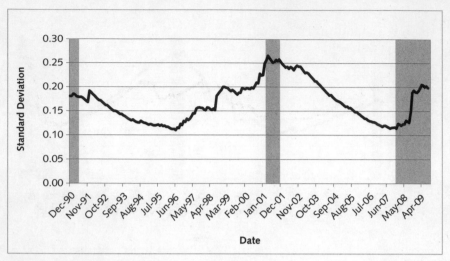

EXHIBIT A.6   Russell 1000 Growth: Volatility
Source: Bloomberg Corporation.

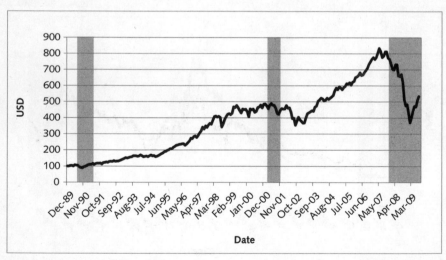

EXHIBIT A.7   Russell 1000 Value: Growth of $100
Source: Bloomberg Corporation.

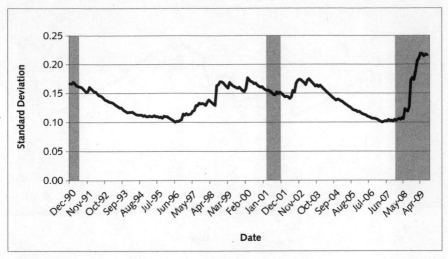

EXHIBIT A.8   Russell 1000 Value: Volatility
Source: Bloomberg Corporation.

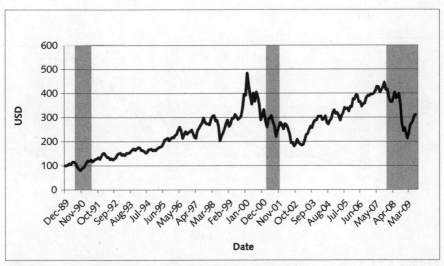

EXHIBIT A.9   Russell 2000 Growth: Growth of $100
Source: Bloomberg Corporation.

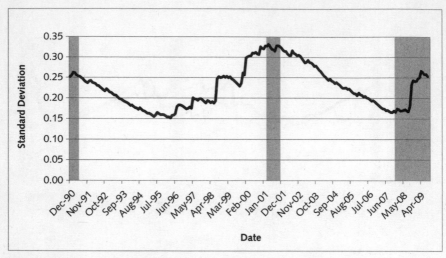

EXHIBIT A.10 Russell 2000 Growth: Volatility
Source: Bloomberg Corporation.

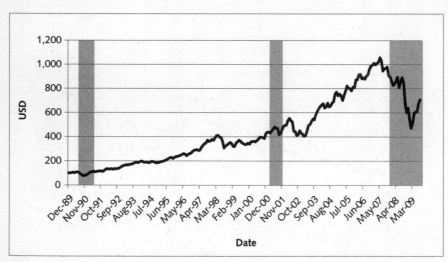

EXHIBIT A.11 Russell 2000 Value: Growth of $100
Source: Bloomberg Corporation.

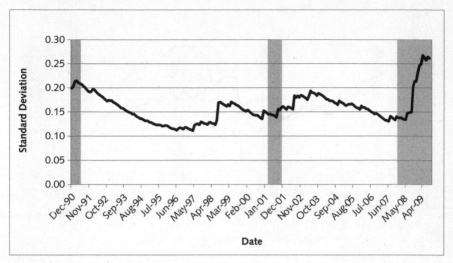

EXHIBIT A.12   Russell 2000 Value: Volatility
Source: Bloomberg Corporation.

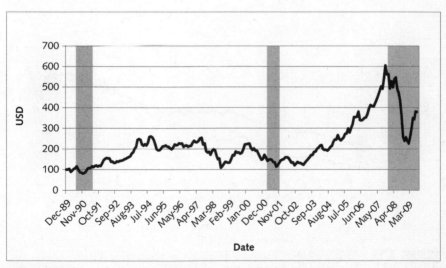

EXHIBIT A.13   MSCI Emerging Markets: Growth of $100
Source: Bloomberg Corporation.

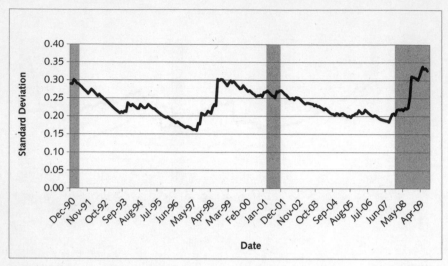

EXHIBIT A.14 MSCI Emerging Markets: Volatility
Source: Bloomberg Corporation.

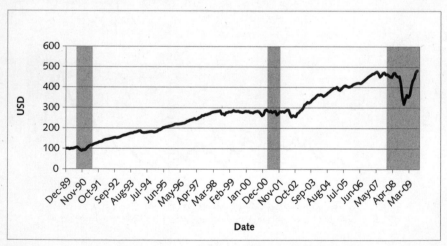

EXHIBIT A.15 BarCap U.S. Corporate High Yield: Growth of $100
Source: Bloomberg Corporation.

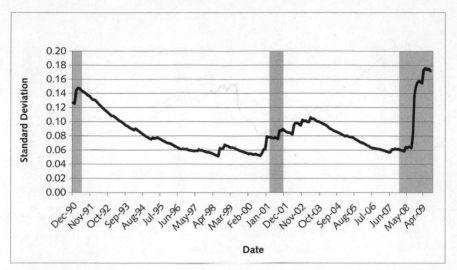

EXHIBIT A.16   BarCap U.S. Corporate High Yield: Volatility
Source: Bloomberg Corporation.

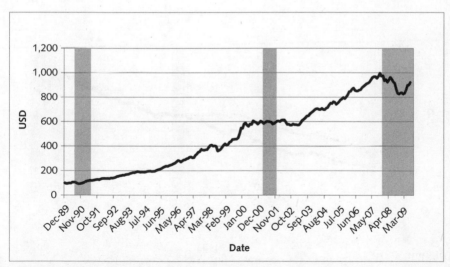

EXHIBIT A.17   CISDM Equity Long/Short: Growth of $100
Source: Bloomberg Corporation.

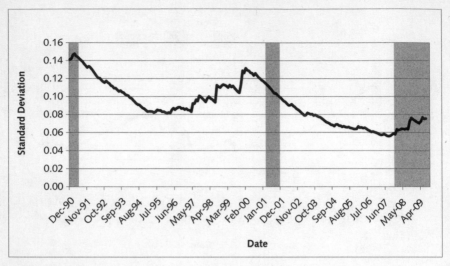

EXHIBIT A.18 CISDM Equity Long/Short: Volatility
Source: Bloomberg Corporation.

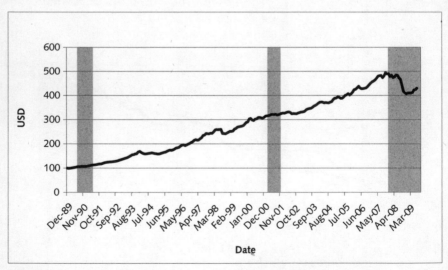

EXHIBIT A.19 CISDM Fund of Funds: Growth of $100
Source: Bloomberg Corporation.

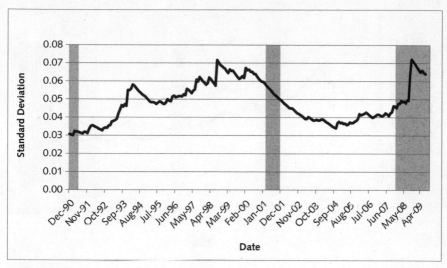

EXHIBIT A.20 CISDM Fund of Funds: Volatility
Source: Bloomberg Corporation.

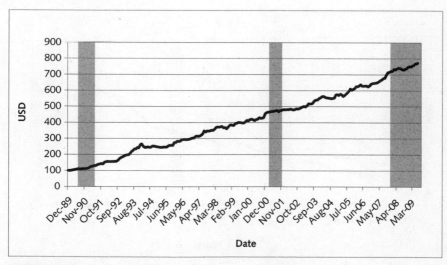

EXHIBIT A.21 CISDM Global Macro: Growth of $100
Source: Bloomberg Corporation.

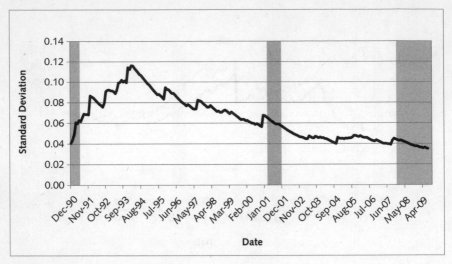

EXHIBIT A.22 CISDM Global Macro: Volatility
Source: Bloomberg Corporation.

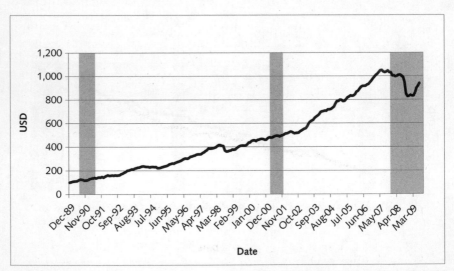

EXHIBIT A.23 CISDM Distressed Securities: Growth of $100
Source: Bloomberg Corporation.

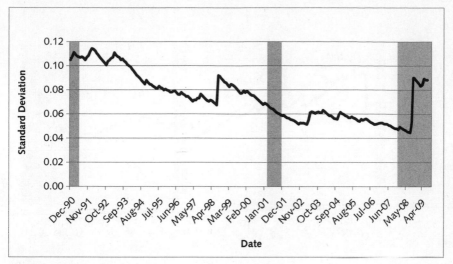

EXHIBIT A.24   CISDM Distressed Securities: Volatility
Source: Bloomberg Corporation.

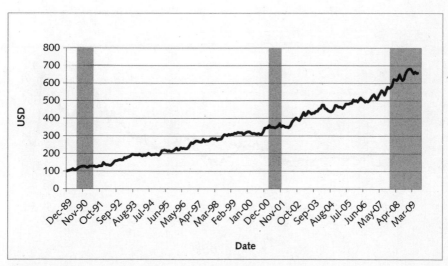

EXHIBIT A.25   CISDM CTA Asset Weighted: Growth of $100
Source: Bloomberg Corporation.

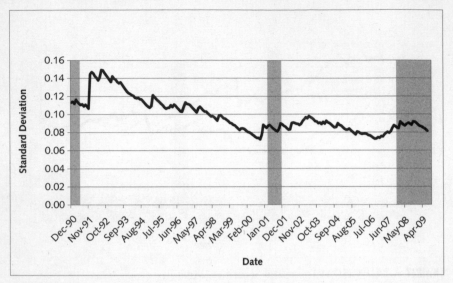

EXHIBIT A.26   CISDM CTA Asset Weighted: Volatility
Source: Bloomberg Corporation.

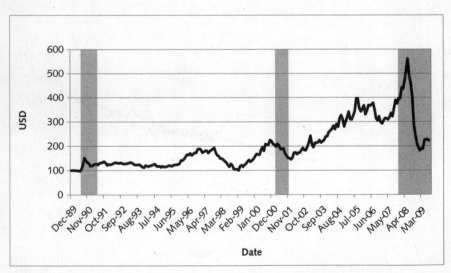

EXHIBIT A.27   Goldman Sachs/S&P Commodity Index: Growth of $100
Source: Bloomberg Corporation.

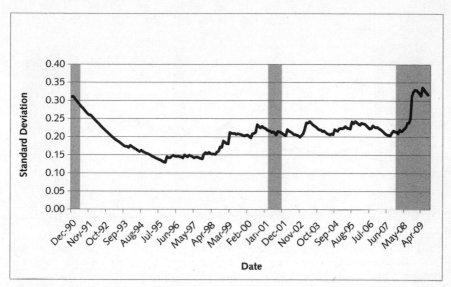

EXHIBIT A.28 Goldman Sachs/S&P Commodity Index: Volatility
Source: Bloomberg Corporation.

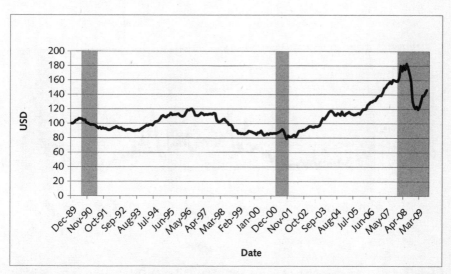

EXHIBIT A.29 Commodity Research Bureau: Growth of $100
Source: Bloomberg Corporation.

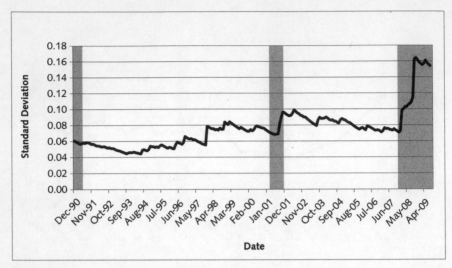

EXHIBIT A.30   Commodity Research Bureau: Volatility
Source: Bloomberg Corporation.

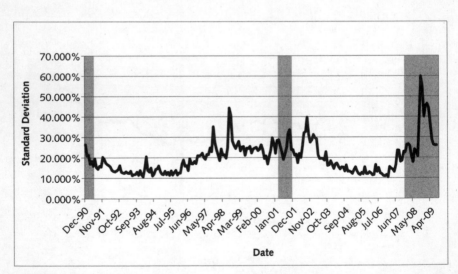

EXHIBIT A.31   Implied Volatility for S&P 500 Index (VIX)
Source: Bloomberg Corporation.

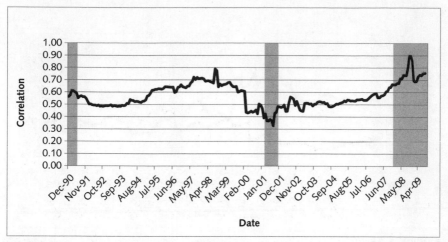

EXHIBIT A.32 Correlation between S&P 500 and BarCap U.S. Corporate High Yield Bond
Source: Bloomberg Corporation.

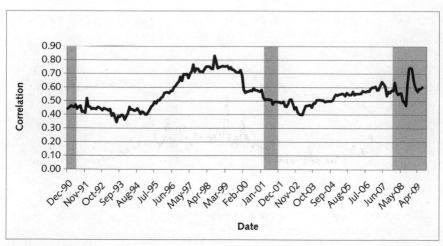

EXHIBIT A.33 Correlation between S&P 500 and CISDM FoF
Source: Bloomberg Corporation.

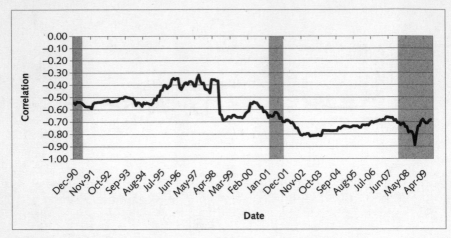

EXHIBIT A.34   Correlation between S&P 500 and Change in VIX
Source: Bloomberg Corporation.

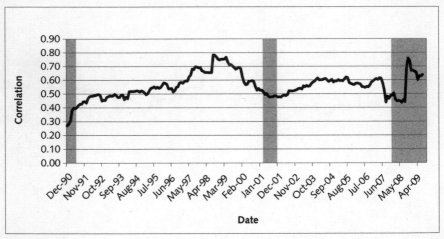

EXHIBIT A.35   Correlation between BarCap U.S. Corporate High Yield and
CISDM FoF
Source: Bloomberg Corporation.

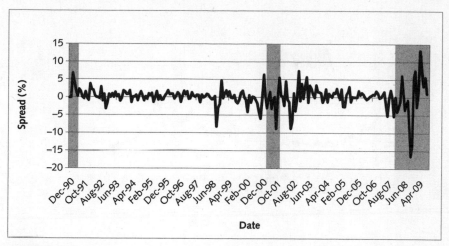

EXHIBIT A.36 BarCap U.S. Corporate High Yield Excess Return Relative to Treasuries
Source: Bloomberg Corporation.

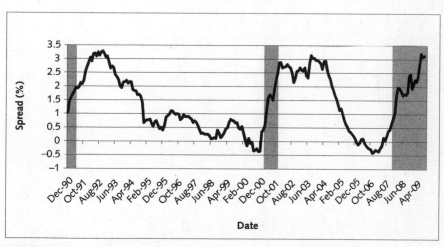

EXHIBIT A.37 Yield Spread between 10-Year and 1-Year Treasuries
Source: Bloomberg Corporation.

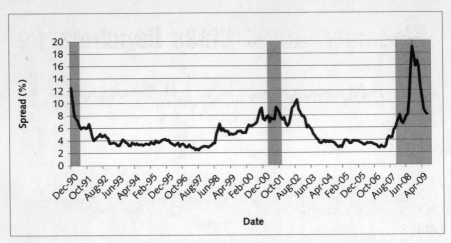

EXHIBIT A.38 BarCap U.S. Corporate High Yield Credit Spread Relative to Treasuries
Source: Bloomberg Corporation.

Glossary: Asset Class Benchmarks

EQUITY

S&P 500:   The S&P 500 is a value-weighted index. The stocks included in the S&P 500 are those of large publicly held companies that trade on either of the two largest American stock market companies; the NYSE Euronext and the NASDAQ OMX. The index does include a handful of non-U.S. companies (six as of July 1, 2009). This group includes both former U.S. companies that have reincorporated outside the United States and firms that have never been incorporated in the United States. The components of the S&P 500 are selected by committee.

Russell 1000:   A market capitalization-weighted benchmark index made up of the 1,000 highest-ranking U.S. stocks in the Russell 3000.

Russell 2000:   The Russell 2000 Index is a small-cap stock market index of the bottom 2,000 stocks in the Russell 3000 Index.

MSCI EAFE: The MSCI EAFE Index (Europe, Australasia, Far East) is a free float-adjusted market capitalization index designed to measure the equity market performance of developed markets, excluding the United States and Canada. As of June 2007, the MSCI EAFE Index consisted of the following 21 developed market country indices: Australia, Austria, Belgium, Denmark, Finland, France, Germany, Greece, Hong Kong, Ireland, Italy, Japan, the Netherlands, New Zealand, Norway, Portugal, Singapore, Spain, Sweden, Switzerland, and the United Kingdom. The index is maintained by Morgan Stanley Capital International/Barra; the EAFE acronym stands for Europe, Australasia, and Far East.

MSCI Emerging Markets (EM) Index: The MSCI Emerging Markets Index is a free float-adjusted market capitalization index designed to measure equity market performance of emerging markets. As of June 2009 the MSCI Emerging Markets Index consisted of the following 22 emerging market country indices: Brazil, Chile, China, Colombia, Czech Republic, Egypt, Hungary, India, Indonesia, Israel, Korea, Malaysia, Mexico, Morocco, Peru, Philippines, Poland, Russia, South Africa, Taiwan, Thailand, and Turkey.

FIXED INCOME

Barclays Capital U.S. Government Index (BarCap US Gov):   The U.S. Government Index is composed of the U.S. Treasury and U.S. Agency Indices. The U.S. Government Index includes Treasuries (public obligations of the U.S. Treasury that have remaining maturities of more than one year) and U.S. agency debentures (publicly issued debt of U.S. government agencies, quasi-federal corporations, and corporate or foreign debt guaranteed by the U.S. government).

Barclays Capital U.S. Corporate High-Yield Index (BarCap US Corporate High-Yield):   Covers the USD-denominated, non-investment grade, fixed-rate, taxable corporate bond market. Securities are classified as high-yield if the middle rating of Moody's, Fitch, and S&P is Ba1/BB+/BB+ or below. The index excludes emerging markets debt. The index was created in 1986, with index history backfilled to January 1, 1983. The U.S. Corporate High-Yield Index is par+ of the U.S. Universal and Global High-Yield Indices.

Barclays Capital U.S. Aggregate Bond Index (BarCap US Agg):   The U.S. Aggregate Index covers the USD-denominated, investment-grade, fixed-rate, taxable bond market of SEC-registered securities. The index includes bonds from the Treasury, Government-Related, Corporate, MBS (agency fixed-rate and hybrid ARM pass-throughs), ABS, and CMBS sectors. The U.S. Aggregate Index is a component of the U.S. Universal Index in its entirety.

HEDGE FUND INDICES

Barclay Hedge Fund Index: A measure of the average returns of all hedge funds (excepting Funds of Funds) in the Barclay database. The index is simply the arithmetic average of the net returns of all the funds that have reported that month.

Hedge Fund Research Indices (HFRI):   Monthly Indices designed to reflect hedge fund industry performance by constructing equally weighted composites of constituent funds, as reported by the hedge fund managers listed within HFR Database. Hedge Fund Research (HFR) also provides the HFRX Indices ("HFRX"), which are a series of benchmarks of hedge fund industry performance that are engineered to achieve representative performance of a universe of hedge fund strategies. In contrast to the HFRX, the HFRX methodology defines certain qualitative characteristics, such as: whether the fund is open to transparent fund investment and the satisfaction of the index manager's due diligence requirements.

CSFB/Tremont Hedge Fund Index: A value weighted index of hedge fund managers that meet a set of methodological restrictions. CSFB/Tremont also provides indices at the strategy level. In addition CSFB provides a series of investible indices which reflect a smaller subset of available managers.

CASAM/CISDM Equal Weighted Hedge Fund Index (CISDM EW Hedge Fund Index):   An equal weighted average of reporting managers to the CASAM/

CISDM Hedge Fund Database. CASAM/CISDM also produces an Asset Weighted version based on reporting managers to the CASAM/CISDM Hedge Fund Database. In addition, CASAM/CISDM provides a series of strategy based indices based on the median of reporting managers.

CASAM/CISDM Equity Market Neutral Index (CISDM EMN Index): Strategies that take long equity positions and an approximately equal dollar amount of offsetting short positions in order to achieve a net exposure as close to zero as possible.

CASAM/CISDM Fixed Income Arbitrage Index (CISDM Fixed Income Arbitrage): The median performance of global macro managers reporting to the CASAM/CISDM Hedge Fund Database Equity market neutral represents strategies that attempt to take advantage of mispricing opportunities between different types of fixed income securities while neutralizing exposure to interest rate risk.

CASAM/CISDM Convertible Arbitrage Index (CISDM Convertible Arbitrage): The median performance of convertible arbitrage managers reporting to the CASAM/CISDM Hedge Fund Database Convertible arbitrage represents strategies that take long positions in convertible securities (usually convertible bonds) and try to hedge those positions by selling short the underlying common stock.

CASAM/CISDM Distressed Securities Index (CISDM Distressed Securities): The median performance of distressed securities managers reporting to the CASAM/CISDM Hedge Fund Database. Distressed securities represents strategies that take positions in the securities of companies where the security's price has been, or is expected to be, affected by a distressed situation, such as an announcement of reorganization due to financial or business difficulties.

CASAM/CISDM Event Driven Index (CISDM Event Driven): The median performance of event driven managers reporting to the CASAM/CISDM Hedge Fund Database. Event driven represents strategies that attempt to predict the outcome of corporate events and take the necessary position to make a profit. These trading managers invest in events such as liquidations, spin-offs, industry consolidations, reorganizations, bankruptcies, mergers and acquisitions, recapitalizations, share buybacks, and other corporate transactions.

CASAM/CISDM Merger Arbitrage Index (CISDM Merger Arbitrage): The median performance of merger arbitrage managers reporting to the CASAM/CISDM Hedge Fund Database. Merger arbitrage represents strategies that concentrate on companies that are the subject of a merger, tender offer, or exchange offer. While there are a number of different trading based approaches, merger arbitrage strategies often take a long position in the acquired company and a short position in the acquiring company.

CASAM/CISDM Emerging Markets Index (CISDM Emerging Markets): The median performance of emerging market managers reporting to the CASAM/CISDM Hedge Fund Database. Emerging markets represents strategies that invest in the debt of sovereign nations, and equities and/or debt of companies located in emerging or developing economies.

CASAM/CISDM Equity Long/Short Index (CISDM Equity Long Short): The median performance of equity long short managers reporting to the CASAM/CISDM Hedge Fund Database. Equity long short represents strategies that take long and short equity positions varying from net long to net short, depending if the market is bullish or bearish. The short exposure can also be a put option on a stock index, which is used as a hedging technique for bear market conditions.

CASAM/CISDM Global Macro Index (CISDM Global Macro): The median performance of global macro managers reporting to the CASAM/CISDM Hedge Fund Database. Global macro strategies employ opportunistically long and short multiple financial and/or non-financial assets. Trading managers following global macro strategies might use systematic trend-following models or discretionary approaches. For systematic trend-following global macro managers who trade primarily in futures and option markets, returns are similar to those of commodity trading advisors.

CASAM/CISDM Fund of Funds Index (CISDM Fund of Funds): The median performance of all hedge fund of funds managers reporting to the CASAM/ CISDM Hedge Fund Database. Its objective is to provide an estimate of the rate of return to fund of funds which invest in hedge fund managers. Fund of funds managers have discretion in creating funds of funds which reflect either a single strategy or a wide range of underlying hedge fund strategies.

CTA INDICES

Barclay CTA Index: A benchmark of representative performance of commodity trading advisors reporting to the Barclay Group. The Barclay CTA Index for the year 2009 is unweighted and rebalanced at the beginning of each year.

CASAM/CISDM Composite CTA Indices (CISDM CTA Index): Asset Weighted (AW) and Equal Weighted (EW) CTA Indices: Asset weighted and equal weighted CTA indices based manager returns are reported for all reporting managers in the CISDM database (CISDM CTA EW Index and CISDM CTA AW Index). Asset weighted and equal weighted indices also exist at the sub-index level.

CASAM/CISDM Equal Weight Discretionary Index (CISDM Discretionary Index): Trade financial, currency, and commodity futures/options based on a wide variety of trading models including those based on fundamental economic data and/or individual traders' beliefs.

CASAM/CISDM Equal Weight Systematic Index (CISDM Systematic Index): Trade primarily in the context of a predetermined systematic trading model. Most systematic CTAs follow a trend-following program although some trade counter-trend. In addition, trend-following CTAs may concentrate on short-, mid-, or long-term trends or a combination thereof.

CASAM/CISDM Equal Weight Currency Index (CISDM Currency Index): Trade currency futures/options and forward contracts.

CASAM/CISDM Equal Weight Diversified Index (CISDM Diversifed Index): Trade financial futures/options, currency futures/options, and forward contracts, as well as commodity futures/options.

CASAM/CISDM Equal Weight Financial Index (CISDM Financial Index): Trade financial futures/options as well as currency futures/options and forward contracts.

CASAM/CISDM Equal Weight Equity Index (CISDM Equity Index): Trade OTC and exchange-traded futures and/or options.

COMMODITY INDICES

S&P Goldman Sachs Commodity Index (S&P GSCI): The S&P GSCI is a quantity based world production-weighted index that currently holds six energy products, eight agricultural products, five industrial metals, two precious metals, and three livestock products. The index has the flexibility to hold any number of contracts as long as the particular contract meets the liquidity criteria. Contracts are weighted by the average worldwide production in the last five years of available data. The S&P GSCI is dominated by energy with around 68% of its weight allocated to the energy sector at the beginning of the year 2009.

Dow Jones-UBS Commodity Index (DJ-UBS): The DJ-UBS is a quantity based commodity index that predefines a set of criteria to prevent any sector from being dominant in the index. Previous to May 2009, it had been known as the DJ-AIG Index. It limits the maximum weight of any commodity to 15% of the index, any sector to 33% of the index, and any commodity along with its downstream products to 25% of the index. This index currently holds 19 commodity futures, of which four are energy products, seven are agricultural products, four are industrial metals, two are precious metals, and two are livestock products. A combination of liquidity and production measures is used to assign weights to individual commodities. Liquidity has twice as much influence as production in deciding the overall weights. Use of the production data has the drawback of underweighting commodities like precious metals that are storable over a longer period and overweighting commodities like agricultural products that must be used over a shorter period.

Bache Commodity Index (BCI): The primary objective of the BCI is to provide broad-based exposure to global commodity markets, with low turnover and strong risk-adjusted returns resulting from multiple return factors. The BCI employs a dynamic asset allocation strategy based on the price momentum of individual commodity markets. This approach to index construction may help reduce transaction costs and turnover, and may increase the risk-adjusted return. This index also incorporates a relative roll strategy that is similar to a synthetic spread trade, which will be profitable if the price of the contract closest to expiration falls in price relative to the longer maturity contracts. With the addition of Gasoil in February 2008, the BCI comprises 19 commodities that are traded on 7 major futures exchanges located in the U.S. and the UK. Commodities in the index are chosen based on their importance to the global economy and on the basis of liquidity measures.

REAL ESTATE

REIT (Real Estate Investment Trusts): A REIT is a company that mainly owns, and in most cases, operates income-producing real estate such as apartments, shopping centers, offices, hotels, and warehouses. Some REITs also engage in financing real estate. The shares of many REITs are traded on major stock exchanges. To qualify as a REIT, a company must have most of its assets and income tied to real estate investment and must distribute at least 90 percent of its taxable income to its shareholders annually. Indices are reported at the composite level (All REIT) as well as at the sub-index level: (1) Equity REITS: Mostly own and operate income-producing real estate. (2) Mortgage REITs: Mostly lend money directly to real estate owners and operators or extend credit indirectly through the acquisition of loans or mortgage-backed securities. (3) Hybrid REITs: As the name suggests, a hybrid REIT both owns properties and makes loans to real estate owners and operators.

NPI (Commercial Real Estate): The NCREIF Property Index is a quarterly time series composite total rate of return measure of investment performance of a very large pool of individual commercial real estate properties acquired in the private market for investment purposes only.

Moody's/REAL Commercial Property Index (CPPI): A periodic same-property round-trip investment price change index of the U.S. commercial investment property market based on data from MIT Center for Real Estate industry partner Real Capital Analytics, Inc. (RCA). The methodology for index construction has been developed by the MIT/CRE through a project undertaken in cooperation with a consortium of firms including RCA and Real Estate Analytics, LLC (REAL). The index is designed to track same-property realized round-trip price changes based purely on the documented prices in completed, contemporary property transactions. The index uses no appraisal valuations. The methodology employed to construct the index is a repeat-sales regression (RSR), as described in detail in Geltner and Pollakowski (2007). The data source for the index is described in detail in a white paper available from RCA.

The Moody's REAL transaction based index TBI index: Complementary information product to the CPPI is also published on the MIT/CRE web site. Both the CPPI and the TBI are based purely on transaction price data. The TBI is based on NCREIF property sales prices data, while the former is based on RCA sales prices data. Thus, the TBI is based on a smaller population of more purely institutionally held properties. The TBI is based on a hedonic regression methodology whereas the CPPI is constructed with a repeat-sales methodology.

S&P/Case-Shiller Home Price Indices: Consists of 20 metropolitan regional indices, two composite indices, and a national index. The indices are constructed using a methodology known as Repeat Sales Pricing, a process that involves recording sale prices of specific single-family homes in any region. When a home is resold months or years later, the new sale price is also recorded and the two sale prices are referred to as a "sale pair." The differences in the sale pairs in any region are measured and aggregated into one index.

PRIVATE EQUITY

Private Equity Index: Based on monthly returns that are based on the S&P Private Equity Index from December 2003 onward. For the period prior to December 2003, firms that were listed in the June 2007 report were used to created an equal weighted monthly returns private equity index back to 1991.

The Cambridge Associates U.S. Venture Capital Index®:   Based on internal rate returns data compiled on funds representing more than three-fourths of venture capital dollars raised since 1981 and nearly two-thirds of leveraged buyout, subordinated debt, and special-situations partnerships since 1986. For the Cambridge VCI Partnership, financial statements and narratives are the primary source for information concerning partnership cash flows, portfolio company investments, and investor transactions. The performance calculation solves for the discount rate (IRR), which makes the Net Present Value of an investment equal to zero. The calculation is based on cash-on-cash returns over equal periods, modified for the residual value of the partnership's equity or portfolio company's net asset value (NAV). The residual value attributed to each respective group being measured is incorporated at its ending value.

LPX index family: Consists of a family of indices similar in construction to the S&P Private Equity indices. The design, development, and delivery of the LPX indices ensure that they are investable, tradable, and transparent. The index construction methodology is manifested and published in the *Guide to the LPX Equity Indices*. Includes global indices (LPX Composite, LPX50, and LPX Major Market); regional indices (LPX Europe, LPX UK, and LPX America) and style indices (LPX Buyout, LPX Mezzanine, LPX Venture, LPX Indirect, and LPX Direct).

Bibliography

Amenc, N., W. Gehin, L. Martellini, and J. Meyfredi. "Passive Hedge Fund Replication—A Critical Assessment of Existing Techniques." *The Journal of Alternative Investments* 11, No. 2 (Fall 2008): 69–83.

Arrow, K., and G. Debreu. "The Existence of an Equilibrium for a Competitive Economy." *Econometrics*. 22, No. 3 (1954): 265–290.

Asness, C., R. Krail, and J. Liew. "Do Hedge Funds Hedge?" *The Journal of Portfolio Management* (Fall 2001): 6–19.

Bansal, R., and C.R. Harvey. "Performance Evaluation in the Presence of Dynamic Trading Strategies." Duke University, Working Paper, 1996.

Bernstein, P. *Against the Gods: The Remarkable Story of Risk*. New York: John Wiley & Sons, 1996.

Black, F., and R. Litterman. "Global Portfolio Optimization." *Financial Analysts Journal* 48, No. 5 (September/October 1992): 28–43.

Black, F., and M. Scholes. "The Pricing of Options and Corporate Liabilities." *The Journal of Political Economy* 81, No. 3 (May/June 1973): 637–654.

Bodie, Z., A. Kane, and A. Marcus. *Investments*. New York: McGraw-Hill, 2008.

Bookstaber, Richard. "Hedge Fund Existential." *Financial Analysts Journal* 59, No. 5 (September/October 2003): 19–23.

Brinson, G.P., L.R. Hood, and G.L. Beebower. "Determinants of Portfolio Performance." *Financial Analysts Journal* (July/August 1986): 39–44.

Brinson, G.P., B.D. Singer, and G.L. Beebower. "Determinants of Portfolio Performance II: An Update." *Financial Analysts Journal* 47, No. 3 (May/June 1991): 40–48.

Case, K., and R. Shiller. "Is There a Bubble in the Housing Market?" *Brookings Papers on Economic Activity* (2003): 299–362.

Chen, P., G. Jiang, and K. Shu. "Fund of Funds, Portable Alpha, and Portfolio Optimization." *The Journal of Portfolio Management* 35, No. 3 (Spring 2009): 79–92.

Choueifaty, Y., and Y. Coignard. "Toward Maximum Diversification." *The Journal of Portfolio Management* 35, No. 1 (Fall 2008): 40–51.

Clauss, P., T. Roncalli, and G. Weisang. "Risk Management Lessons from Madoff Fraud." http://ssrn.com/abstract=1358086, Working paper 2009.

Davis, J., F. Kinniry, and G. Sheay. "The Asset Allocatin Debate: Provocative Questions, Enduring Realities." Vanguard, 2007.

Dempster, M., M. Germano, E. Medova, J. Murphy, D. Ryan, and F. Sandrini. "Risk-Profiling Defined Benefit Pension Schemes." *The Journal of Portfolio Management* 35, No. 4 (Summer 2009): 76–93.

Dusak, Katherine. "Futures Trading and Investor Returns: An Investigation of Commodity Market Risk Premiums." *Journal of Political Economy* 81, Issue 6 (November/December 1973): 1387–1406.

Fama, E. "Efficient Capital Markets: A Review of Theory and Empirical Work." *Journal of Finance* 25, No. 2 (May 1970): 383–417.

Fama, E., and K. French. "Business Cycles and the Behavior of Metals Prices." *Journal of Finance* 43, Issue 5 (December 1988): 1075–1093.

Fama, E., and K. French. "The Cross Section of Expected Stock Returns." *Journal of Finance* 47, No. 2 (June 1992): 427–465.

Fama, E., and K. French. "Size and Book-to-Market Factors in Earnings and Returns." *Journal of Finance* 50, No. 1 (March 1995): 131–155.

Fernandez, P. "Market Risk Premia Used in 2008 by Professors: A Survey With 1,400 Answers." University of Navarra, IESE Business School, April 2009.

Fernandez, P. "Betas Used by Professors: A Survey With 2,500 Answers." University of Navarra, IESE Business School, May 2009.

Ferson, W.E., and K. Khang. "Conditional Performance Measurement Using Portfolio Weights: Evidence for Pension Funds." NBER Working Paper No. W8790, February 2002.

Ferson, W.E., D. Kisgen, and T. Henry. "Evaluating Fixed Income Fund Performance with Stochastic Discount Factors." EFA 2003 Annual Conference Paper No. 486, April 2003.

Friedman, Milton. *Essays in Positive Economics*. Chicago: University of Chicago Press, 1953.

Frost, P.A., and J.E. Savarino. "For Better Performance: Constrain Portfolio Weights." *The Journal of Portfolio Management* 15, No. 1, (Fall 1988): 29–34.

Fung, W., and D. Hsieh. "Asset Based Style Factors of Hedge Funds." *Financial Analysts Journal* 58, No. 5 (September/October 2002): 16–27.

Fung, W., and D. Hsieh. "Hedge Funds: An Industry in its Adolescence." Atlanta: Federal Reserve Bank of Atlanta, 2006.

Geltner, D., and H. Pollakowski. "A Set of Indexes for Trading Commercial Real Estate Based on the Real Capital Analytics Transaction Prices Database." MIT Center for Real Estate, September 2007.

Geman, H. *Commodities and Commodity Derivatives*. Hoboken, NJ: John Wiley & Sons, 2005.

Graham, J., and C. Harvey. "Market Timing Ability and Volatility Implied in Investment Newsletters' Asset Allocation Recommendations." *Journal of Financial Economics* 42, Issue 3 (November 1996): 397–421.

Grubel, Herbert. "Internationally Diversified Portfolio: Welfare Gains and Capital Flows." *The American Economic Review* Vol. 58, No. 5 (December 1968): 1299–1314.

Harris, L. *Trading and Exchanges: Market Microstructure for Practitioners.* New York: Oxford University Press, 2003.

Hill, J.M., V. Balasubramanian, K. Gregory, and I. Tierens. "Finding Alpha via Covered Index Writing." *Financial Analysts Journal* 62, No. 5 (Sept./Oct. 2006): 29–46.

Hryshko, D., M.J. Luengo-Prado, and B.E. Sorensen. "Childhood Determinants of Risk Aversion." www.ssrn.com, 2009.

Ibbotson, R.G., and P.D. Kaplan. "Does Asset Allocation Policy Explain 40, 90, or 100% of Performance?" *Financial Analysts Journal* (Jan./Feb. 2000): 26–33.

Ibbotson, R.G., and R.A. Sinquefield. "Stocks, Bonds, Bills and Inflation: Update." *Financial Analysts Journal* 35, No. 4 (1979): 40–44.

INGARM. "Benefits of Alternative Investments Series." Institute for Global Asset and Risk Management, 2009.

Jaeger, L., P. Cittadini, and M. Jacquemai. "Case Study: The SGFI Futures Index." *The Journal of Alternative Investments* 5, No. 1 (Summer 2002): 73–80.

Jaeger, L., C. Wagner. "Factor Modeling and Benchmarking of Hedge Funds: Can Passive Investment in Hedge Fund Strategies Deliver?" *The Journal of Alternative Investments* 8, No. 3 (Winter 2005): 9–36.

Kapadia, N., and E. Szado. "The Risk and Return Characteristics of the Buy-Write Strategy on the Russell 2000 Index." *The Journal of Alternative Investments* 9, No. 4 (Spring 2007): 39–56.

Kazemi H., and T. Schneeweis. "Conditional Performance of Hedge Funds." CISDM Working Paper, 2009.

Kazemi, H., F. Tu, and Y. Li. "Replication and Benchmarking of Hedge Funds." *The Journal of Alternative Investments* 11, No. 2 (Fall 2008): 40–59.

Kritzman, M. "Are Optimizers Error Maximizers?" *The Journal of Portfolio Management* 32, No. 4 (Summer 2006): 66–69.

Kritzman, M., and S. Page. "Asset Allocation versus Security Selection: Evidence from Global Markets." *Journal of Asset Management* 3, No. 3 (December 2002): 202–212.

Kritzman, M., and S. Page. "The Relative Importance of Asset Allocation and Security Selection." Comment: *The Journal of Portfolio Management* 33, No. 4 (Summer 2007): 111.

Kritzman, M., and L. Thomas. "Reengineering Investment Management." *The Journal of Portfolio Management*, 30th Anniversary Issue 30, No. 5 (September 2004): 70–79.

Kuhn, T.S. *The Structure of Scientific Revolutions.* 2nd ed. University of Chicago Press, 1970.

Leland, H. "Portfolio Insurance and October 19th." *California Management Review* (Summer 1988).

Leland, H., and M. Rubinstein. *The Evolution of Portfolio Insurance*, in D. Luskin (ed.) *Portfolio Insurance: A Guide to Dynamic Hedging.* New York: John Wiley & Sons, 1988.

Levy, H., and M. Sarnat. "International Diversification of Investment Portfolios." *American Economic Review* 60, Issue 4 (September 1970): 668–675.

Markov, M. "Madoff: A Tale of Two Funds." *MPI Quantitative Research Series* (December 2008).

Markowitz, H. "Portfolio Selection." *Journal of Finance* 7, No. 1 (March 1952): 77–91.

Martin, G. "Alpha and Pseudo-Alpha in Hedge Fund Returns: A Note on Admissible Measures of Portfolio Performance." CISDM, 2005.

Merton, R. "Theory of Rational Option Pricing." *Bell Journal of Economics* 4, Issue 1 (Spring 1973): 141–183.

Merton, R., and R. Henriksson. "On Market Timing and Investment Performance Part II: Statistical Procedures for Evaluating Forecasting Skills." *Journal of Business* 54 (October 1981): 513–533.

Modigliani, F., and L. Modigliani. "Risk-Adjusted Performance." *Journal of Portfolio Management* 23, No. 2 (Winter 1997): 45–54.

Olan, E., E. Sorensen, and R. Hua. "Global Value Investing Delivers Diversification: A Multi-Strategy Perspective." *The Journal of Portfolio Management* 35, No. 2 (Winter 2009): 42–49.

Redington, F. "Review of the Principles of Life-Office Valuations." *Journal of the Institute of Actuaries* 78 (1952): 286–340.

Reilly, F.K., and K. Brown. *Investment Analysis and Portfolio Management*. 6th ed. South-Western College Publishing, 2008.

Roll, R. "Ambiguity When Performance Is Measured by the Securities Market Line." *Journal of Finance* 33, Issue 4 (September 1978): 1051–1069.

Rosenberg, B. "From Concept to Function: Converting Market Theories into Practical Investment Tools—A Discussion with Barr Rosenberg, Ph.D." *The Journal of Investment Consulting* 7, No. 3 (Winter 2005–2006): 10–20.

Ross, S. "The Arbitrage Theory of Capital Asset Pricing." *Journal of Economic Theory* 13, Issue 3 (December 1976): 341–360.

Sabal, J. "The Determinants of Housing Prices: The Case of Spain." (2005). Available at www.sabalonline.com.

Schneeweis, T. "Dealing with Myths of Managed Futures." *The Journal of Alternative Investments* 1, No. 1 (Summer 1998): 9–17.

Schneeweis, T. "Dealing with Myths of Hedge Fund Investments." *The Journal of Alternative Investments* 1, No. 3 (Winter 1998): 11–15.

Schneeweis, T. "Frequently Asked Questions on Hedge Funds." INGARM (2009).

Schneeweis, T., H. Kazemi, and R. Gupta. "Eurex Derivative Products in Alternative Investments: The Case for Hedge Funds." Eurex, June 2006.

Schneeweis, T., H. Kazemi, and V. Karavas. "Eurex Derivative Products in Alternative Investments: The Case for Hedge Funds." Eurex, 2003.

Schneeweis, T., H. Kazemi, and G. Martin. "Understanding Hedge Fund Performance: Research Issues Revisited—Part I." *The Journal of Alternative Investments* 5, No. 3 (Winter 2002): 6–22.

Schneeweis, T., H. Kazemi, and G. Martin. "Understanding Hedge Fund Performance: Research Issues Revisited—Part II." *The Journal of Alternative Investments* 5, No. 4 (Spring 2003): 8–30.

Schneeweis, T., H. Kazemi, and R. Spurgin. "Momentum in Asset Returns: Are Commodity Returns a Special Case?" *The Journal of Alternative Investments* 10, No. 4 (Spring 2008): 23–36.

Schneeweis, T., and R. Spurgin. "The Benefits of Index Option-Based Strategies for Institutional Portfolios." *The Journal of Alternative Investments* 3, No. 4 (Spring 2001): 44–52.

Schneeweis, T., R. Spurgin, and G. Georgiev. "Benchmarking Commodity Trading Advisor Performance with a Passive Futures-Based Index." CISDM Working Paper, 2000.

Schneeweis, T., R. Spurgin, and H. Kazemi. "Eurex Derivative Products in Alternative Investments: The Case for Managed Futures." Eurex, June 2003.

Schwarz, E., J. Hill, and T. Schneeweis. *Financial Futures: Fundamentals, Strategies, and Applications.* Homewood, IL: Irwin, 1986.

Sewell, Martin. "Behavioural Finance." University College London (Rev. August 2008). www.behaviouralfinance.net/.

Sharpe, W.F. "A Simplified Model for Portfolio Analysis." *Management Science* 9, No. 2 (January 1963): 277–293.

Sharpe, W.F. "Capital Asset Prices: A Theory of Market Equilibrium Under Conditions of Risk." *Journal of Finance* 19, Issue 3 (September 1964): 425–442.

Sharpe, W.F. "Mutual Fund Performance." *Journal of Business* 39, No. S1 (January 1966): 119–138.

Sharpe, W.F. "Asset Allocation: Management Style and Performance Measurement." *The Journal of Portfolio Management* 18, No. 2 (Winter 1992): 7–19.

Siegel, J.J. *Stocks for the Long Run: The Definitive Guide to Financial Market Returns and Long-Term Investment Strategies*, 4th ed. New York: McGraw-Hill, 2008.

Szado, E., and T. Schneeweis. "Loosening the Collar." CISDM Working Paper, 2009.

Taleb, N. *The Black Swan.* New York: Random House, 2007.

Tobin, James. "Liquidity Preference as Behavior Toward Risk." *Review of Economic Studies* 25, Issue 2 (February 1958): 65–86.

Tokat, Y., N. Wicas, and F. Kinniry. "The Asset Allocation Debate: A Review and Reconciliation." *Journal of Financial Planning* 19, No. 10 (2006): 52–63.

Treynor, J.L. "How to Rate Management of Investment Funds." *Harvard Business Review* 43 (1965): 63–75.

Williams, J. *The Economic Function of Futures Markets.* Cambridge University Press, 1986.

Yale Endowment Report 2005, Yale University

Yau, J., D. Downs, H.-G. Fung, and G.A. Patterson. "The Linkage of REIT Income- and Price-Returns with Fundamental Economic Variables." *The Journal of Alternative Investments* 6, No. 1 (Summer 2003): 39–50.

Yau, J., and T. Schneeweis. "Financial Futures: A Review." INGARM, 2010.

About the Authors

Thomas Schneeweis, Ph.D., has more than 30 years' experience in investment management. Professionally, he is a Director and co-founder of the non-profit Institute for Global Asset and Risk Management (INGARM). He was also a co-founder of Alternative Investment Analytics (a commodity investment firm that helped create the Bache Commodity Index) and of White Bear Partners (a hedge fund/managed futures trading firm). He was also associated with the creation and development of the Zurich and Dow Jones Investable Hedge Fund Indices. He has acted as director of research at Ursa Capital, one of the first managed account based hedge fund platforms. He is the Michael and Cheryl Philipp Professor of Finance and director of the Center for International Securities and Derivatives Markets at the Isenberg School of Management, University of Massachusetts-Amherst. He is the founding editor of *The Journal of Alternative Investments* and is co-founder of the Chartered Alternative Investment Analyst Association. He received his Ph.D. from the University of Iowa in 1977, an M.A. from the University of Wisconsin, and a B.A. from St. John's University. He has published more than 100 articles in the area of investment and asset management. He has presented at major conferences globally, has been quoted in major financial press, and has spoken on many financial news programs. He has been credited in part for the creation of asset allocation breakthroughs such as portable alpha and the development of hedge fund replication products.

Garry B. Crowder, J.D., M.M., has more than 20 years' experience in investment management. Professionally, he is a co-founder of the non-profit Institute for Global Asset and Risk Management (INGARM). Garry Crowder was the founder and managing partner of Ursa Capital LLC and Lyra Capital LLC, both of which he sold to a multi-national

European based investment bank. Garry Crowder created one of the first managed account hedge fund platforms, which form the basis for many structured products based on managed account hedge fund investments. In addition, he led the development and creation of the Zurich Hedge Fund Indexes and the Dow Jones Hedge Fund Benchmark Series, both of which were based on the Lyra money management platform. Previous posts include managing director at Zurich Capital Markets, Inc., managing director at Tiger Management LLC, and managing director at Morgan Stanley Asset Management. He began his career at Sidley Austin Brown & Wood LLP in 1983. Garry Crowder was a law clerk to the Honorable Thomas Gibbs Gee, United States Court of Appeals for the Fifth Judicial Circuit and is a member of Northwestern University's Law Board. He has spoken at hedge fund and alternative asset conferences around the world and is regarded as a noted expert in the development and creation of multi-asset portfolio products. Mr. Crowder holds a J.D. degree from Northwestern University School of Law, a master of management at J.L. Kellogg Graduate School of Management, Northwestern University, a Masters of Science from the University of Louisville, and a bachelor of science from the University of Missouri.

Hossein Kazemi, Ph.D., CFA, has over 15 years of investment management experience. He is regarded as a leader in the area of asset allocation. He has published more than 20 academic articles in the area of asset pricing and asset allocation. Professionally, he helped create Alternative Investment Analytics (a commodity investment management firm that helped create the Bache Commodity Index) and White Bear Partners (a hedge fund and CTA trading firm). He is professor of finance as well as associate director of the Center for International Securities and Derivatives Markets at the Isenberg School of Management, University of Massachusetts-Amherst. He is also director of research and curriculum at the Charter Alternative Investment Association. He received his Ph.D. from the University of Michigan in 1986, an M.A. from Eastern Michigan University, and a B.A. from the NIOC.

Index

Absolute risk, 65
Academics, 228
Algorithmic models, 14, 120–122
Alpha, 39–57
  alternatives, 54–55
  determination, 42, 46–48
  problems in determination, 48–50
  transfer, 12
  what it is, 39–45
Alternative assets, 219–221
Alternative benchmarks, 42
Alternative investments, 59. *See also* specific
    investment, i.e. Commodities, Real
    estate
  commodity indices, 184
  defined, 134
  groupings of, 115
  modern, 65
  myths about, 223
  sources of risk and return, 134–166
  and spot market prices, 217
  and TAA modeling, 101–102
  traditional, 65
Alternative REIT investments, 179, 181
Angel investors, 151, 153
Arbitrage, 10–11, 40
Arbitrage pricing model, 214
ARCH models, 95
Asset allocation:
  academic discussions, 228
  benefits of, 58
  core quantitative tools, 62–63
  defined, 20
  determining optimal, 100

fundamental directives, 3
future of, 239–248
history of, 1–19
importance of discretion in decision-
  making, 226–239
in the modern world, 14–15
myths of, 212–225
optimization models, 92–98
overview and limitations, 59–61
preliminary steps, 60
and risk budgeting, 195–211
and risk tolerance, 117
theory and implementation of, 226–230
traditional and alternative investments,
  61–66
traditional stock/bond *vs.* multi-asset,
  70–71
types of, 91–109
what it is, 1
Asset classes, 58–90
  benchmarks, 194, 271–277
  core, 114
  determining number of, 112
  performance, 135–139
  primary, 66
  return and risk among similar
    benchmarks, 167–194
  risk and return through business cycles,
    251–270
  traditional and alternative breakdown, 65
Assets:
  alternative, 219–221
  illiquid, 63, 98, 217
  marginal risks, 17

Assets (*Continued*)
  myths about value, 213–214
  pricing, 6–11, 46
  return distribution, 29
  traditional, 66
Attribution analysis, 34
Averages, historical, 94

Bache Commodity Index (BCI), 182
Backfill bias, 192, 194
Banks, investment, 227–228
Barclays Capital U.S. Aggregate, 36, 37, 141,
    147, 156, 185, 258, 259, 267, 268
  benchmark returns ranking, 80
  portfolio returns ranking, 83
  and Treasuries, 267, 268
Bear market, 111
Behavioral economics, 13
Benchmark returns, 136
  aggressive and conservative portfolio
    management, 77
  and beta, 64
  commodities, 162, 165
  and CTAs, 147
  differences among similar asset classes,
    167–194
  performance in alternative investment
    periods, 75
  private equity, 152
  ranked by BarCap US Aggregate, 80
  ranked on change in VIX, 121
  real estate, 157
  and S&P 500, 79, 138, 165
  and standard deviation, 64, 76
Benchmarks, 48–49, 56–57. *See also*
    Indices
  alternative risk-adjusted, 42
  alternatives, 104
  asset, 194
  asset class, 271–277
  biases, 192
  commodities, 179–185
  correlation, 137
  determining appropriate, 111–117
  and equity exposure, 135
  investable alternatives, 54
  performance, 105
  principal in determination of, 54
  private equity, 170–173
  real estate, 173–179

stocks and bonds, 168–170
  and strategic asset allocation, 99–100
Beta, 10, 38, 39–57, 97
  and benchmark return, 64
  benefits and limitations of, 40
  determination, 46–48, 48–50
  and market changes, 41
  and traditional alternative investments,
    67
Biases, 141, 143, 192, 194
Bid-ask spread, 197
Biggs, Barton, 216
Black, Fisher, 11
Black-Litterman model, 95
Bonds, 58, 70
  indices, 168–170
Bootstrapped portfolios, 94
Bottom up replication, 123
Break-even analysis, 43
Business cycle, 160, 250–270
Buy-write strategies. *See* Covered call

Call option, 11
Cambridge Associates, 170
Can-risk capacity, 117–118
Capital Asset Pricing Model (CAPM). *See*
    CAPM (Capital Asset Pricing Model)
Capital International Stock Indices, 168
Capital Market Line (CML), 5–6
CAPM (Capital Asset Pricing Model), 4–6,
    18, 62–63
  acceptance of, 28
  and efficient market hypothesis, 6–10
  and market risk, 43
Cash flow, 98
Casualty insurance, 98
CISDM CTA indices, 149, 150, 261, 262
CISDM ELS index, 193
CISDM Fund of Fund indices, 267, 268
CISDM Hedge Fund indices, 55, 131, 142,
    144, 145, 185
CISDM indices, 259, 260, 261, 262, 263
Clustering, volatility, 95
Collar strategy, 234
Collateralized debt obligations (CDOs),
    228, 229
Commodities, 59, 61, 65, 129, 130,
    143–148, 160–165
  benchmarks, 179–185, 275
  futures, 12

return and risk performance, 162–163
volatility, 182, 185
Commodity Futures Trading Commission
(CFTC), 11
Commodity pool operators (CPOs), 143
Commodity Research Bureau, 265, 266
Commodity risk, 196
Commodity trading advisors. *See* CTAs
(commodity trading advisors)
Conditional model, 41
Conditional performance evaluation, 53–54
Constant proportional portfolio insurance
(CPPI), 107
Convexity, 49–50
Core allocation, 110–133
Correlation analysis, 34, 116
Correlations, 24, 68–69, 214
between Barclays Capital U.S. Aggregate
and S&P 500, 267
benchmark, 137
betwen cash and futures price changes,
204
CISDM CTA indices, 149
between CISDM Fund of Fund indices
and BarCap U.S. Corporate High Yield,
268
between CISDM Fund of Fund indices
and S&P 500, 267
CISDM hedge funds, 144
commodity sector, 164
FTSE REITs, 160
intra-asset, 135
passive collar, gateway feeder funds, 237
and private equity, 152
between real estate indices and S&P 500,
175, 178
between S&P 500 and VIX (CBOE
Volatility Index), 268
Cost of carry arbitrage, 11
Counterparty risk, 196–197
Covariance. *See* Variance-covariance matrix
of returns
Covered call, 206–208, 210–211
Credit risk, 103, 196–197, 198
Credit spread, 52, 139
CTAs (commodity trading advisors), 59, 61,
143–148
indices, 189, 190, 274–275
Currencies, 63
Currency risk, 196

Decision-making, 120–122
and discretion, 226–239
Decomposition, 34, 202–203
Derivatives, 6–11, 37, 217
Deutsche Bank Liquid Commodity Index
(DBLCI), 182
Dhar, Madav, 216
Diapason Commodities Index (DCI), 182
Differential return, 232
Discretion, 226–239
Distressed debt investing, 151
Diversification, 4, 122, 156, 214–215
Dow Jones-UBS Commodity Index
(DJ-UBS), 182
Down markets, 134
and commodity performance, 163
and hedge fund performance, 143
and managed futures performance,
148
and private equity performance, 153
and real estate performance, 158–160
Due diligence, 232–235
Dynamic asset management, 2, 107–108
Dynamic portfolio insurance, 12
Dynamic trading strategies, 92, 197

Economic model based estimates, 95
Efficiency, 4, 31–32, 33, 85, 101
Efficient market hypothesis (EMH), 6–10
EMN indices, 236
Endowment, 98
Energy sector, 182
Equilibrium, 40, 99
economic models, 95
returns, 100
Equity benchmarks, 271
Equity beta, 67, 73
Equity bias hedge funds, 141, 143
Equity markets, 11, 59, 65
Equity REITs, 157–158
Equity risk, 196
Equity securities, 214–215
Estimating, 94–95, 103
Estimation errors, 25, 85, 93–94
Excess break-even rate of return (EBK),
43–44
Excess return to market factor, 45
Exchange traded equities, 63
Exchange traded funds (ETFs), 55, 122,
123–124

Expected return, 4, 24, 31, 46, 93, 230
Expected risk-adjusted return, 9

Factor mimicking portfolios, 44–45
Fairfield Sentry, 234
Fama-French 4-factor models, 45
Fees, 54, 88
Feynman, Richard, 245
Fixed income securities, 12, 24, 63, 65, 270
Floor, 107
Forecasting, 215
Friedman, Milton, 18
FTSE NAREIT indices, 173, 180
FTSE REITs, 160, 161
Fundamental Indices, 169
Futures, 10–11
    commodities, 12
    financials markets, 12
    managed, 65, 68, 143–148
    returns, 220
    and risk management, 203–206

GARCH models, 95
Goldman Sachs/S&P Commodity index. *See*
    S&P Goldman Sachs Commodity Index
    (S&P GSCI index)
Groupings, 111–117, 126–132
Growth in Corporate Earnings, 52

Hedge funds, 13, 43, 54, 59, 61, 65, 68,
    89, 129, 131–132
    benchmarks, 270–272
    index vs fund investment example,
        189–194
    indices, 185–189
    myths about, 219–223
    return and risk performance, 140–143,
        220
    and risk, 118
    sources of return, 139–140
Hedge ratio, 204, 205
Heuristic models, 120–122
HFRX indices, 189
High book value minus low book value
    (HML) factor, 45
Historical data, 94, 215
Hybrid REITs, 158

Illiquid assets, 63, 98, 217
Indices. *See also* Benchmarks

alternative hedge funds, 186–188
biases, 192
buy-write, 206
commodity, 182–185
hedge funds, 185–189
passive security-based, 140
private equity, 171, 174
problems in creation of, 168–169
replication-based, 122–126
S&P/Case Shiller Home Price, 175
stocks and bonds, 168–170
Inefficiency, 101
Inflation risk, 96–97, 163, 196
Informational uncertainty, 214
Initial Portfolio Theory (IPT), 3
Inputs, estimating, 94–95
Insurance, 12, 98
Interest risk, 196, 198–199
Investable manager based hedge fund
    indices, 185
Investable securities, 123
Investment banks, 227–228
Investment horizon risk, 19
Investment managers, 25, 216–217, 218
    active *versus* passive, 46
    evaluation and review, 232–233
    and fund returns, 215
    hedge funds, 185
    skill of, 139, 146
    value of discretion, 230–232
Investments:
    alternative (*See* Alternative investments)
    correlations strategy, 68–69
    descriptive statistics, 67
    passive alternatives, 54
Investors, 218–219
    attitudes and asset value, 213–214
    and hedge funds, 139
    objectives, 59–60, 99
    protecting, 243–245
    risk tolerance, 89, 117–119

J-curve effect, 151

Kurtosis, 29, 223

Lagging, 175
Lead-lag relationship, 103
Leverage, 218
Leveraged buyouts, 151

Liabilities, 96, 99
Linear factor models, 124
Linear regression, 7, 40, 198
Liquidity, 62, 64, 98, 122, 127
Liquidity risk, 197
Long collar, 208–210

Madoff, Bernard, 233–235
Managed futures, 65, 68, 143–148
Managers. *See* Investment managers
Marginal risk, 17
Market:
  efficiency, 85
  risk, 7, 65, 196
  risk analysis, 34
  segment, 70–71, 82–84
  sensitivity, 74–84, 89
  timing, 50
  volatility, 139
Market/manager allocation strategies,
  110–133
Market model, 8, 40
Market risk premium, 47–48
Markowitz, Harry, 3–4, 15, 92, 214
Mathematics of diversification, 4
Maturity, bond, 169
Maximizing over the errors, 95
Mean, 29, 30, 93, 99
Mean-variance asset allocation, 92
Mean-variance efficient portfolios, 4
Mean-variance optimization, 94, 97, 100
Merrill Lynch Commodity Index eXtra
  (MLCX), 182
Mezzanine investing, 151, 153
Microsoft Excel Solver, 200
MIT Transactions-Based Index (TBI), 173,
  175
Mixed (security/algorithmic based)
  replication, 123
Modern alternative investments, 65, 66, 68
Modern Portfolio Theory (MPT), 3–4, 18,
  214
  myths about, 223–224
Mortgage REITs, 158
MPT. *See* Modern Portfolio Theory (MPT)
MSCI Emerging Markets, 257, 258
Multi-asset allocation, 70–71, 133
  performance, 148, 153, 158
  principal concerns, 167
Multi-factor model, 41, 42, 43, 44, 50–54

Multi-factor regression model, 51
Multivariate linear regression, 198
Mutual funds, 129

NAREIT Domestic Real Estate Index, 179
NASDAQ, 250, 251
NCREIF National Property Index (NPI),
  173, 175
Non-linear payoffs, 197

Old Portfolio Theory (OPT), 3
Operational risk, 197
Opportunity cost risk, 210
Optimization models, 92–98, 200
Options, 11, 197
  and return distribution, 27
  and risk management, 206
  trading, 12
Option theory, 10–11, 231, 238, 246
Order, definition of, 242–245
Oversight, 243–244

Parameter estimation error, 25
Peer group creation, 126–132
Performance alpha, 46–47
Performance attribution, 34
Performance evaluation, conditional, 53–54
Political risk, 197
Portfolio insurance strategy, 92, 107
Portfolio management:
  active *versus* passive, 46–47
  convexity of returns, 49–50
  market segment weightings, 70–71
  performance comparison between
    aggressive and conservative, 72–73
  risk based, 66
Portfolio returns:
  differences in aggressive and conservative
    management, 86–87
  ranked by BarCap US Aggregate, 83
  ranked by S&P 500, 81
  weightings, 84–85
Portfolio risk, 11, 30–34
Portfolios:
  bootstrapped or resampled, 94
  measuring exposure, 198
  model, 102
  quantitative construction models, 93
  rebalancing, 15, 107, 201
  return volatility, 99

Portfolios (*Continued*)
  risk based, 106
  risk decomposition of, 202–203
  tactical asset, 106
Portfolio weights, 94
Price risk, 33, 219
Private equity, 61, 65, 118, 148–153
  benchmarks, 170–173, 174, 275
  performance of indices, 171
  return and risk performance, 151–153
  returns ranked by S&P 500, 154, 172
  sources of return, 151
Probability, 2, 20
Product development, 15–16
Pro forma performance, 167, 169
Protected investment strategy, 107
Pure security, 62
Purity, style, 126–132
Put-Call Parity Model, 11
Put option, 11
Put protected investment strategy, 107

Quantitative model, 102–103

Rate of return:
  annualized S&P 500, 93
  excess break-even rate, 43–44
  and risk, 197–198
Real estate, 61, 65, 129, 153–160, 176
  benchmarks, 173–179, 274
  comparison benchmark performance, 157
  correlation with S&P 500 indices, 178, 181
  international and FTSE returns, 177
  prices, 155–156
  return and risk performance, 156–158
  sources of return, 155–156
Real estate investment companies (REITs), 155
Reallocation strategy, 103
Reasonable man theory, 60
Rebalancing, 15, 107, 201
Regression coefficients, 52
Regression model, 51, 52
Regulations, governmental, 127, 197, 244–245, 247–248
REITs (real estate investment companies), 155, 157–158, 179
Replication-based indices, 122–126, 223
Reporting bias, 192

Return and risk:
  of asset classes through business cycles, 251–270
  characteristics of alternative investments, 61–62
  characteristics of indices, 169
  commodities, 162–163
  differences among similar asset class benchmarks, 167–194
  hedge funds, 140–143
  historical attributes and strategy allocation, 66–70
  historical comparisons, 71–74
  managed futures, 146–148
  models post-1980, 11–13
  multi-factor estimation, 50–54
  performance results, 66
  predictability of, 95–96
  private equity, 151–153
  real estate, 156–158
  sources in alternative investments, 134–166
  and strategic asset allocation, 99
Return estimation models, 50–54
Return generating models, 46
Return intervals, 36
Returns:
  benchmark, 136
  CISDM hedge funds, 145
  commodities, 160–162
  hedge funds, 139–140
  and managed futures, 146
  and performance of investment managers, 215
  real estate, 155–156
Return to risk, 2, 18, 19
Return volatility, 61, 99
Risk, 1–2
  absolute, 65
  and alternative investments, 134–166
  assessment, 28–30
  aversion, 98, 100, 133
  budgeting and asset allocation, 195–211
  decomposition, 34, 202–203
  determinants, 23
  and expected return, 230
  factor weightings, 54–55
  individual *vs.* portfolio, 69
  and liabilities, 96
  management of (*See* Risk management)

measurements of, 20–38, 96–97
measures of exposure, 63
qualitative, 63
and rate of return, 197–198
tolerance, 89, 117–119
and tracking error, 97–98
what it is, 22–24
Risk factor sensitivity analysis, 34
Risk-free assets, 4
Risk hedge ratio, 204
Riskless rate of interest, 7
Risk management, 1–2, 3, 11, 107, 214, 247
benefits of reduction, 74
goal of, 199
models, 247
multi-factor approach to, 195–200
using futures, 203–206
using options, 206
and volatility, 200–202
Risk premia, 7, 214
Robertson, Julian, 222
Rogers International Commodity Index
    (RICI), 182
Roll returns, 166
Rosenberg, Barr, 10
Russell Growth, 120, 207, 251
    volatility, 254, 255, 256, 257

Salomon Brothers Bond Indices, 168
Sample selection, 38
Satellite allocation, 110–133
Scholes, Myron, 11
Securities:
    fixed income, 12, 24, 63, 65, 272
    investable, 123
    pure, 62
Securities and Exchange Commission (SEC),
    229
Securitization, 155
Security market line, 6
Seed capital, 153
Selection bias, 192
Semi-standard deviation, 97
Semi-variance, 30
Sensitivity, market, 74–82, 82–84, 89
Sharpe Ratio, 18, 26–28, 37, 43
Skewness, 29, 62, 97, 223
Slope of the yield curve, 101
Small minus big (SMB) factor, 45
Smoothing, 28, 175

S&P 500, 36, 37, 185
    annualized rate of return, 93, 168
    annualized standard deviation, 93
    benchmark returns, 79, 138
    CISDM CTA indices, 150
    commodity benchmarks, 165
    correlations with real estate indices, 175,
        178, 181
    correlation with Barclays Capital U.S.
        Aggregate, 267
    correlation with CISDM Fund of Fund
        indices, 267
    correlation with VIX (CBOE Volatility
        Index), 268
    forecasted returns for, 52–53
    FTSE REITs, 161
    growth of *.116100, 249
    performance, 2004–2008, 111
    portfolio returns ranking, 81
    private equity returns, 154, 172
    volatility, 103, 250, 264
S&P/Case Shiller Home Price indices, 175
S&P Goldman Sachs Commodity Index
    (S&P GSCI index), 179, 182, 264, 265
Split-strike conversion strategy, 234–235
Spot market, 217
Standard deviation, 4, 20, 26, 30, 31,
    32–33, 35, 70
    aggressive and conservative portfolio
        management, 78
    annualized rate of return, 93
    benchmark performance in alternative
        investment periods, 75
    and benchmark return, 64
Stocks, 58, 70, 96, 168–170
Strategic asset allocation, 91, 99–100, 113
Strategic asset management, 2
Style purity, 126–132
Subprime market, 228–229
Surplus-at-Risk (SAR)/Liability Driven
    Investment (LDI), 34
Survivorship bias, 192, 194
Swaps, 15

Tactical asset allocation (TAA), 2, 12,
    91–92, 101–106
Taxability, 62
Tax codes, 197
Term premium, 103
Term spread, 52

Thomson Financial, 170
Timing, 50
Tobin, James, 4
Top down replication, 123
Tracking error, 34, 97–98
Traditional alternative investments, 65, 66, 67
Transparency, 62, 64, 122, 127, 222, 240
Treasuries, 10, 11, 24, 52, 269, 270
Treynor measure, 28

UBS Bloomberg Constant Maturity Commodity Index (CMCI), 182
Uncertainty, 2, 214
Up equity markets:
 and commodity performance, 163
 and hedge fund performance, 143
 and managed futures performance, 148
 and private equity performance, 153
 and real estate performance, 158–160
Up minus down (UMD) factor, 45

Value at risk (VaR), 34–36, 202, 248
Values of the means, 93
Variance, 30, 96
Variance-covariance matrix of returns, 7, 93, 94, 124
Variance of the return, 92

Venture capital, 151, 153
VIX (CBOE Volatility Index), 14, 42, 103, 120, 266, 267
Volatility, 4, 14, 18, 24, 27, 93, 249. *See also* VIX (CBOE Volatility Index)
 Barclays Capital U.S. Aggregate, 259
 CISDM CTA indices, 264
 CISDM indices, 260, 261, 262, 263
 commodities, 182, 185
 Commodity Research Bureau, 266
 comparison performance measures, 56
 Goldman Sachs/S&P Commodity index, 265
 market, 139
 and modern alternative investments, 68
 MSCI Emerging Markets, 256
 NASDAQ, 251
 NCREIF returns, 175
 predictability in, 96
 return, 61, 99
 and risk, 197, 200–202
 Russell Growth, 254, 255, 256, 257
 S&P 500, 103, 252
 and traditional alternative investments, 67
Volatility clustering, 95

Weights, portfolio, 70–71, 84–85, 94, 104
Will-risk aversion, 118–119